Golden Threads
Women Creating Community

Faculty Women's Club
University of Calgary

Editors
Polly Knowlton Cockett
Eileen Lohka
Kate Bentley

DETSELIG
ENTERPRISES LTD

Detselig Enterprises Ltd.
Calgary, Alberta

Golden Threads: Women Creating Community

© 2009 Faculty Women's Club, University of Calgary

Library and Archives Canada Cataloging in Publication

    Golden threads : women creating community / Polly Knowlton Cockett, Eileen Lohka, Kate Bentley, editors.

Includes bibliographical references.
ISBN 978-1-55059-377-8

    1. University of Calgary. Faculty Women's Club – History. 2. University of Calgary – Public services – History. 3. Civic leaders Alberta – Calgary – Biography. 4. Community life – Alberta – Calgary – History. I. Knowlton Cockett, Polly, 1954- II. Lohka, Eileen, 1953- III. Bentley, Kate, 1949-

LE3.C32G64 2009   378.7123'38   C2009-905398-5

Detselig Enterprises Ltd.
210, 1220 Kensington Rd NW
Calgary, Alberta
T2N 3P5

DETSELIG
ENTERPRISES LTD

www.temerondetselig.com
temeron@telusplanet.net
Phone: 403-283-0900
Fax: 403-283-6947

    We acknowledge the support of the Government of Canada through the Book Industry Development Program (BPIDP) for our publishing program.

    We also acknowledge the support of the Alberta Foundation for the Arts for our publishing program.

Cover design by Bree Horel

ISBN 978-1-55059-377-8   SAN 113-0234   Printed in Canada

Contents

Teacups – *Bree Horel*

Drunkard's Path Quilt Square – *Vera Simony* . . . . . .in Cover Design

References

Norris, Marjorie (October 23, 1981). *The Faculty Women's Club, University of Calgary: A Commemorative History*. 38 p. UARC 86.022.01.12.

University of Calgary Archives UARC 86.022. Faculty Women's Club, 1956-1986.

Glenbow Museum Archives M.8220. Campus Preschool Association, 1973-1988.

A New Day – *Judith Hall*

Threading Together a Community

Polly Knowlton Cockett, Eileen Lohka, Kate Bentley

Golden Threads acknowledges, in a variety of genres, the intimate link between women, the University of Calgary, the Calgary community, and the landscapes we share.

Having come from all corners of the world and from around the corner, a small group of women founded the Faculty Women's Club on October 23, 1956. Over the years, our behind the scenes contributions have enabled the University of Calgary to grow at various levels: Faculty Women's Club members were the forerunners of today's fundraisers, alumni and faculty associations, support services, counsellors, daycare providers, and more. These same women fulfilled countless roles assisting the budding institution and a growing city. For the first time in their own voice, we hear women's stories anchored in the University and the city's past, and continuing through to the present. They explore the legacy of the first women academics and spouses of academics who were fundamental in the development of a sense of place and community, both on and off campus. Their contribution to community is as relevant today as it was 50 years ago.

The idea for this book started innocently enough when, anticipating the new millennium, we planned a Tea and asked for personal reflections on our organization, its meaning for us and for the greater community. Recognizing how profound some of these memories are, we slowly changed our focus and the project evolved into a more ambitious undertaking which saw us applying for a grant from The Calgary Foundation in association with our Golden Anniversary in 2006, and then working intermittently over three long years toward the completion of this book. We acknowledge the tenaciousness of Polly Lee Knowlton Cockett who, from the start, worked tirelessly to weave together the various threads of our common story.

Writers have offered personal or historical narratives, from the present or the past; they have spoken through their artwork and their poetry; they have inserted themselves in the landscape, and discussed various aspects of their relationship with the University and the wider Calgary community. The variety of voices reflects the multifaceted contributions of several generations of women while the relationship between history, geographic space, and community outreach provides the underlying unity to the publication. Through testimonial, anecdotal, and archival material, over fifty years of community building comes alive. Contributors include past, present, and potential members of the Faculty Women's Club, the Faculty Babysitting Swap, Campus Preschool Association, and the broader University of Calgary community.

Our heartfelt thanks go out to all our contributors, not only for the thoughtful way you shared your experiences with us, but also for everything you did for the Faculty Women's Club, the University of Calgary, and greater Calgary over the years. Our warm thanks also go to FWC Charter Member Marjorie Barron Norris, whose 1981 commemorative history of the first twenty-five years of our organization is freely excerpted and liberally sprinkled throughout, thus providing introductory and contextual commentary for this "sequel."

The last three executive committees of FWC have been unstinting in their support; in particular Ann Elliott, Brinsley Fox, Marie Gailer, Kate Jullien, Elizabeth Solecki, and Lynn Williams. Countless others, although nameless, have all contributed to the vision of this book in their own way. We love the intergenerational connections represented in so many ways throughout the book, including through our talented cover designer, Bree Horel, and her grandmother, Carol Marica, an FWC Alumna. We are most appreciative of the friendly support and generous permissions to reprint articles and images we received from the University of Calgary and Glenbow Archives; the University's publications: *On Campus, Gazette*, and *U* magazine; and *The Calgary Herald*.

We are extremely grateful for the invaluable Community Grant we received from The Calgary Foundation without which this book would not be possible, nor would our grant have been realized without the vital partnership of the SEEDS Foundation and Margo Helper. Last but not least, our thanks go to Ted Giles and his team at Detselig Enterprises Ltd. for making this dream into a very real book!

Golden Threads illustrates the way women favor collaborative teamwork to accomplish a project. Be it a quilt or a book, we have banded together to ensure that memories stay alive, that stories are told, and, at last, that the contributions of countless women are celebrated.

Polly Lee, Kate, and Eileen

Imagining

The Source of the Idea
The Birth of the Faculty Women's Club

Our own Madge Aikenhead was the source of the idea which resulted in the birth of the Faculty Women's Club on October 23, 1956. Twenty-five years ago we were a very young University known then as The University of Alberta in Calgary and headed by Vi's husband, Dr. Andrew L. Doucette, designated its Director. From its beginnings in 1946 as a branch of the University of Alberta faculty meetings were held in private homes with the staff (mostly men) gathering in one room and their wives moving to another part of the house for a social get-together. By 1955, the staff had grown to over twenty, so "Andy" moved staff meetings to the campus, located in the west half of the Collegiate Gothic neo-Tudor style block of the Institute of Technology and Art (now SAIT). Madge felt that the cessation of home meetings left a social void which warranted a structured kind of association for the women. Over coffee one day with Audrey Allen, she proposed the idea and Audrey liked it very much. So it was passed up to Vi Doucette who gave it her enthusiastic support, suggesting an initial meeting to be chaired by Madge.

When the time came to elect officers in the spring, Madge was the logical choice for President, Audrey Allen became Vice-President and Bernice Gibb, the Secretary-Treasurer.

Norris, p. 1

October 23, 1956 - Meeting 1
Meeting Host – "should provide coffee"
Co-hostesses appointed – will bring simple refreshments

November 27, 1956 - Meeting 2
Vi Doucette agreed to ask Mrs. Denny [secretary of the Wauneita Society] for the use of the coffee urn.

March 19, 1957 - Meeting 3
Wauneita Lounge
It was decided that evening refreshments would be served in the lounge instead of the Cafeteria from now on. We were reminded to book the lounge well ahead of our meetings. We were all agreed that we would like to present a gift to the Wauneita Society in return for the use of their room. An electric coffee-maker was suggested. After considerable discussion Shirley Goodwin moved that we investigate the prices of electric coffee makers. Honor seconded; carried. The executive is to look into the matter during the summer and report in the fall.

We hope to rent the coffee urn from Mrs. Denny for the occasion as this has been done for other social events.

October 24, 1957 - Meeting 4
Wauneita Room
First order of business: Shirley Goodwin reported on the price of coffee urns. In view of the financial state of the club, it was suggested that a decision on purchasing an urn be postponed until the new university buildings are ready. It was moved by Shirley Goodwin, seconded by Shirley Bagley, that a coffee urn should not be purchased, but that borrowed coffee pots be used for the present. Carried.

March 12, 1958
Report from the Social Committee – regarding plans for Spring Tea:
Mary reported that the cafeteria will supply a tea urn and five metal jugs for approximately $1.00.

Wearing Our Hats
Elizabeth Challice

We came to Calgary in 1957 and were warmly welcomed by all the members of the Faculty Women's Club, which at that time was a year old. I was speedily initiated into such things as the Wauneita Tea, a social occasion when the girl students learned about wearing hats, heels, and gloves and balancing teacups while eating!

In those days, if there was a student hop, many of the staff and wives also went and danced. At the end of the event, we often gathered at someone's house where we all fitted!

The FWC filled various social needs. We served at the Tea after Convocation (of course wearing our hats!), and our regular meetings every month had not only interesting speakers, but were times of getting together when we all knew each other. In the 1960s we were all YOUNG and babies' arrivals were quite frequent with the accompanying showers.

Barbara Wilson was the prime mover in establishing the University Ball, held several years in the 60s. The aim was to get "Town and Gown" to mingle and to get to know each other. Among special guests, the Lieutenant Governor and the Mayor accepted our invitations. The Balls were great affairs, taking much work but were successful in achieving their aim. We had our moments of crisis including when one of the "Town" guests surreptitiously changed our carefully organized seating plan. Fortunately this was rearranged by an alert committee member before dinner was announced!

Many members have done great work connected with the social needs of the city. The Local Council of Women has benefited enormously from the contributions of Faculty Wives. However, we were concerned chiefly with the needs of the University. We did a great deal in connection with day care for the children of students, and for several years, helped with "Adopt a Family" at Christmas. This led to sad, touching, and also exasperating happenings (did a student family *really* need a garment from a particular shelf in the Gap store?).

When we acquired our first baby, I was finishing a B.Ed. and was President of FWC. Dr. Armstrong had just been appointed President and I remember pushing the "pram" (a real English coach-built one) over from St. Andrew's Heights in order to welcome Kay Armstrong both to the University in general and as Patron of FWC.

Early on we acquired a logo, noted by an eminent classics professor to be a phallic symbol. The retiring FWC President was given a silver spoon or a silver salver with the logo engraved on it. Then we became very grand and had a golden pin made for the retiring president. Many of these were made until they became too expensive. Dorothy Vernon gave me hers when she left for England and it is now handed on to each succeeding president for her term of office.

It is great that we have reached another milestone: our 50th Anniversary. Although the FWC has changed over the years, it is good that we keep together and enjoy the various things we do together. May we continue for many years to come.

Presidents and Mayor are Piped In at the Ball

The Faculty Women's Club second annual University Ball was held at the Palliser Hotel, February 1965. Guests included, from the top, Calgary Mayor Grant MacEwan and his daughter Mrs. Heather Foran, University of Alberta, Calgary President Dr. Herb Armstrong and Mrs. Armstrong, Faculty Women's Club Honorary President, Dr. Cyril Challice and Mrs. Elizabeth Challice, Faculty Women's Club President, all led down the stairway by Calgary Highlander Piper William Hosie.

Image courtesy of the University of Calgary Archives. UARC 82.010.01.62.01

That Most Ambitious of All Our Undertakings
The University Ball

Now, back to the origins of that most ambitious of all our undertakings – the University Ball, held first on February 8, 1964. From the outset, the concept was staggering. But then, with people like Mary Winspear as a Past President and Barbara Wilson as Special Events Chairman to promote it, the mind could boggle. Barbara and Mary decided it was time we 'branched out' to a town-and-gown type function. The time for entering the City social scene was right for a dressy affair. Our Honorary President was Vi Taylor, recently recognized as one of Canada's ten best dressed women, and as charming as she was beautiful. People were most aware of the University now we were on our new campus and growing rapidly. The proposal was that a list should be drawn up of people prominent in the Calgary volunteer community or interested in the University (not necessarily one and the same). As President, I felt the latter category would sort itself out, but I was apprehensive as to who the prominent ones were? The crucial list was drawn up and the chosen courted to come to the ball. That they did and in greater numbers than our own reluctant staff. In those days University salaries covered only the bare essentials, so, because of the cost of raiment required we conceded that the men could come formal or informal. You could buy a tuxedo for $60.00 at Tip Top Tailors, but then you could also buy other longed-for items. . . .

The money for our early expenses was met, in part, by each member of the Ball Committee staking $12.00 on a favorable outcome (this was the cost of a month's utilities then.) As time grew near and income versus expenditure accounting ran close, we felt that wine-with-dinner was an impossible touch of grace. But Principal Malcolm Taylor christened our first ball with a $100.00 donation to launch us properly. Since then that heady benefice has not been equalled!

We followed through with a social coup – the surprise table seating. With a staff couple at each table to act as hosts, the city guests were seated alphabetically. The committees stayed with a 'mixer' approach through all 12 balls, feeling that, in this way, couples who came alone would automatically be included; town and gown would not be able to stay in cliques. Behind-the-scene pressure did occur. One year, as Ball Chairman, I stuck to our guns during an outraged barrage of protest from a dean who wanted to sit with his party. After the ball was over he sent the following complimentary message to our President:

This is just a note to congratulate you on the extremely successful Ball last Friday. As you may know, I had several guests from downtown and they enjoyed this opportunity to meet people from the University very much.

Our function became so popular that in 1968, when Joni Chorny was Chairman, the attendance had risen to over 400 with a waiting list. The immense and early success of these functions was due in no small part to the tremendously impressive pictures and flowery language used in a remarkable amount of press publicity. In advance of our third annual Ball, both the *Calgary Herald* and *The Albertan* carried photos of Elizabeth Challice – Ball Chairman – and Jenny Brown and Pat Buckmaster admiring exhibits from the UAC permanent art collection selected for display as part of the Ball theme. That year even our committee meetings were noted in the society columns! Next year in the January 7 edition of *The Albertan*, Eva Reid predicted in her column – The Party Line: "The 1967 version of the University Ball promises to top all social events of the season." A stunning photo of Mussarrat Ariz wearing a beautiful hand-woven midnight blue and silver silk sari, attended in the background by Helen Tavares and Barbara Glyde, caught the attention of social aspirants reading the January 27 edition of *The Albertan* in 1968. One all-encompassing picture of our receiving line appeared in the *Calgary Herald* on February 5, 1968 showing 17 people in all – the titled ones being: Alberta's Lieutenant-Governor Grant MacEwan and his daughter Mrs. Max Foran; Dr. H. S. Armstrong (our President) and Mrs. Armstrong; Alderman Lou Goodwin and Mrs. Goodwin; Chief Justice C. C. McLaurin, University of Calgary Chancellor, and Mrs. McLaurin; and Dr. and Mrs. Malcolm Brown. (Jennie Brown was our club President.)

I am not certain that *all* of our publicity was assigned to the society page. A case in point is the write-up which appeared on page 63 in the Friday, April 26, 1974 edition of the *Calgary Herald.* Our heading, *U of C women taking action for annual ball* (in modest type), was surrounded by an all-embracing article headed (in bold type), *Chastity belt business is booming!*

We sited these 'gala' occasions downtown for seven years, negotiating intensely with the Palliser Hotel and the Calgary Inn. I am reliably told that one of our eminent Past Presidents used to set a meal price with the Palliser, then clarify in a prestigious manner that, as our professors came from all over the world, the menu should reflect a suitable level of gourmet sophistication! The price did not increase but the chef's items on the menu did. As a matter of historic interest, the Hotel in 1964 provided this menu at a cost of $4.25 per person. Quote:

Coquetel Crabe et Crevettes – Sauce Favorite
Essence Madrilène au Sherry
Grenadines of Beef Tenderloin – Béarnaise
Pommes Mignonettes (that meant French fried)
Broccoli Polonaise
Tomate Grillée
Gateaux de Fromages aux Fraises – Chantilly Coffee

Mary Winspear was an admirable negotiator!

In 1971 we took the town to the campus, holding University Ball Number 8 at the Dining Center. The food was a gourmet triumph with cherries jubilee lighting the darkened dining area as they were paraded in by chefs in full attire. Meanwhile the off-campus hired bartenders were getting flambéed on our liquor at the bar in the Blue and Gold Room.

Moving from the hotels to the functional structure of the Dining Centre provided a special challenge for the decorating committees. However, as the balls now took place in April and May, springtime themes of flowers and greenery provided a fresh haven from the still bare spring world outside. A delightful theme of "Sunset and Sea" came close to reality when President Berta Fisher and Ball Chairman Pamela Morrow completed their nautical theme with a 12-foot sailboat used as the main center floor piece. Although the months of careful planning produced an outstanding ball most years, finally the effort was not worth the problems of staff turn-out and break-even budgeting. The Ball was discontinued in 1976 after a survey indicated low response. If we have to recollect on a regrettable change over the years, the demise of our University Ball would be it (in my opinion).

Although the Ball is over, there are some legacies. From an original start on a low budget and the hope we could be financially self-sustaining, the balls soon became such a success that we were able, over the years, to contribute to the University through support of our scholarship fund; the purchase of a complete set of Chronicles of Canada for the library, Canadiana section; art; and funds to the Campus Child Care Co-op.

Norris, p. 9-14

Elephant Stew

Madge Aikenhead

ONE Elephant (medium size)
2 rabbits (optional)
Salt and pepper

Cut the elephant into small bite-size pieces. This should take about two months. Add enough brown gravy to cover. Cook over kerosene fire for about four weeks at 465ºF.

This will serve about 3800 people. If more are expected, two rabbits may be added, but do this only if necessary, as most people do not like to find hare in their stew.

(Lifted from Frankfurt International School H & S recipe book.)

Faculty Women's Club Favorite Recipes (1969). (2)1, p. 3

Madge Aikenhead was a Charter Member and the First President of the Faculty Women's Club. She served as President again ten years later, in 1966.

Women Students at the University of Calgary
Ethel King-Shaw

Anniversaries are a time for nostalgia and remembering highlights from the past. Within the student body the roles and activities have undergone many changes, some perhaps reflecting societal changes and others may be unique to university life.

To put the tremendous growth of the University of Calgary into perspective it is important to note some significant dates. Alberta became a province in 1905. A year later the University of Alberta was formed in Edmonton and Calgary became the home of the Normal School. Two other Normal Schools were established in Edmonton and Camrose. In 1945 Alberta became the first province in Canada to transfer all teacher education to the University of Alberta. At this point the Calgary Normal School became the University of Alberta, Calgary Branch. That is the year I began my program of studies which, at the time, was housed in the Southern Alberta Institute of Technology. Only Education courses were offered in the first year and then students continued on to the University of Alberta in Edmonton. Arts and Sciences courses were added in Calgary soon after.

I returned to accept an appointment to the staff in 1955. Dr. Andrew Doucette was the Director. Courses followed the programs offered at the University of Alberta and, while there was much cooperation, Calgary was not autonomous.

Three years after the University of Alberta was established, the female students formed a group in 1908 which they called "The Wauneita Society." It is believed that the word "Wauneita" is a Cree word meaning "kindhearted." The main purposes of the Wauneita Society were to promote friendly understanding among the campus coeds and to create a spirit of active interest in student affairs. Each faculty elected student representatives. The Wauneita Society was formed in Calgary under the leadership of Miss Mamie Simpson, Dean of Women in Edmonton, but with its own adviser to the Wauneita Society. Mrs. Eunice Hannah, who had worked with the Dean in Edmonton, was appointed initially for a year. On her departure I was asked to assume this role in 1958 which included activities before and after the move to the new campus. Later in 1961, Mrs. Aileen Fish was appointed Advisor to Women Students.

The Calgary girls had their own lounge and their own handbook based on the University of Alberta publication. Each year an initiation ceremony was held for the incoming girls. They all gathered around the campfire as the drums beat loudly. The senior girls led the juniors around the campfire where they each received a feather. These feathers, when crossed, were the symbol of the Wauneita Society. The President then read the initiation ceremony which ended with the motto, "Payuk Uche Kukeyow. Kukeyow Uche Payuk" (Each for all and all for each.)

Calgary students had their version of the Wauneita Song.

> Soft o'er the campus
> Gleam the lights of Calgary
> Home of Wauneitas
> Payuk uche kukeyow
> Kukeyow uche payuk
> This the ancient battlecry
> By the ruddy campfire's glow,
> Neita, Wauneita
> Payuk uche Kukeyow

The little handbook that was given to all women students when they registered included descriptions of some activities including:

1. Big sisters – during the week all women students were phoned by the returning students to welcome them.
2. Wauneita tea – an opportunity to meet other women students, women faculty, and faculty wives. The appropriate dress was a suit or afternoon dress, hat, and gloves.
3. Wauneita initiation – new members were admitted in a tribal ceremony around a campfire. Each one brings her own blanket. Slacks and sweaters are worn.
4. Wauneita formal dance – this is the social highlight of the year and the girls invite the boys. No corsages are worn but boutonnieres are provided by the Wauneita Society. Dress is semiformal.
5. Several Christmas activities, including a benefit drive for needy families, were annual events.

The Faculty Women's Club which included faculty women and faculty wives was formed in 1956. Faculty wives supported the Wauneita Society in many ways, notably serving as honorary president or patrons at social functions. Later the Club raised money for scholarships for deserving students.

To read the Wauneita Handbook today is to realize how much social conventions have changed in the last half century. The rules of etiquette outlined might either be applauded or scorned in some social circles today: introductions, receiving lines, formal dinners, writing formal and informal invitations, letters of thanks, and even appropriate wording to accompany a corsage.

The first Wauneita tea on the new campus was held in September 1960. Unfortunately the electricity went off and boiled water had to be carried from a laboratory to the Lounge. There were rumors of the infamous "tunnel of love" between the first two buildings on campus. Some activities had a short life but others were so popular that they became traditions such as Bermuda

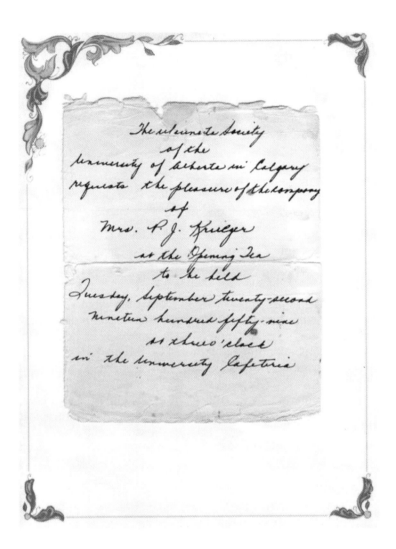

Requesting the Pleasure of Your Company

Shorts Day. These examples are just a few of many anecdotes that alumni share at reunions.

Associated with most of these activities there were many human interest stories, many of them suggesting that some students were adjusting to life away from home for the first time, to testing just how different university was than high school.

In the early 1960s the Wauneita tradition began to fade away and one could speculate on many reasons for this. Some would say there was a growing awareness of the political implications of the ceremonial significance of another culture. Others would say it was the so-called sexual revolution of that decade or the feminist movement. The role of the advisor to the Wauneita Society became one of Advisor to Women Students.

Prior to autonomy, faculty devoted a lot of time serving as advisors to student organizations. After the University of Calgary became autonomous, course offerings expanded greatly and included the addition of graduate programs. More students from foreign countries added to the diversity in the student population. Faculty women became more involved in research and in related scholarly organizations. For many faculty women it meant less opportunity to participate in the increasing number of activities of the Faculty Women's Club.

The proportion of female to male students has increased greatly in recent years in many faculties. Increasingly women students were elected to more committees and leadership roles in the Students' Council. Similarly the number of female faculty members has increased significantly in some areas. Opportunities for faculty women continue to increase with the appointments to senior positions in administration followed by the appointments of women as Deans.

The interaction among women students, faculty women, and faculty wives has been ongoing for over fifty years from involvement in social activities, assisting at convocation, providing scholarships, and perhaps, in some small way, encouraging the development of leadership skills.

From the inherited traditions of the University of Alberta, numerous changes have occurred to the University of Calgary during the last forty years. From the Wauneita Lounge to the newly open Women's Resource Centre there are new roles, resources, responsibilities, and challenges from women students. Interaction among women on campus may still be guided by the traditional motto:

"Each for all and all for each."

Ethel King-Shaw is a Charter Member and was an Honorary Co-President for the Faculty Women's Club Golden Anniversary year, 2006-2007.

A Woman of Firsts

Memory Maker: Ethel King-Shaw

Ethel King-Shaw was the first woman to receive full professorship at the U of C, the first advisor to female students, and the first woman elected to the General Faculties Council.

Years earlier, she was one of the first students in what would eventually become the U of C.

In 1945, fresh out of high school, King-Shaw enrolled in education at the newly launched Calgary Branch of the University of Alberta.

After graduating in 1949, she returned to the U of C as a faculty member in the 1950s and was there when the university received autonomy in 1966. "We weren't locked into the traditions of older universities," King-Shaw recalls. "We were very receptive to innovation. It was a good place to test out new ideas."

Education Dean Dr. Annette LaGrange was one of King-Shaw's students. "Her care and attention to me as a student has served as a model as I work with my own graduate students," she says.

King-Shaw says the growth of the university was a foregone conclusion. "From the beginning of when Alberta was a province, Calgary wanted a university. Its growth has been amazing – but it was not unexpected."

Reprinted with generous permission from University of Calgary: Frazer-Harrison, A. (Spring 2006). Memory Makers. U *magazine, p. 27*

Places Imagined / Place à l'imagination
Gisèle Villeneuve

La folle du logis

Let me tell you the story of la folle du logis. The madwoman of the house.

The house where she lives is in perfect order. Picture her storming through the rooms, upsetting everything. Something compels you to follow her, but soon, you catch yourself tidying up. You still hear her, up and down the stairs of past centuries, back to the present, off to the future, at times, light on her feet, often, staggering.

Throughout the ages, she has been much maligned. She's been gagged, oh gagged so many times we lost count. She's been vilified, mocked, imprisoned, raped. She's been hanged, shot, hacked to death, burned at the stake.

She is maddening, la folle du logis. No matter how often she is pushed underground, she rises back, fresh and strong as the day she was born. How is it possible?

Despite so many enemies ready to strike, she has always been surrounded by armies of champions. Everywhere, many gave their lives for her and yet, new champions continue to close ranks around her. Without them, she would lie dormant. She would atrophy, crumble to ashes and disappear forever.

How did she acquire that name? La folle du logis. Is she truly a mad-woman?

Meet the man who baptized her: Nicolas Malebranche. A seventeenth century French philosopher and theologian. The same year he is ordained priest, he discovers Descartes. Descartes is a fine fellow, right? *Cogito, ergo sum* and all that. We have no quarrel with Monsieur Descartes. However, Monsieur Malebranche, lui, soon distances himself from Descartes to get closer to God.

In his own brand of Cartesian philosophy, he states that God is the only true will in nature and the only one from which everything derives mechanically. Our own will, debased by the original sin, is the source of our mistakes and passions. Only Christ and the love of immutable order shall free our minds.

Can you hear him? Nicolas, hard as nails, God firmly on his side: "Rational mind. Order! Order!" Can you see the womanphoenix striding toward him from the other side of his well-ordered house? Can you see the casuist in black robes, meeting her in all her glorious flesh, ready to strike? She hasn't a hope in hell. Now, she disturbs his dreams. She makes him feel. Feel! "Mon Dieu! Non!" She shows him worlds from within, worlds not so mechanically ordered anymore. She shows him what? The true nature of his desire! "Mon Dieu! Quelle horreur!"

He is terrified. The seductress. He is angry. The witch. It has to stop. How? Let's declare her mad. She is, anyway, n'est-ce pas? Folle! Folle! Folle! Sabotaging God's beautiful, mechanical order. Let's brand her la folle du logis. Then let's execute her. No trial, not even a little inquisition. This is urgent.

Gag her. Burn her. Scatter her to the four winds. Bon débarras. End of story.

End of stories.

Fiction Feindre Mensonge To Lie

La folle du logis, you guessed it, is Malebranche's metaphor for imagination. Such a derogatory coinage implies that imagination is untrustworthy, while logic is the cornerstone of sanity. That brings us one step closer to fiction writing, or storytelling, such as the novel, the novella, the short story, theatre, poetry and sundry related genres, which is imagination's domain par excellence. We are entering uncharted territory indeed.

In his *Dictionary of Literary Terms and Literary Theory*, Cuddon defines fiction as "a vague and general term for an imaginative work, usually in prose," adding that it is "moulded and contrived – or feigned." An unfortunate quirk of language that the word fiction, closely related to lie or mensonge in the old meaning, should label such a creative act. Notre pauvre folle du logis is twice bedevilled. First, la fiction and l'imagination, both feminine nouns in French, are as irremediably linked as conjoined twins; second, they share dubious credentials, one a liar, the other insane. To add insult to injury, not only do we pit imagination against logic, lie against truth, but also we deny works of the imagination their place in the "real" world. Constantly, readers and not a few journalists want to know what, in fiction, is real.

L'imaginaire as opposed to la réalité. As if imagination was not real. I choose to refer to the real world as the concrete world. Hence, the word real can be applied to fiction writing, as well as non-fiction writing, to rational mind and imaginative mind.

However, creative writers themselves are caught in the tug-of-war between rational mind and imaginative mind. Even in our most heroic efforts to break free from conventions, text escapes to realign itself with logical order through at least a modicum a linear narrative, chronology, memory/history.

We waver between the subversion of and the faithfulness to memory. We are in an agony of choice between storytelling, the privileged place of imagination, and the need to state the facts of history/memory – what is "real" – as ordered by the inquisition court: the truth, the whole truth.

Why presume that telling stories is the same as telling lies? To tell a lie, we must have the intention to deceive. When fiction is written, the contract between writer and reader is clear: I, the writer, am telling you, the reader, a story which is the gateway to another world.

Story is the house of imagination, not a lie, not falsehood. Imagination bores through the concrete world to expose its many layers, rich with meaning and correlations not immediately apparent on the surface. Without the solid world, imagination cannot exist; without imagination, the concrete world remains as dull as a finance committee meeting. Finally, let me reassure the proponents of the "real" world that telling stories does not lead to madness.

The Enigma of Arrival

Rewind September 1st, 1978. Three a.m. Calgary.

Tom picks me up at the airport in his second-hand red Beetle. We arrive at the corner of our street in University Heights. The area is cordoned off, police cruisers flashing, police officers in full alert mode. "Where are you going?" one of them demands. "Home. Just up the street." "Okay, drive through and stay inside." "What's going on?" "There's a shooting in progress."

Welcome West, young woman. The basic facts of the incident of my arrival in Calgary belong to history. They are committed to memory. But history can be interpreted in countless ways and memory, that unreliable entity, will reweave endlessly the threads of story. For instance, the dialogue above cannot be accurate since I did not carry a tape recorder that night of my arrival.

Leap of faith or leap of imagination? Gunfight at the U.H. Corral may have been a quaint welcoming to the land of cowboys and other misfits, but Montréal also has its established gunslingers, there, gang related, especially in the glory days of the local Mafia. The point is: I landed with a minimum of luggage. I came here with an uncluttered mind. Travel light and allow the place to work itself into the creative mind.

Québécois Abroad

Fast-forward. Fall 1991. Between referendums. From Calgary, revisiting the place of origin.

For many Québécois, "abroad" means everywhere outside Québec, including the rest of Canada (ROC). At home, to protect themselves from the perceived threats of other cultures, they have created a close-knit society where language acts as a fortress, and where the dicta of the social contract laid first by the Catholic Church, then by the state, have nurtured their fear of the unknown, represented by everything foreign. That is history.

Nevertheless, when I left Montréal in 1974 to roam the world, I rarely encountered Québécois. Should I meet them, I presumed I would find my compatriots in enclaves around the old church steeple, as was the custom with French-Canadian pionniers, in Western Canada, at the turn of the last century. My perception changed when I started to meet Québécois in Calgary shortly after my arrival.

They came to work and to live a different experience. They came with an open mind and as individuals, not as emissaries of a cultural group. They elected to live in various parts of the city, whether other French-speaking people were established in those neighbourhoods or not. They participated in the cultures of the many without fear of losing their identity. If they attended cultural events in French, they did so for their own pleasure and interest, not to wage a crusade for survival.

Québécois form a curious ethnic group. At home, they follow, often passionately, the political, social and cultural trend du jour, at the expense of their individuality and without questioning their place in the larger picture. Outside their natural habitat, they regain their freedom of expression, which enables them to form strong bonds with non French-speaking people. As dogmatic as they can be at home, they are well-liked in other countries, because they don't seek to convert others to their point of view.

The contemporary Québécois living abroad remind me of the ancient voyageurs who explored the uncharted regions of North America. On their travels, those early French Canadians recovered their true sense of independence and their spirit of discovery – letting loose, at it were, la folle du logis living within – that had been gagged by the rigid society of their day. They did not fear to lose their culture, but sought new knowledge and learned to speak many native languages.

It is often dans l'ailleurs, in those places imagined, that the expression of self surfaces best. Félix Leclerc – whose international career as a Québécois folk singer was launched in Paris, not in Montréal, in the early nineteen fifties – wrote, in his 1961 book of maxims, *Le calepin d'un flâneur*, that we leave our country for the same reasons we leave our father's house.

The Proposal

Rewind. April 1978. We were living in Ottawa when Tom landed a position as assistant professor in the Chemistry Department at the University of Calgary. We had been together for seven years, living in Montréal, travelling through Asia, then working in London, England, before moving to the capital. Of Calgary, I knew nothing. A place barely imagined somewhere at the edge of the world. A place for me? What was I going to do there? For twenty-four hours, I went into a catatonic state of deep reflection, not sleeping, not eating, simply sitting in a dark room and imagining a place called Calgary with me in it. Or not.

After such a mental marathon, Tom felt that I needed sustenance. A steak would do nicely, so he took me to a restaurant. I have no recollection of the place. We ate our entire meal in perfect silence. A young couple, visibly in love, was sitting at the table next to ours. They were in a good mood, but we could tell they had not failed to notice our dour silence. No doubt, they thought we had had a fight and were now seething with anger. Any moment, we would explode into a fit of rage. They were bracing for the impact.

Our coffee arrived at the same time as theirs. I took a sip and said to Tom: "If I'm going to Calgary with you, it means I'd probably go anywhere in the world with you. We might as well get married."

The young man at the next table nearly choked on his coffee.

This is story recollected. In story imagined, a character choking on his drink in surprise has become such a cliché that, to work in a good piece of fiction writing, it would have to be deleted or carefully redrawn in order to subvert the readers' expectations.

Fast-forward to the here and now. Remembering the 1978 anecdote of the proposal, an image comes to mind. I imagine a two-year-old Czech boy escaping with his parents, in 1949, the newly communist country of his recent birth and establishing himself in Montréal, the city in which I had yet to be born. History, the big one, intersects our personal history and we meet as young adults across the French/English divide still prevalent in the Montréal of the early 1970s. The odds of such events ever occurring are staggering.

Eight years following that improbable encounter in a Montréal bar, Calgary loomed unimaginable on the far horizon. Recollecting that April evening in 1978, in the no-name Ottawa restaurant, I am glad I had the good sense of not throwing out the Czech baby with the bathwater of my trepidation.

First Landing

Rewind. July 1978. Calgary. Gorgeous weather. The Stampede, a distant thunder.

Gazing at the famous big sky, I declared: "Oui. I can live here."

Despite the boom – one of many – we quickly found and rented a town-house in University Heights. I still had a few days left before flying back to Ottawa to finish a contract. Tom would be staying, as his appointment began in August.

We had a rental car, time on our hands, so we drove farther west.

We saw the Rockies.

If Calgary then could not be imagined, the mountains became for us the dwelling place of imagination constantly renewed.

Job Connection

I had been freelancing as a writer, translator and researcher in Ottawa, our previous port of call. Freelancing suited my temperament very well. So, I wanted to continue the practice in the land of oil and money. First contract: a six-month job with Com/Media at the university. I worked as a researcher assigned to a weekly public affairs television program produced on campus.

In this city of confluence, where so many come from elsewhere, I discovered a connection with an earlier port of call.

Rewind. London, 1974-1976. I was working for English by Radio, a department of the BBC's World Service. I proposed an idea for a series of radio dramas to the program director, an easy-going Scot who pretty well gave me carte blanche to write and produce my own series, inviting me to use the resources at hand.

Fast-forward. University of Calgary. At my job interview, the director of the weekly television program in wild west Calgary, a Welshman, told me that he had worked for the BBC in England. He knew the Scottish man who had given me my first chance at writing for professional radio.

The Big Question

Rewind. The early years. "What brought you here?" "Pourquoi êtes-vous venue en Alberta?" Mirror-image questions in our bisected Canadian tongue.

In the early years, in a bar in English or in interviews in French, the standard question kept recurring, asked like an accusation. As if landing in Calgary was a sin. As if the place was unworthy of consideration. You lived in London! Why come here? In French, of course, the question was: pourquoi ne pas vivre à Paris?

Nobody ever asked Gertrude Stein or Hemingway why they lived in Paris. Nobody questioned Anne Hébert's wisdom when she moved to the French capital in the early 1960s and stayed for thirty years. Or Mavis Gallant and so many other writers.

Paris, New York, London; the classic cities. So much so that they have become clichés. Or for a touch of exotica, Hong Kong perhaps, or Tangier. Think about Jane and Paul Bowles. But Calgary? As a Montréal friend – a writer and producer – told me years ago when I persisted in staying: "Il n'y a rien là." For her who had never ventured here, it was obvious that I lived in a cultural desert. For Calgary to work itself into people's imagination, people's expectations first had to be subverted.

Simply put: the mythology of the place had yet to be invented by novelists and poets, filmmakers and storytellers, in songs and in visual arts. Slowly, Calgary is being written. Slowly, the place imagined is rising.

In the early years, whenever I returned to Montréal for a visit, miscellaneous Montréalais were equally flummoxed. "Comment peux-tu vivre là-bas?" I forged a standard answer: "Je prends ce qui m'intéresse et j'ignore le reste." I did not arrive in Calgary with a suitcase full of comparisons. I was not living here to reproduce what I had left behind. No excess bagage.

Fast-forward. 1988. The Winter Olympic Games. People stopped asking the big question. The final education of the Easterners was completed when the media covering the Olympics explained the chinook to them.

What were they perceiving? The chinook captured their imagination. A wind of good fortune was blowing warm. Les Québécois, along with so many from other cultures, have since been flocking here in greater and greater numbers.

Fast-forward. Since 2000, I routinely hear Québécois French spoken on the street, in stores, on campus and, particularly, in the mountains. Nobody asks pourquoi anymore.

A Friends Factory

Rewind and play. Making lifelong friends in the city by the Bow has always been easy. The process began shortly after my arrival with my first contract at the university and has continued ever since through other contracts in the city, various workshops and university creative writing courses. Calgary's mood makes it possible to meet like-minded people from around the world and with whom we are instantly on a first-name basis, a curious phenomenon belonging to Alberta and often remarked upon by newcomers. I surmise that we connect along the margin of imagination, in a place that we are all building with the bits and pieces of treasures we brought from elsewhere. But without, in my experience, the excess bagage.

Fast-forward. In the last few years, comments from newcomers have surprised me: "I can't find friends here. People are straight-laced here." That remark came from a fellow writer, a woman working downtown, surrounded by, to use Auden's words, "the short-haired mad executives" running amok in the city core canyons.

Or this: "If you talk to someone in a café, he looks at you funny." From a young teacher used to chat strangers up in her native Québec without anyone taking umbrage.

Interesting, because in Calgary, connections happen like nowhere else I've lived.

Rewind. In 2004, I was attending an international literary festival in Montréal. A Québécois man chatted me up (I took no umbrage!). He told me he knew three people in Calgary. Jokingly, I asked him who they were, I might know them. In a city of one million people, what were the odds . . . Eh bien! Of the three people he knows in Calgary, I know two of them!

Writing

I came with my partner. Side by side. Not like une pionnière reluctantly following her husband, tripping in the folds of her long skirt. I came here to write. To rearrange the song a little: if I can write in Calgary, I can write anywhere. That was the conclusion I reached back in 1978 that led to the famous marriage proposal. Bring pen and paper and carry only the essential, not the entire household. Let la folle du logis loose in the city and the mountains. Sooner or later, this place will course through your bloodstream into your unfettered mind. Then you can recreate it as place imagined.

Rewind. 1987. When I read "The Journey," the second section in V.S. Naipaul's *The Enigma of Arrival,* I was astounded to discover so many similarities between the author's experience as an Indian born and raised in Trinidad and my own experience as a Francophone growing up in Québec. (Although *The Enigma of Arrival* is billed as a novel, I have always read it as a scrutiny of self; the writer's progress thinly disguised as fiction, but certainly greatly enriched by his creative mind.)

On the surface, our worlds should never have meshed. V.S. Naipaul grew up on a tiny island in a remote corner of the British empire; I grew up in the second largest country in the world, with Québec alone being three times larger than France. V.S. Naipaul was schooled in English; I in French. He shouldered the ancient culture of India, which was often at odds with his formal English education; I, on the other hand, had no sense of cultural genealogy as a North American, a situation further confused by references in the classroom to our short-circuited connection to France.

Cependant, these differences in upbringing between Naipaul and me are inconsequential compared with our shared progress; unknowingly, as individuals we travelled the same road, because as individuals we struggled to extirpate ourselves from inherited cultures that failed to provide answers.

Naipaul writes of himself: "He was close to the village ways of his Asian-Indian community. [. . .] Yet there was another side to the man: he did not really participate in the life or rituals of that community. [. . .] Unhappy in his extended family, he was distrustful of larger, community groupings."

Although raised in Montréal, I could have lived in a small village, so uncosmopolitan was our life then. But most importantly, at an early age, I too became deeply suspicious of a society that trained us in the fear of living. Ideas, initiative and creativity were all duly discouraged, whereas intellectual limbo was elevated to a desirable goal.

To that effect, I share Naipaul's distress over the unavailability of books in his hometown. To him the iron roofs of the general stores that sold but a few books became a metaphor for his sense of isolation. In the Montréal of my childhood, books of substance were banned in the name of religion. Until the age of sixteen, we were prohibited access to the adult section of our public libraries. French-speaking Québécois had access to fewer public libraries than English-speaking Quebeckers. And so, in my Montréal disguised as a village, we lived in a rarified atmosphere where our own depleted stores reaffirmed our colonialism of the mind.

At the age of eighteen, Naipaul left Trinidad to study in England and to become a writer. I too elected to live in London for a while, although my trajectory as a writer took a very different arc. Until his arrival in London, since his formal education failed to reflect his personal life, V.S. Naipaul rejected as trivial any theme connected with his tropical island. As he puts it, "And then this idea of abstract study had been converted into an idea of a literary life in another country."

I too wanted to become a writer, but my background never provided me with suitable material. If I failed to decode the elements of memory, if I failed to chart its inner landscape, I blamed our formal education, which emphasized French culture, while belittling Québec cultural and social life. Indeed, the latter occupied so trivial a place in our schooling that we were turned into cultural living dead. Therefore, like V.S. Naipaul, I was looking toward un ailleurs to create a whole cultural identity from which to write.

Ironically, but perhaps not, in my novels, short stories, plays, radio works, in French or in English, now that I was living in the place imagined, I ended up writing exactly about that which had been hidden when I was still living in the place of origin. This land between mountains and prairie affords the wild mind the long view, the necessary distance of geography to explore, unimpeded.

Today, every ethnic group throughout the world shouts over the rooftops how different it is from its neighbour; how partition is the only solution against extinction; how the memory – real or sometimes fabricated – of past humiliation calls for redress. Québec has not escaped this agitation over cultural assertiveness, this obsession with extinction, no more than Naipaul's Trinidad had many years ago.

However, while I am not advocating a worldwide monolithic culture, I believe that, in the words of V.S. Naipaul, "a political stimulus, a communal rhetoric of sentimentality and anger" manipulates those various cultural entities into emancipation with complete disregard to the much deeper similarities that unite us. We must be strong enough to sustain exposure without losing our own cultural personality, flexible enough to welcome influences from abroad, and yet wise enough to recognize that cultural mélange is vital to enhancing our humanity.

Of Exile and Exogamy

Words that had never entered my vocabulary. Fast-forward. I recently learned that exogamy is an object of serious research at the national level in this country. In that context, those of us who have married outside our cultural/linguistic milieu are said to live in a state of exogamy. As in a state of mortal sin? Or as to live with a terminal illness? That turn of phrase sounds suspiciously like labelling imagination the madwoman of the house and less like a freeing of the human spirit. As for exile, I am grateful that I am not acquainted with it.

Library Days

Rewind. In the early days, the university library was open to all in the community, free of charge. During my six-month contract assigned to the television program, I often haunted the floors of the library. Borrowing plenty of books. Acquiring knowledge through the works of countless authors. Searching my way through forests of facts, rivers of words, oceans of imaginary worlds. I sought to discover how to tell stories my own way and in a voice that could accommodate two languages, now beckoning.

When the contract ended, I continued to borrow books, free of charge. Until a convergence of bust, budget cuts, ill-conceived politics, a general gagging of imagination and creativity on the hill in favor of "deliverables" turned the library into a place where knowledge was no longer freely accessible.

Fast-forward. Nevertheless, I still find solace within its crowded rooms – crowded with students who have no concept of silence in such a place and with more and more books and no more shelves on which to stack them. I find solace especially in summer when the student body is greatly reduced and blissful silence returns to la grande bibliothèque. When gardeners yielding horticultural tools from hell shatter the quiet days of summer in my neighbourhood, making writing at home impossible, the library then is un havre de paix.

Landscape and Cityscape

Play. In *Places Far From Ellesmere,* Aritha van Herk labels Calgary "this growing graveyard." This, the city I agreed to enter when, thirty years ago in an Ottawa restaurant, I made a pact with my beloved.

Calgary, the Rockies. The place, concrete and imagined, has changed the blood chemistry. From afar, stories stored in the genes started to form. I wrote them all here, from first novel in French to the latest one in English spiced with French, a hybrid of languages and cultures that continues to modulate my writer's voice. It is dans l'ailleurs d'ici, in this place of light and vast spaces that imagination has been growing wild and free, but not mad.

Toward an Ending – Imagining a Remote Future

Recording in progress. The fast-growing city ever since the first tent was pitched by a barkeep or a land speculator or a prostitute or a preacher. The fast city of stone and black gold, graveyards and businesses. A city compressed along its frenzied trajectory, dangerously wound up.

The Tower on the Hill, a lot worse for wear. Tightly moored southward to Calgary's corporate downtown, northward to Edmonton's wanton governance, the Tower, à la recherche of its lost identity where joyous creativity and intellectual rigour – not rigor mortis – should fill the daily agenda. The Tower, where the binary mind should coalesce, not rational mind and imaginative mind circle each other in a gunslingers' showdown. Leap of faith or leap of imagination?

Speaking of imagination, let's go find la folle du logis one last time. She's still here, roaming rooms and streets, rushing up staircases and across courtyards, scaling the landscape, excavating, weaving meanings, turning everything upside down, challenging expectations. Don't be too quick tidying up. Look at her! She's wearing nothing at all. But look carefully. She's carrying whole worlds. Ignoring Nicolas Malebranche cowering in the corner, caressing his mechanical order, she is transmuting from lead into platinum those places that live in our collective memory into the scintillating places of the imagination.

Beginning of stories.

References

Auden, W.H. "The Climbers" in *The Collected Poetry of W.H. Auden.* New York: Random House, 1945.

Cuddon, J.A. *The Penguin Dictionary of Literary Terms and Literary Theory.* London: Penguin Books, fourth edition, 1998.

Leclerc, Félix. *Le calepin d'un flâneur.* Montréal: Fides, 1961. In this 1971 edition, the original quote (on p. 59) reads: "On quitte son pays pour les mêmes raisons qu'on quitte la maison de son père."

Naipaul, V.S. *The Enigma of Arrival.* London: First published by Viking, 1987. Penguin Books, 1987.

van Herk, Aritha. *Places Far From Ellesmere. A Geografictione: Exploration on Site.* Red Deer: Red Deer College Press, 1990.

Nose Hill: The Hill That is Shaped Like a Nose
Karen Gummo

Nose Hill has a distinctive profile in the northwestern corner of Calgary. Gaze north and eastward when you cross over Crowchild Trail on Charleswood Drive on a fall afternoon, when the winds have pushed dark grey-blue clouds above, and the setting sun highlights the golden undulating hill. Golden slopes set against a smoky blue sky catch my attention. Winding pathways beckon. Soft copses of aspen huddle in humility along the way. I see subtle hues of mauves, taupes, faint and deep greens and golds in patches gently stitched together. There is a figure on the hill! It is a single wanderer. How is it up on the Nose, I wonder?

I want to go there too. If I follow the wagon trail made by early travellers, I would soon find myself in another world. Early travellers such as my great grandparents, Ofeigur Sigurdsson and Astridur Tomasdottir likely made their way up that hill seeking their new Valhalla, their promised land. I wonder if they stopped to look back at the wide open river valley and the long line of mountains stretching westward and northward? The river valley looked a little different in 1889 without the wide expanse of newly planted trees, not to mention the ever expanding built landscape that we see now.

Ofeigur and Astridur were headed on foot to the Tindastoll and Markerville area north of the Red Deer River. They would join other Icelanders there. They would make the territory not far from the Medicine River their final home, after much searching and travelling. But Ofeigur was lured back to the Nose Creek Valley in the summers of 1890 and 1891 to earn some much needed cash.

He made the four to five-day journey on foot to the Nose Creek Valley to work as a sheep shearer in the spring and then took his flock of sheep over the prairie hills to find good pastureland and to protect them from predators. He worked as a shepherd for three to four months and then walked home again with a little pay in his pocket and groceries for the family slung across his back.

One day, I'll make a pilgrimage and try to trace his footsteps. For now, I have the hill to wander. It is a place where I can make a connection with the earth and with those who came before me.

One of the things that I love to do on Nose Hill is to pick saskatoons. Since my forbearers for many generations were people who lived off the land and who out of necessity picked wild berries and preserved them for the winter so that they could get much needed vitamins and nutrients, berry picking has been a vital task. I am happy to keep up the tradition. What follows is my tribute to the work of gathering saskatoons. It starts with a little song, or a chorus. You can sing it if you like. It came to me on a hot July day, not long ago.

Saskatoons, oh saskatoons!
Time to go a berrying with Marion today!

How do we find the berries?
We follow the path.
Sunny faces of gaillardia beckon
Look for the pink pincushion Bee Balm
Long lanky lupines
Their cups of blue hanging on until new beans
Push them off.

Saskatoons, oh saskatoons
Time to go a berrying with Marion today!

Ant hills frantic with activity,
The very best saskatoons grow over top.
Forgot your berry picking boots?
Sandals on bare feet?
Hope your toes aren't ticklish,
Or you'll be doing the berry picking dance,
The syncopated Saskatoon sashay!

Saskatoons, oh saskatoons,
Time to go a berrying with Marion today!

Those ants are biters
I throw them the odd berry
In recompense.

Fall's Final Glory – *Karen Gummo*

I don't mean to trample their homes.
The lure of succulent berries just takes over.
Rains have been plentiful
The sun shines down brilliantly.
Green berries turn to red then to purple.

Saskatoons, oh saskatoons,
Time to go a berrying with Marion today!

cont.

Fingers reach out for perfect berries, the ones that pop easily
   off the stem.
Under that leaf is a beauty,
Oh, there's another under my nose.
Close up and far away. . . .
How is your depth perception?
Peripheral vision is always needed.
"Pick me! Pick me!" the ripest berries say.
And I do.

Saskatoons, oh saskatoons,
Time to go a berrying with Marion today...

Who is Marion?
You ask?
She is the one who shows me the way
To the very sweetest berries.
Thank you Marion.
Because of you I am singing a Saskatoon solo tune

Saskatoons, oh saskatoons,
Time to go a berrying with Marion today!

So what about you?
Are you a berry picker?
Seeker of sweet treasures?
God's gift to those who embark on the hunt?
Nose Hill is ever generous with offers of tranquility, beauty, and sweet
fruits. I am grateful, and willing to share the gifts that I find with
friends and beasts alike. Come with me sometime!

A Mother's Verse

Victoria Reid

My husband, David Reid, and I immigrated to Canada from Belfast in
1968 and there was rarely a week, until David's mother, Meta Mayne Reid,
died in 1990, that long letters were not exchanged. She lived for the sound
of the postman pushing mail through her door. Most people dislike writing letters, but she anticipated joyfully when she could steal time from a busy schedule to write to the myriad of friends and acquaintances she had around the
world. She liked to tell us that she wrote almost 500 letters a year, and not
short jottings, but long detailed celebrations of the ordinary details of her life
– such as the contents of the compost pile – which leaped into life on the end
of her Biro, making the ordinary extraordinary. As a busy housewife, garden-
er, community activist, caregiver to her father, and mother, like Mary Pratt who
painted what was in her kitchen, a carton of eggs or fish on tinfoil, Meta wrote
about what she experienced in her day to day activities.

She once wrote:

We travel not at all
we do not socialize
nor entertain the great
I nourish myself on trifles
I wait for the roving cat
To roll on sun warmed flags
Beseeching a caress
Upon his ermine pelt.
I listen to the collared dove
As he coos and ruffles on the roof.
Such things are now my bread.

Or, in another poem:

I have not fought the barricades
nor taken a dozen lovers
I live in landscapes of my own contriving.

. . .

Oh yes I want happiness
but my true needs are different
the unlikely, the unreachable,
the bird who sings far out of sight
the fish who darts into depths
which I cannot fathom.

On another occasion, she said, "from such small things spring a story, which with a little good fortune may find a resting place on the printed page, then in the reader's mind." So it was not surprising that when in answer to a weekly letter with details of our life in Calgary, the changes of the seasons, or flora and fauna in our back yard, she would respond with a poem such as "After Receiving a Canadian Letter," printed here.

Meta and David, my husband, were very close and shared a passion for mountains and all things living and breathing (not humans especially). When she was dying and David was to climb Mount Kilimanjaro, she insisted that he not cancel the trip. The day he returned from Africa he was at her bedside where he held her hand and talked for hours about the beauty of the mountain and its plants and animals. She refused to die until she had heard every last detail of the climb. She was living through his words and died content. Through her imagination and David's vivid description, she bridged the gap between Tanzania and a Northern Ireland hospice. She *was* in Africa. Just as when David wrote of the Canada geese, she actually *saw* them. Such is the power of the well written and well spoken word.

So from Northern Ireland to a Bowness backyard is not so very far at all, is it?

After Receiving a Canadian Letter
Meta Mayne Reid, May 1982

I have never seen
the migrating geese
upon your garden shore,
which the Bow River sweeps,
as, fed by glacier snow,
it hustles winter ice.

Yet, in my mind's eye
they stand clear cut as cameos.
Had another told the tale
imagination would not have stirred
upon her lazy bed.

The geese like snowflakes,
would have melted in the flood.
You are the sorcerer
who prints the scene upon my retina.

The birth-cord, cut so long ago,
still, willy-nilly, carries messages.
What you see, widens my eyes,
what you hear, rings in my ears.

Your geese - my geese -
We share their springtime rituals,
as we share blood and birth.

Not a Tree in Sight!
Josephine Prescott

We arrived in Calgary from Australia in 1961. At that time the University was still a branch of the University of Alberta and Calgary was just beginning to expand. As my husband said, the campus looked like an abandoned airfield. There was not a tree in sight! We were able to build a house within sight of the University; I could put the vegetables on to cook when my husband's office light went out.

The academic staff of the Physics Department consisted of Professor C.E. Challice, Fred Terentiuk, Harvey Buckmaster, and Brian Wilson. Our three children were the only ones of the Department. The Department Head's wife was extremely conscientious in making each newcomer welcome and held Christmas parties for us all. The Faculty Women's Club was, of course, small and it was nice to be able to know people in other disciplines. We certainly supported one another as so many of us were far from former friends and relatives. I remember, particularly, taking food to a sick family, and helping a husband shop for nappies and garments for a new baby. At the time, I did not hold any sort of office in the Women's Club that I remember, largely because I was too busy with other commitments, such as Brown Owl for my daughters' Brownie Pack. For physical exercise I took swimming lessons at the local YMCA since there were no University facilities available at the time. My efforts at skiing or skating were generally regarded with hilarity by my family. This was also part of settling in a new country – even sports were different!

My husband's field of Cosmic Rays meant that he went off to biennial International Conferences around the world, without me at the beginning since I had to mind the children. In 1967 an International Cosmic Ray Conference was held in Calgary. We hosted a barbecue at our house, which was attended by a big contingent of Russians. This experience, followed by others in Plovdiv, Moscow, and Kyoto helped me greatly when, in 1990, the Conference was held in Adelaide, my native city, to which we had returned in 1971. It was my turn to be in charge, as, years ago, someone had done for us. As wife of the Chairman of this Conference, I was responsible for the Women's Program. I will always be grateful to friends and relatives who rallied to my assistance. I had come a long way from the shy faculty wife who had arrived in Calgary from halfway around the world.

We look back to our time in Calgary with pleasure, our daughters speak a hybrid language, and our son remained there. I must admit, however, that I never really adjusted to so much winter!   Now I garden, walk, and play croquet all the year round!

A Bit of a Rebel
Judith Hall

What was life like at the University of Calgary, then UAC or the University of Alberta in Calgary? When I began my studies, attitudes towards the education of women were not the same as they are today. There were only three widely accepted choices: teaching, nursing, and secretarial. Many times I heard, "She's only gone to University to find a husband" or "You'll only get married and have children." Being of a somewhat perverse nature, that only made me more determined to get a degree and not find a husband. Fortunately, my parents supported my decision to attend UAC. When my mother was young, Grade 11 was as far as most people could go. Already more opportunities were opening up for us.

I have always had three main interests in life: art, music, and science. Neither of the first two seemed like a practical way to make a living, and so it was that I registered for a degree in chemistry. It was the fall of 1959, the year before the move to the present campus. UAC occupied the west half of the main SAIT building and two or three army huts located just to the west of it. Times were different. When we registered, we were given a handbook which included precise instructions on how to dress. Some social occasions required a hat and gloves. Girls were not allowed to wear slacks to lectures which meant that the ladies' washroom would be crowded after Phys Ed class, as we quickly changed into skirts so we could attend the following physics lecture. Lab equipment for undergraduates was adequate but basic. When ice was required it was found in the form of snow outside the army hut door.

Most of the students were in education at that time. Classes in the other disciplines were small and girls were scarce in the sciences. There were three of us in chemistry, one in physics, and one in mathematics. Many friendships that have lasted until the present day were made with classmates. It was not possible to complete degrees in Calgary but every year, as I went along, the next year of courses was added, allowing me to graduate from the University of Alberta without ever having gone to Edmonton. This was important to me as I could not afford to go there.

In the fall of 1960, UAC moved to the present campus on the flat, treeless prairie. There were two new buildings, Science and Engineering (Science A) and Arts and Education (Administration Building). When the wind blew there were unpleasant dust storms that we avoided by travelling between buildings through the utility tunnel, even though the practice was frowned upon.

From 1962 to 1964 I was a graduate student in chemistry. As a girl I was totally accepted as part of the group. During these years there was a lot of stress and a lot of fun. The graduate students were a close knit group that socialized and hiked together. Popular diversions were noon hour croquet games on the level expanse of lawn between the two original buildings. (Imagine my surprise on returning several years later to find it all hilly and landscaped.) I have fond memories of field trips to the south end of Barrier Lake with my supervisor. It was there that we would inject delphinium plants with radioactive precursors, tie a ribbon on them, and return to harvest them eight days later. It's hard to imagine now that Kananaskis Country has become a popular recreation area. In those days it was Forest Reserve that one registered in and out of and not very many people visited the area. By this time the campus had grown to four buildings with the addition of a Library and a Physical Education building. The summer of 1964 was quite jarring as the piles for Science B were driven into the ground and that definitely interfered with the balances and other equipment in the laboratory.

For the next few years I lived elsewhere. First I attended the University of British Columbia for three years where I obtained my PhD and, in spite of my resolve, a husband, thus confirming the predictions of many of my parents' generation. It was at UBC that I discovered that girls were unwelcome in chemistry: one professor told me that he did not accept any. Fortunately, the other natural products professor did, but the eleven males in the laboratory made it known that they did not want a girl there. I informed them that I'd only be there for three years. At first they did not speak to me but when I didn't disappear they came around, and by November, I was invited to go fishing with them. From then on, everything was fine. Relief from studies was found in practicing the piano in the music department every day. I had purposely not taken my art supplies with me so that I wouldn't be tempted to spend time painting but my mother sent them out with a friend at Easter the first year and of course, I used them when I should have been studying.

In 1967 we moved to Liverpool, England for two years of postdoctoral studies and in 1969 we relocated to Washington, D.C. where my husband was a visiting scientist at the National Institute of Mental Health in Bethesda. Shortly after arriving there, our first son, Kevin, was born and my daughter-in-law, Debbie Hall, can attest to the fact that he was my next experiment as documented by the "lab" book I kept about him.

In 1971 my connection to the University of Calgary was re-established as I returned as a faculty wife. I became a member of the Faculty Women's Club for a few years, as well as their Book Group and the Babysitting Swap. Both of our sons attended Campus Preschool.

Over the years I worked off and on as a research associate in both the Chemistry and Chemical Engineering Departments but I was never as dedicated a scientist as I suppose I should have been. As I have spent less and less time with Chemistry, my other interests have taken precedence. I am now a professional artist and I have fulfilled a lifelong desire to play the violin. That being said, I have never felt that my education was wasted. The skills I learned can be applied other places and it has helped me to better understand much about the world I live in, to learn on my own, and to think critically.

The association with U of C has continued in our family as both of our sons have studied here. The elder one obtained a BSc and MSc in geophysics. His family has been a member of the Babysitting Swap and both of their children attended Campus Preschool. Our younger son graduated with a BMus. Thus, links continue to be forged, generation after generation.

Looking at the current campus, which continues to expand, I realize the University has come a long way since I attended it. The change is phenomenal. It is wonderful to see that there are more girls in science and engineering, and in many other disciplines. A number of years ago at my High School reunion, I was horrified to see, posted on a display board, an article I had written for the school newspaper about the engineering profession entitled, "For Boys Only." How could I have ever thought such a thing? I may have been a bit of a rebel but I was also obviously influenced by the attitudes of that time.

Otherwise, I might have studied engineering myself.

The Color of Spring – *Judith Hall*

The aspen trees in spring remind me of the little grove of trees where I would go to eat lunch when a student, somewhere near to the current engineering building.

Plastic Wine Glasses

Cathy Wagner

Based on conversations with Polly Knowlton Cockett, Kate Bentley, and Eileen Lohka

It is my pleasure to be included in this publication in celebration of the 50th Anniversary of the University of Calgary Faculty Women's Club (FWC). My husband, Dr. Norman Wagner, was appointed President of the University of Calgary in 1978. We arrived here in August with two teenagers. Before we moved here, my husband was Dean of Graduate Studies at Wilfrid Laurier University. I was pleased to be asked to be Honorary President of the FWC since I had enjoyed my association with the group at Wilfrid Laurier. In those days, very few women worked outside the home. I had three small children at home and really enjoyed getting out for an evening of fellowship and stimulation. When I came to Calgary, I was delighted to know that women faculty members also belonged which was not the case at Wilfrid Laurier.

Every year, in the first week of September, the President would have a welcoming reception for all new faculty and their spouses. In mid September, I would have a welcoming tea at the President's Residence for all new faculty wives and women faculty. The wives of senior administration and the FWC executive would also attend. There were silver tea services at each end of the dining room table. The Dean's wives would rotate with pouring the tea and coffee. Eventually, the first woman dean was appointed as Dean of Nursing. You have to find different ways to connect with community. One difficulty we encountered was the privacy rules in effect at that time (pre-FOIP). I could not easily contact new faculty wives or female faculty directly with an invitation to my welcoming tea. The invitation was sent out with welcoming material given to new faculty. It sometimes got lost or it never went home. Another difficulty in trying to build community!

About thirty-five or forty people would come to most of the regular monthly meetings. I would reiterate what I said earlier, that these meetings were very important for me. I would attend as many as I could because I felt that I was part of the community. There were many times when I couldn't attend because we had other obligations representing the university, but I always enjoyed the meetings very much. FWC had several special interest groups at that time, and some of them continue today. There was Book Club, Hiking Club, and Out to Lunch Bunch which I still attend. Many of the spouses have now retired, and I know these people quite well. The Town and Gown Balls were before our time and there was no longer fundraising going on by the FWC for the University – although we once had a fashion show in which I was involved. We also met with the Faculty Women's Club of the University of Alberta. We invited them here and they invited us back to Edmonton. We used to exchange thoughts because by that time, bit by bit FWC numbers were diminishing because the new people coming in would often be professional women. They didn't feel they either needed FWC or had the time, which I understand. So we thought perhaps we could get some fresh ideas from each other. At that time we were still having monthly meetings in the evening in the Faculty Club. On occasion, I would invite the executive to meet at the President's Residence for their meetings.

Since then, FWC is no longer as visible on campus. For example, space for meetings in my time wasn't an issue. I really don't remember that we had any hassle – space was there and it was available. We always had permission to meet in the Faculty Club, which was then in the Social Sciences Building. I understand that the arrangements when Anne Fraser and Sue White were Honorary Presidents enabled FWC to use a room at the Olympic Volunteer Centre. Since they have recently renovated, this arrangement is no longer available for FWC, nor for the Emeritus Association.

When I came here in 1978, I think what was expected of me was mainly entertaining and we did rather a lot of that. My husband and I always hosted a reception in June for members of the General Faculties Council (GFC) and their spouses. We tried garden parties for several years because it was too large to accommodate everyone in the house, but unfortunately, June is a rainy month in Calgary, so we reluctantly moved to the Blue Room in the Dining Centre. Following the final GFC meeting came Convocation a week or so later. I always loved attending these, and I never missed one in ten years. I usually sat with the families of the Honorary Degree Recipients; I always thought Convocations were wonderful ceremonies.

Every institution has different customs. I was so appreciative of the help and guidance of many people when I first arrived. I was used to hosting and entertaining. My husband always had his students to our house once a year (to eat us out of house and home I might add). When he became Dean of Graduate Studies, we also held receptions and dinners at our home.

Before coming to Calgary I worked at the Wilfrid Laurier University Press. My hours were flexible enough that I could work during my children's school hours. When we came here I did not pursue my career but became more involved in volunteer work. There were also times when I informally represented the University since my husband had to attend another function.

Nowadays, hosting functions for the University is a complex job involving many people. I think a lot of large companies are finding the same thing. The federal government is selling off a lot of the ambassadors' residences because they are no longer used for receptions. It's now dinners in clubs, or receptions in hotels. There is an organization called the Council of Universities and Colleges of Canada. They meet once a year, rotating around universities in Canada. At one point one of the president's wives suggested we have an informal discussion to compare notes on what is done in each other's university. It was most educational. I discovered that there were several president's wives who actually had contracts and they were paid x number of dollars for the duties that they performed.

When I entertained, I was not necessarily reimbursed for all my expenses. There was some equipment that belonged to the university, some dishes for example, but most of the stuff was mine, even the tea towels. But it was catered by University Food Services. They would come with their big truck and bring in the food and a bartender. There was enough room in the house to accommodate about sixty people for a stand up reception. For a sit down dinner I used to spread people all over the house, in front of the fire, in a small dining room, and then we could accommodate about thirty-five. I much prefer sit down dinners. I am very old fashioned. I would have them served, with someone to pour the wine instead of plopping the wine bottle on the table. That was all paid for, and part of our budget. There was, however, wear and tear on our personal things, e.g., broken dishes and glasses. There was one cupboard that housed university stuff and it had plates, cutlery (which was brass and had to be polished all the time!), a few serving bowls, cups and saucers, and plastic wine glasses!!!

As to the university house, it was taxable. Many people think that as it was owned by the University, that it was free, but it was a taxable benefit. The house was located at 1356 Montreal Avenue, almost at 14th Street, just on the fringe of Mount Royal. It was bought for Fred and Jean Carrothers; it was a wonderful family home, and also great for entertaining.

We came here in 1978 with two of our three children. My oldest daughter was married but still in university, so she and her husband stayed in Ontario for a year. When she finished her degree they moved out here, and then her husband went to the University of Calgary. My son was sixteen when we moved here, and both my younger daughter and son went to Western Canada High School. My youngest was fourteen then, and she found the transition very difficult. When in Grade 2, the principal phoned us just before Easter that year and said, "You know she's absolutely bored. Would you consider putting her in the next grade?" She was only in Grade 3 from Easter to June and then in September went into Grade 4. So when we moved here, although she was only fourteen, she was already in Grade 11, and the cliques had already formed. So she was very lonely, and when she finished Grade 12 she went back to Wilfrid Laurier for her undergraduate degree. Later on she did her Bachelor of Education degree here.

When our tenure with the university ended, we moved out to Springbank where we lived for ten years. We moved back into town because my husband's health started to fade. He had prostate cancer surgery in November, and in June of the next year a heart attack. It was just easier being back in Calgary. I couldn't take care of all the work involved with the house in Springbank. A lot of it was treed and in the country you could hire somebody who would ride around on the tractor and cut the grass but they would not trim, and they wouldn't do any weeding or tending to the flowers. I am really very happy living downtown in the Ranchmen's complex.

I must tell you an amusing story; a couple that we know very well in Edmonton took me out to dinner not long after Norm died. She said, "Are you going to stay here?" I said, "Of course I am." She said, "What about the memories?" and I said, "They're good memories." I also said, "Besides that, I can walk everywhere," and she said "I didn't know you didn't drive a car." She just assumed that because I walk everywhere that I don't drive. I can walk down to Bow Valley to my bank, my doctor is in Gulf Canada Square; my lawyer is on 7th Street. I just walk and it's so funny because people say, "I suppose you walked again," and I respond, "Yes, of course I walked." I've always admired European cities where you walk nearby to all the services one might need or want. That's the way I feel about living where I live. The only major thing missing is a farmers' market.

I now live in the Estate at the Ranchmen's Club, a beautiful facility that is 118 years old. My first visit was an uncomfortable experience. Soon after we arrived, we were invited to a private dinner at the Club. My husband warned me the Club had restrictions for women. I was only allowed to enter by the back door. My husband assured me it was not a problem since the parking lot was at the back of the building. We tried to find the room where the dinner was being held, but not knowing the Club very well, we walked down a hallway that went through the billiard room to the front entrance. The receptionist quickly advised us I was not allowed at the front entrance and promptly escorted us out of there. I was so embarrassed. Soon after that they began to change rules. Eventually you could become a lady associate member, and slowly but surely, as more women demanded to be members they changed their policies, built a new entrance for everyone, and women were welcomed as full members.

As an afterthought, before the rules changed, the one time each year that ladies could come in the front door facing onto 6th Street was on New Year's Day, when the President of the Club hosted a reception. It wasn't until about 1981 that women were allowed through the front door on an ordinary day. Here I am now, living next door and a full voting member.

The same thing happened to the Petroleum Club; it had a really difficult time being a men's only club. In the early 1980s when Mulroney was Prime Minister and Pat Carney was the first woman Minister of Energy, the Petroleum Club would not allow women into the Club before 2:30 in the afternoon. Pat Carney came to Calgary for a meeting with the energy people but was not able to go to the Petroleum Club for lunch, even though she was the Federal Minister of Energy. They ended up postponing the lunch, but right after that a lot of companies resigned their memberships in protest. Not long after, they changed their policy.

Times have changed. Women's lives and careers have changed. We still have a way to go but we are now being acknowledged for our own accomplishments.

I was very pleased to attend the FWC 50th Anniversary dinner. It brought back a lot of memories, and I saw friends I had not seen in years. Ethel King-Shaw and Marjorie Norris did a great job as co-hostesses. I have known both of them since my arrival in Calgary. I am especially happy for the older members who were there from the beginning. They were able to see fifty years later, that we were basically celebrating their achievements.

Cathy Wagner was Honorary President of Faculty Women's Club from 1978-1988.

Heading West

Sue White

April 30, 1996 the University of Calgary Gazette Bulletins around campus announced, "Dr. Terrence White appointed sixth president of U of C." Just days before, we had learned of Terry's selection as the University of Calgary's new President and we were thrilled to be finding ourselves moving west.

Early in May of that year we received a welcoming letter from the outgoing president Murray Fraser and his wife, Anne. Anne was kind enough to enclose a series of photographs of our new home – the university owned a residence in Varsity. It's very inconspicuous from the street, but have you ever lived in a house with four furnaces? Thank goodness the forty plus foot living room came with some furnishings; we could never have filled it.

Joining on the welcome was a lovely letter from Tannis Teskey, then president of the Faculty Women's Club. She was asking if I would consider being the Honorary President of the Faculty Women's Club. I was pleased to be asked and so excited about the prospects, I decided not to write, but phoned Tannis right away. "Yes," I said, and I looked forward to meeting everyone.

Both Terry and I were glad to be back in Alberta (we had lived in Edmonton for thirteen years). We were thrilled to be at the University of Calgary, a university with great people and lots of prospects. So, on October 16, 1996 at the request of Ann McCaig, Chancellor, and J.E. Newall, Chair, Board of Governors, Terry was installed as sixth President and Vice-Chancellor of The University of Calgary. It was a fabulous evening with dinner beforehand at The University Club – an evening we will remember forever.

We had come from the presidential position at a smaller university in Ontario, so we definitely had an idea of what our lives would be like. We jumped in with both feet and Terry began a life of at least ninety-hour weeks. I did not work outside the home when we came, but just keeping up with the daily social agenda, entertaining at the university and our residence, and attending university sporting events filled most of my days. We met presidents and premiers, princesses and pundits – we were very fortunate to have many unbelievable opportunities. All of this kept me very busy. I was glad to have the Faculty Women's Club where I met women who were so welcoming and who knew a lot about the university. I was involved with many of their activities and interest groups and was glad to be associated with so many people who were (and still are) dedicated to keeping the Faculty Women's Club alive. It is a small group, but made up of friendly women with so many interests, you can't help but want to be a part of it.

We have many wonderful memories of Terry's five years as the University of Calgary President and then his subsequent five years in the

Haskayne School of Business and the Faculty of Education. He retired from the university on December 31, 2006, and has gone on to other endeavors, but Calgary and the mountains of Alberta will always be our home.

Sue White was Honorary President of Faculty Women's Club from 1996-2001.

Getting to Calgary
Sally Goddard

Getting the dogs to Calgary was the most difficult part of the experience of moving here. We had to get them to the kennels just outside of Halifax so they could be loaded on the plane when one of the girls flew. It was determined that I would drive the dogs on the day a professorial colleague arrived from London to teach summer school. It was also the day the packers were arriving. The plan was that I would drop off the dogs, have lunch with a friend, and then pick up the Open University professor from the airport and return to Antigonish.

It sounded so simple.

I got the dogs in the car. They were three years old and had never been in a car for longer than twenty minutes. I had a box of dog treats to lure them into the kennels. Just as I was about to leave, the phone rang. I raced back inside and dealt with the caller. By the time I returned to the car, the treats were just a pleasant memory. So we began our two hour trip.

All went well for the first one and a half hours. Just as we reached the four lane highway outside of Truro, one of the dogs started circling the front seat of the car. He then had projectile diarrhea against the dashboard of the car. He jumped into the back seat of the car and had another episode. I was driving at 110 km/hour and thought, "If I stop, what am I going to be able to do?" So I kept on driving.

It was a hot day in early July and you can only imagine what the smell was like. I arrived at the kennels. The dogs jumped out of the car and ran straight in. The woman sniffed the air and asked if I needed something to help clean.

"Yes," I said. "That would be lovely."

She brought out a bowl of disinfectant and a cloth. I did what I could do but the car still smelled.

I drove off trying to figure out how I was going to meet my husband's colleague from the Open University and drive him the two hours back to Antigonish. I parked the car in a multistory car park in Halifax and left all the windows open. There was a sign that said, "Please lock your car and take all valuables with you. This is a high crime area." I also left it unlocked. I thought that was one solution. If someone stole the car, then I would just rent another. At least it wouldn't smell.

I had lunch with my friend, all the while trying to figure out what I would do if the car was not stolen. Then I remembered that there was a car wash at the airport. I would pick up shampoo, air freshener, and some paper towels. I would slip the car wash attendant $20 extra to clean the inside of the car. Once I had a plan, I was more relaxed. When I returned to the car park, no one had stolen the car so I proceeded with my other plan. I stopped at a department store on the way to the airport and picked up the necessary supplies.

The car wash at the Halifax airport was a welcome sight. I pulled up outside the entrance way and a man came out.

"Can I help you?" he asked.

I proceeded to explain what had happened. It took me a while and then he said, "Lady, I'd love to help you but we have no power. There was an electrical storm about half an hour ago and it knocked out the electricity in this area."

So, I thought to myself, "What to do?" I knew there was another gas station at the next exit but I wasn't sure if there was a car wash. I had about twenty minutes before the London plane arrived. I left the airport and whipped up to the next exit. Unfortunately, there wasn't a car wash. It was up to me. I opened all four doors and proceeded to use the shampoo and the air freshener. In my enthusiasm, I completely soaked the front passenger's seat. I looked around. I had about five minutes to get back to the airport. I saw a dime store in the strip mall across the street from the gas station. I drove there, parked the car, and ran inside. I bought two beach towels and draped them over each of the front seats so they looked like seat covers.

I got back to the airport just in time. I had never met the professor but he was looking for me and I for him. As we walked towards the car, I said, "Are you allergic to dogs?"

He said, "No, why?"

I replied, "The dogs sometimes ride in the car."

It Was Actually the Women

Angela Rokne

Looking back now it becomes clear what a remarkable group of women they were. Smart, unaffected, and full of fun; only through the prism of memory do I see how their courage made it all work.

They followed their husbands' academic careers, arriving in Calgary where they expected to stay for a few years as the new university was forming . . . and ended up staying a lifetime. They came from university communities around the world: Singapore, Hong Kong, Chicago, Salzburg, Cambridge, Lahore, Prague, Gaza, New Delhi, and San Francisco. These women were well educated and articulate. One might think it was their husbands who made the university but it was actually the women.

They arrived to the dusty calm of Calgary's mid sixties and were left each day by their preoccupied husbands to find and furnish homes, raise children, suffer and sustain themselves. In the early days, the men were rarely home. They trundled off daily to a bald prairie campus to write their papers, argue theorems, give lectures, and complicate any sense of tranquility by going on cross continental jaunts, sabbaticals, or by inviting adjunct professors who in turn needed help with cars and residence.

Most of the women were used to compact, textured cityscapes with everyday needs met within walking distance or a short bus ride. They arrived to Calgary's bland suburban landscapes, brown lawns, and long winters. The general lack of amenities came as a surprise. Undaunted, the women learned to love the winter, the snow, and the mountains. They learned to ski, to drive, and to create for themselves a remarkable social network to hold one another safe. They created the Faculty Women's Club with its container-full of meeting places: the Hiking group, the Book group, the Bible Study group, the Bridge group, the Out to Lunch Bunch, and the Babysitting Swap are a few in which I participated as a young woman.

What I remember of these years was the enduring sense of welcome. The late sixties and seventies was a time of great social change. The first group of faculty women came with close memories of the war years. Most of them had foregone careers. To this early group were added new groups of younger women, some of whom were the free spirits of the "hippie" years. There never seemed to be a clash of cultures between the two groups. They seemed to find ways to meet happily together. I remember they once put together a book of favorite recipes. To everyone's delight, one young woman contributed a recipe for tossed green salad. Their lack of harsh judgment and their appreciation of difference has informed me throughout my years in Calgary.

I remember hikes where whomever walked the slowest would always be waited for and where lunches were generously shared. No matter who you were or where you came from someone would recognize the good you brought to the group.

I remember house parties where everyone was welcome. The host was supported by the others. No one cleaned or prepared alone. Louise Guy made the most fantastic layer cakes and Edna Lancaster made Christmas cakes that were practically addictive. There was almost always dancing, singing, and piano playing. They knew how to have fun. Edna Lancaster's husband Peter was my husband's supervisor and when they went on sabbatical, Jon went too. He became part of their family, Jon driving through Switzerland in a flower painted Volkswagen with their daughters in tow.

Many of the great women of those early days are gone now but they have left an inheritance of community building. Even now, when I go through my recipe box I pause over the recipes they shared with me as I wobbled my way into learning how to run a home.

Looking back I realize how privileged I was to be part of it all.

Living Links: Edna Lancaster's Christmas Cake
Angela Rokne

Recipes provide a living link from one person to the next. As you prepare the food you perform the same steps and wonder the same things about the same ingredients and you taste, smell, and sense the same experiences as your kitchen billows with the aromas of cooking. In preparing these dishes you practice the same form of care for your family and friends. All in all a fully evocative memory as one generation joins hands with the next.

Edna Lancaster's Christmas Cake

1 lb	currants
1 lb	seedless raisins
1 cup	mixed fruit
½ lb	glace cherries
1 cup	pecans
2¼ cups	warm water
2¼ cups	granulated sugar
1 lb	margarine
3 tsps	mixed spice
1 tsp	salt
3	beaten eggs
3¼ cups	flour
1 tsp	baking soda
2 tsp	baking powder

Put all ingredients till salt in pan, boil 1 minute. Cool.
Add eggs to cooled fruit mixture.
Stir dry ingredients into the above mix.

Bake in 2 well lined (3 layers) 8 inch square pans at 275°F for about 3 hours.

Have a pan of water low in the oven during baking.

When Edna gave me the recipe she told me that she used walnuts instead of pecans.

I leave out the cherries and use butter instead of margarine.

Settling

Arriving as Total Strangers
Welcoming Letters and Gatherings

Soon after we formed, the rapid growth in staff began. With many families arriving as total strangers in our city, Pat Buckmaster headed a Hospitality Committee which inaugurated our "Welcome Letter," first sent to new staff in the spring of 1962. A copy of the draft includes the following helpful suggestions:

1. Moving expenses include lodging, food and travel. If you should experience any difficulty in paying movers, write to Dr. E. Oetting, University of Alberta, Calgary to ask about an advance payment. He can, if necessary, have a cheque ready for you when you arrive.

2. For those of you coming from the United States:

(a) do read very carefully the enclosed leaflet from the Department of National Revenue, Customs and Excise, Canada.

(b) do bring with you cottons of all kinds (household, clothing, etc.) as they are more expensive in Canada.

(c) do bring your own piano, organ, and large electrical appliances. These are also more expensive in Canada.

4. Kindergartens are not part of the school systems and are privately operated in community centers . . .

6. The members of the Faculty Women's Club have arranged to supply drivers, advisors, and to find baby-sitters for you until the end of September. Please let us know when you will arrive, by what means of transportation and how many there will be in your family.

11. Social events in the latter part of September which you will be asked to attend include:

(a) The Principal's Tea for faculty staff and their wives or husbands

April 6, 1964
The Club coffee urn is to be found and a plaque to be placed on it.

June 2, 1964
Jo Prescott is to check with Rosemary Plotnick about the coffee urns.

September 16, 1964
Jo Prescott reported that we have 2 coffee urns which are not in very good condition. They have yet to be located.

Jan 11, 1965
Jo Prescott is to obtain a quote for the repair of the coffee urn.

January 27, 1965
Jo Prescott reported that Moody's gave her a quote of $4.00 for the replacement of a washer in the coffee urn. Jo was asked to obtain just the washer.

March 29, 1965
Jo Prescott reported that the repair of the switch and washers on the coffee urn cost $5.00.

May 10, 1965
Jo Prescott reported that coffee urns were repaired, and have been labelled, by W.A. Jones.
L. Wright is to write him.

April 1966
A Coffee Convener became an Executive Position.

September 1967
Coffee urn repairs $7.85

(b) The Wauneita Tea (Club for Women Students) for faculty staff wives

(c) The Executive of the Faculty Women's Club Tea for all new staff wives

(d) An evening cocktail party for all staff and their wives and husbands.

Our President, Elizabeth Challice, arranged to have each new staff member or his wife receive a personal letter from one of our members. By 1964 the Calgary Faculty Women's Club had been nationally recognized for this effort. We received honorable mention in Chatelaine's Club Project contest for our hospitality extended to the wives of new members of staff.

We continued to elaborate on information supplied, by 1969 even listing motel prices (daily summer rates). The 1978 letter prepared by Carol Marica recommends reading: *Calgary Cavalcade; Kid Stuff in Calgary; Calgary's Natural Areas; Cow Town*; and *Alberta - A Natural History*. We are thorough!

Whereas the Welcoming Letter was a viable preliminary contact with prospective staff, the Welcoming Tea and the Welcoming Party were two on-arrival super social introductions. Even before our Faculty Women's Club became a reality, the Welcoming Tea was already a tradition at our young University. Dr. and Mrs. A.L. Doucette co-hosted with all of the staff and their spouses invited to their Rosedale area home in northwest Calgary. The wives of permanent staff introduced new members appointed to the same subject area as their husbands because, although Dr. Doucette, as Director of the University of Alberta Calgary Branch, lived in Calgary, all deans and department heads resided in Edmonton. The president of our University now lives in the prestigious Mount Royal area of Calgary where the University purchased a spacious home upon the arrival of President and Mrs. A.W.R. Carrothers. For some years now, this formal event has become the Honorary President's Welcoming Coffee Party, reflecting our co-hostessing responsibilities through the years. At the beginning of each Fall term, the Honorary President and the Executive of the Faculty Women's Club invite the wives of new staff appointments and new women appointments to attend a morning Coffee Party at the President's residence. Our deans' wives are invited to pour!

For the first few years, our Welcoming Party was held out at the RCAF Officers' Mess, McCall Field, and subsequently at the newly opened Allied Arts Center on 9th Avenue. At that time it was not possible to serve liquor at a function held on campus. For an authentic Western setting, the 1977 Welcoming Party moved 40 miles west of Calgary to the Rafter Six Guest Ranch. To give some idea of the number of people involved in organizing these parties, I will list the acknowledgements as they appeared in our newsletter for the one held at the Faculty Club in 1976. No one was overlooked:

> The Committee would like to thank John Kendall who acted as M.C., Jennifer Abouna for the excellent work on posters, Loraine Seastone for providing all the flowers and Caroline Cole for doing the flower arrangements on the serving tables. Thanks also to

Laura Baecker, Penny Bayer, Christine Bewley, Holly Bourne, Judi Kendall, Cynthia Kubinski, Edna Lancaster, Kay Limbird, and Marg Mohtadi for helping with the food, decorating, typing, etc., . . . Finally, thanks to Ches Loov and Frances McLachlan who chaired this event and to their committee of Beth Davies, Christine Slater, Diane Zissos and Burdette Brown; last but not least thanks to Regina Shedd who put in many hours supervising. . . .

The records show that this event earlier on was co-sponsored by the Faculty Club and TUCFA, a University recognition of the need for the function.

Norris, p. 19-22

Sister Heroines
Marjorie Barron Norris

I first saw the light of day on Sunday, February 11th, 1923, at a farmhouse near Oak Lake, Manitoba. At age six my twin and I moved west with our parents, Oliver and Jessie Parsons, to Nanton, Alberta, where we completed our schooling during the years of the Great Depression. Upon matriculating, I enrolled at the University of Alberta, during World War II, and received my Bachelor of Education in 1944. My first teaching position was Vice Principal at Rocky Mountain House, west of Red Deer. That next summer I married Stanley Norris, a Petty Officer in the Royal Canadian Navy, who was stationed at Halifax. After his demobilization, we returned to Alberta where I continued teaching until he also graduated from the Faculty of Education in Edmonton.

From then on, I chose to spend most of my life as homemaker, giving time to our two daughters so that my husband was free to further his studies. After his appointment to the young University of Calgary, I joined the Faculty Women's Club upon its founding and from there served as a delegate to the Calgary Local Council of Women – a lobby organization which addressed social and political issues. After a term as its president, I was elected to the Provincial Council and from there served at the national level. My efforts were generously recognized when the National Council of Women in Canada awarded me the Queen Elizabeth Silver Jubilee medal, in 1977.

Sometime after that, my preoccupation with the writing of history began. The Council of Women experience provided the background for my first major endeavor, *A Leaven of Ladies – A History of the Calgary Local Council of Women,* published by Detselig Enterprises Ltd., Calgary in 1995. The book, which represented five years of in depth research, highlighted the organization's triumphs and tribulation while its leading ladies lobbied for suffrage and municipal improvements.

Previous to *A Leaven of Ladies,* I prepared the twenty-five year commemorative history of the earlier mentioned Faculty Women's Club, in addition to the municipal history of the Summer Village of Half Moon Bay – where I had served on the Council, since its inception, a decade earlier.

The inspiration for my latest history, was my mother, Jessie Barron, a World War I nursing sister who served first with the British Queen Alexandra's Imperial Military Nursing Service Reserve in Malta, then with the Canadian Army Medical Corps in England, and finally at the Tuxedo Military Hospital, Winnipeg. Although she never reminisced about her wartime experiences, she kept her personal autograph album, badges, and other reminders of Malta and England, which my twin sister and I, while still children, were allowed to examine, carefully.

I knew mother was a 1910 graduate of the Calgary General Hospital, even though I could not find her name on the Hospital's Honor Roll or in the local papers of the time. This early effort was by no means wasted, however, because it became a beacon. During my search, I encountered references to other Calgary nurses who enlisted – a precious few of them enhanced by accounts of their wartime service. The details inspired me to include the graduates of Calgary's two training hospitals as well as others who were nursing in the city when they enlisted. The biographies, including my mother's, total twenty-eight, enhanced by honor rolls. All carefully traced.

Some six years later, before mid June of 2002, the great day arrived. Geoff Todd, President, Bunker to Bunker Publishing, Calgary, delivered *Sister Heroines – The Roseate Glow of Wartime Nursing 1914-1918,* to me. It weighed fourteen ounces.

Marjorie Norris is a Charter Member and was an Honorary Co-President for the Faculty Women's Club Golden Anniversary year, 2006-2007.

One Small Cog
Eileen Lohka

This was not my first transcontinental or transoceanic move; I was hoping it might be one of the last. To pack up everything again, to pull out the tree that had been blossoming in the warm, friendly earth of Colorado, to loosen the roots that had taken hold, to see the long move up I-25 wither the deep green leaves of belonging to a community, to start from scratch in a new, forbidding space – too wide, too flat, too empty – was sending shivers down my spine.

Once again, I would be too far away from my identity-sustaining ocean brine. Once again, I would shiver for months on end, longing for a sun that stays awake more than a few hours at a time and that means business, a sun ready to warm me up, inside and out. Once again, I'd be different, with a foreign accent when speaking either official language. Once again, I'd be told "Congratulations, you speak very good French." . . . for an "Eileen," understand . . . I'd be asked where Mauritania is, when I hail from Mauritius. I'd have to start all over again, for the sixth time in my life. In a cold, flat, empty space with a university that was younger than me . . .

And so it was that my family moved to Calgary, Alberta, Canada – as people seem to say here – in 1992. One of the two Dr. Lohkas got paid, as per his newly minted contract, by the Department of Biological Sciences, while the other earned peanuts teaching Continuing Education classes in the evening before being "promoted" to working as a sessional instructor in the Department of French, Italian and Spanish – a "sessional" appointment that lasted eight years until, by a quirk of bargaining, the lowly doormat was "converted" into a second class citizen, an Instructor. The capital *I* makes all the difference here. Now, you can become one of the good guys, an "ongoing" faculty member, albeit in a slightly less venerable stream than the professoriate since one is supposed to teach more than most and is not supposed to do research, other than "maintaining currency in the field." If I am using an overabundance of inverted commas, it is in part to underline the irony of academe: how can such bland vocabulary end up taking such exclusionary meaning?

After such a long introduction, let us hail back to reality, Calgary 1992-style. The city is still relatively small, a quasi-rural *bourg*. Housing prices are steep however, and, having teenage children in dire need of space, preferably away from our own, we settle for a bi-level, of the cheap modern variety, in dreary suburbia. Having spent my childhood in a tropical environment, where every house is always open, where large families gather at the drop of a hat, and where one's sense of belonging hails back generations in a small handkerchief-size island hemmed in by the vast ocean, and having lived in bustling cities since, I felt totally lost. How does one put down roots in such a dry environment, perched as we are on an old quarry? How does one meet people, make friends, when all houses are locked tight against the claws of winter for so many months, not to mention the fact that some summers never materialize either and the cool dampness keeps fellow citizens in malls or far away from here, somewhere warm? How welcoming are houses that offer their large, foreboding, ever-closed double- or triple-car garage doors as façades to passersby? Can one ever find one's way in neighborhoods with similar names: Scenic Acres Boulevard, Scenic Acres Drive, Scenic Acres Close, . . . Hill, . . . Crescent, . . . Gate, . . . Mews, . . . Glen, . . . Way, . . . View, . . . Landing? Will I ever belong here?

Enter Faculty Women's Club. My first open door in Calgary, other than family, was actually an opened envelope – opened with a quizzical frown pasted on my brow. After my stint in the USA, where anything offered for free out of the blue surely must be suspicious, I wondered whether to accept the friendly invitation to all faculty wives and women to a welcoming Coffee Morning at such and such an address. My brilliant deductive mind whispered that, since the name and phone number matched the same in the official city phone book and that the last name did match an equivalent faculty member on campus – oh yes, I checked that too – it would probably be all right for me to phone and "judge by the voice" whether to say yes or no to the invitation. You must have realized by now that the voice was as sweet and welcoming as can be because, as they say, the rest is history. I have been inwardly smirking at the "two boobs and big behind" of the Faculty Women's Club logo ever since.

In the fourteen years since that angst-ridden move, the tree that is our family *has* managed to put down some semblance of roots. Although I am still asked where I come from, because I don't quite speak like "us," I seem to have found my place in this city, which to me is still a Far West frontier town, with its yearly Stampede, White Hats, and vast expanses. I seem to have found my place on this University of Calgary campus, where I am now tenured *and* doing research, in spite of the categorization that says "thou shalt not do research but maintain currency etc., etc., etc." After all, my French blood comes quickly to a boil and, like my compatriots before me, I tend to resist *fiats* from above. "To the barricades!" gives impetus to much that I do on campus: from going against the tide before interdisciplinary endeavors became fashionable, to starting experiential learning courses before the term gained currency, to working within the Faculty Association to try and improve conditions for sessional instructors on campus.

Faculty Women's Club became the first of many clubs, groups, and committees on which I have sat, served, deliberated, to which I have belonged. Yes, I belong – in a small way; I feel part of this vast land I have not quite fathomed yet. My heart swells when I travel the long grey ribbon toward Lethbridge and watch the sun at play on the undulating waves of blond wheat, with the majestic, rugged, snowcapped mountains standing out against an impossibly blue, impossibly huge, sky. My children and nieces smile at me when I get excited over a patch of mountain avens or gentians, when I bend their ears with lessons on U- or V-shaped valleys and moraine lakes. Glimpses of black bears, moose, or bald eagles have become my specialty. I seem to know instinctively where to find them. I have come to understand that, in spite of the dark, frigid winters – which I still hate – I am comfortable here. Like Calgary, I tend to sprawl on any seat I occupy. I take my space. I tame it in my own way. I wear down its rough edges until it becomes like a pair of old slippers: they become so comfortable you don't even remember they are on your feet!

And so, I share Alberta's big skies with babbling brooks pregnant with melting snow. With crows and meadowlarks. With chipmunks and coyotes, pumas – cougars, I should say since I am a Canadian – and Herr Rabbit in my backyard. Chief Crowfoot, Victoria Belcourt Callihoo, the Famous Five. Lakes as green as my brother's eyes. Tumbling waterfalls on stark cliff faces. Saxifrage, skunk cabbages, larches' gold. Glaciers' deep blue crevasses, orange grain elevators, solitary sentinels of the prairie. The mystique of the 1988 Olympics. Speed skaters at the Oval. Joggers on the river path, hockey fans on the Red Mile, farmers in their big combines, drivers at the wheel of monster dumptrucks with $53 000 tyres – oops, that should be "tires" – in the tar sands. I do not pretend to understand all of them. I certainly do not understand Alberta politics, probably never will. I still do not participate in the Stampede. But little tendrils, bursting with sap, now link me to the territory, to the history of this area.

On the University of Calgary campus, trees have grown and hidden bare spots. Buildings have sprouted in the most unlikely places. Like the plus-fifteen-style corridors that allow me to walk from one side of campus to the other, I have established links within the academic community. My office in dreary Craigie Hall is as overcrowded with books, papers, and mementos as that of the long-timers on campus. I have taught hundreds of students to "throw up" their French *r* and to pucker up for a perfect *u*. I have made friends, held seminars, participated in conferences, found my way in the maze of offices, paperwork, and regulations that govern an unwieldy institution such as this one. I have marveled at the intellect of my colleagues, applauded their success, and worked hard at resolving grievances through my involvement with the Faculty Association. Since there are no more phone directories at this "on the edge and leading the way" campus, I must assume that the fact that my name is listed in the online directory means that I *must* belong to this community. Like the *Cheers* song, I tell myself that this is my neighborhood bar, my territory, since here, everybody knows my name.

And when, then, will I finally come to the purpose of this collection of testimonials? When will I connect the dots between the geographical space, Alberta's landscape, the University of Calgary, who is celebrating its fortieth anniversary, and the Faculty Women's Club, basking in the golden glow of its Jubilee? Once again, a resourceful academic will find a way to weave artfully various threads of thought in a magnificent tapestry. Just watch . . . The third element of the trinity mentioned above, the friends I made in Faculty Women's Club, are the cement, the glue, the grout that hold everything together. Although I do not always participate in the various interest groups, as I did when I was a sessional woman of leisure, I still keep in touch with many and I know that I can count on any, should the need arise.

Over the years, I learnt more about the women who started FWC so many years ago. I would like to herald the many unsung services they performed for the University of Calgary in its gestational stage as well as in its infancy. I have heard many stories and I cannot believe that most on campus ignore completely the contributions of the pioneer women who participated at the periphery of campus life, giving of their time freely at a time when volunteer work was almost expected of them, while their husbands dedicated their lives to "loftier" pursuits. In spite of the Famous Five one of our own wrote so extensively about, faculty wives could maybe work as nurses or teachers, but mostly they dedicated themselves to the University community. While others might be the rivets, leather tethers or money-belts, they became the pastel ribbons that tied the ivory tower on the bald hill to the Calgary community.

Although I will leave this aspect of the Faculty Women's Club history to those more cognizant than me, I cannot help but repeat what our book proposal states, that FWC members were the forerunners of today's fundraisers, support services, counsellors, daycare providers, fulfilling countless roles to assist the budding institution. Case in point, it was U of C Faculty Women's Club who began Campus Preschool, originally called Campus Child Care Co-operative, back in 1965. Faculty Women's Club members "supported the view that a childcare facility was needed to enable mothers to attend University while their preschool children met nearby in a centre which afforded their children creative and intellectual development. After a successful summer and winter season, the Co-operative moved off campus" *(FWC Archives)*.

I have also listened, fascinated, when senior members have told about getting down on their hands and knees to clean, wax, and shine floors, bringing their polished silver from home, baking goodies for days and finally changing into their long gowns for the Town and Gown Ball fundraisers they used to sponsor. I can barely imagine the days they talk about when the whole professoriate and administration met at a faculty member's house for Senate (or General Faculties Council) meetings while all the wives cooked the meal everybody would share afterwards. Today's 2500 academics, together with the countless University of Calgary administrators, would need the Jubilee Auditorium and several caterers to be so collegial. Imagine also, if you will, faculty women scouring the town to find a house, buy pots and pans, groceries and bedding so a newly hired academic, hailing usually from Britain, would find shelter and a modicum of comfort for his family upon arrival. A majority of these women, having come from all corners of the world, thus created a strong network, providing the opportunity for friendship and social interaction. Those were the days when the institution still functioned on a human scale.

I never had to break barriers or work so hard at establishing an institution I believed in and cared for. Unheralded pioneers blazed the trail for me. Faculty members like Dr. Ethel King-Shaw, faculty wives like Marg Oliver who stood by her man and still today participates in Hiking Groups when she is not, with fellow hikers, blazing up Katmandu trails to Mount Everest's Base Camp. Like Louise Guy who, at 90+, still attends U of C functions of all kinds, hosts Coffee and Chat, hikes, and so gracefully shares her sharp intellect. Like Sally Goddard whose strength and generosity garnered the admiration of all when her eldest daughter, Captain Nichola Goddard, died in action on the dry sands of Afghanistan.

My task, in relation to Faculty Women's Club, is quite modest by comparison. One October morning, a few months after our arrival here, I was asked to help at a special convocation: Mikhail Gorbachev, then president of the Soviet Union, was coming to town to receive an honorary degree and inaugurate the new Gorbachev Foundation. The Chancellor's office needed volunteers. My task that day was to ensure that attendees had the proper tickets, that nobody ate or drank in the gymnasium, and that those who approached the platform to take pictures left their backpack behind. Jack Simpson Gymnasium was crawling with RCMP and security agents of all sorts, mumbling in their headpieces while never making eye contact. Actually, their eyes darted from one side to the other throughout the ceremony. And my new career was born: Convocation Usher.

The Faculty Women's Club has provided countless volunteer ushers over the years, women who hand out official programs to families at the entrance, who direct traffic, answer questions and generally ensure the public can enjoy Convocation to the fullest while allowing the ceremony to proceed with the proper pomp and circumstance. Since that first day, I have attended over ninety consecutive convocations, with only a sabbatical leave hiatus in 2005 . . . and counting. For the baseball aficionados, my husband calls me the Cap Ripken Jr. of Convocation . . . when he is not ribbing me about my "Catholic martyr complex." And yet, despite the long tiring days, the sometimes long boring speeches, I enjoy volunteering in this small way, following in the footsteps of the FWC women who did much more for the university over the years. I even have stories to tell.

Take the Master's Degree graduand I was to watch closely during the ceremony. She rightfully wished to walk across the stage and shake the Chancellor's hand but her enormous tummy hinted without any subtlety at impending disaster – for convocation that is. She was already in labor and I was to judge which of her grimaces was profound enough to warrant escorting her to the back on her way – do not stop, do not pass GO, do not collect $200 – to the delivery room, preferably at the hospital. Of course, I had my other tasks to accomplish as well . . . And how about the fracas on the platform one rainy June day. An honorable colleague of mine had dozed off during one particularly droning speech – or was he fidgeting too much? – at any rate, he pushed his chair just enough for the back legs to slip off the platform. The chair, with him on it, came crashing down behind the podium while the ceremony continued as if nothing had happened. Those of us on the sidelines are supposed to deal with this sort of emergency while the show, the graduation ritual I mean, must go on.

My favorite story concerns a sweet little old lady, no heavier than a wet canary, whose eyesight had deteriorated to the point where she could see no farther than the tip of her nose. Her favorite (great?) granddaughter was graduating and her pride was refreshing to see. She wanted to come close enough to see – or most probably guess at – her granddaughter crossing the stage. Softie that I am, I helped her up the first row of bleachers and sat her down in the seats usually reserved to 'park' the numerous dad-, boyfriend-, mom-photographers that swarm the area, affectionately known as the "scrum pit," hoping to take the million dollar picture in the mêlée of arms, legs, and heads. I told her not to move and that I'd stop her granddaughter so she could give her a hug. Which I did. In her excitement, grandma opened wide her arms . . . and her finger having caught in her strand of pearls, snapped the necklace. Pearls pinged, pinged, pinged their way all over the floor, right under the feet of the procession of newly minted graduates walking back to their seats. I am thankful for the fact that the TV cameras had already left after the honorary degree recipient's speech. Otherwise, on the six o'clock news, Calgary would have been treated to a middle aged woman, holding a partly blind lady by the arm, while frantically reaching between the graduates' legs to collect pearls that she deposited in the old lady's cupped hands, while at the same time warning graduates not to go sliding on said pearls and "gently" suggesting that parents keep the aisle open for the procession to move smoothly. Multitasking at its best!

I never did get danger pay for working my corner. Should have. Parents get so frantic wanting their pictures, that they would walk over slow movers, bulldoze passing graduates, jump over seated officials, dive through the crowd, scale bleachers, slide down banisters, anything to get to the very front, much too early. And they do. And so it was that this hefty, refrigerator of a gentleman, intent on the smile of his progeny, missed the last step and went flying through the air. And so it was that, instead of moving to the side with my hand extended in a "please, after you" kind of gesture, I reached out to stabilize him. His weight and impetus were no match for my arm which promptly clunked out of its socket, before popping back in, in a flash of agony. The rest of the ceremony went by in a blur of smiles, gentle prodding and verbal exhortation. The hot shower felt good that evening! To this day, the creaking sounds in my left shoulder bring back visions of the gentleman's surprised face as his body turned into an awkward catapult.

No convocation ceremony is complete without the rebel who lifts his gown to flash his fellow graduands, the sentimental who sneaks her cat under her gown so her beloved pet can share the moment, or the grateful who spells "hi mom" in masking tape on her mortarboard. We have seen it all and more. At least now, the zipped up gowns make it more difficult for graphic shows of independence, rebellion, or simple air conditioning. I have smiled my way through it all. Through the interminable fire alarm, when we were told to wait while safety personnel investigated. Which we did, anxiously tracking disabled guests, and the crowd we would have to usher out, in a supposedly orderly parade, following a preordained escape route, into the pouring rain outside. I must say I was very glad not to have to test the hypothesis! The alarm was turned off and the speech droned on without any further ado.

My reward is simple. I am positioned in the best possible spot, right down the ramp where new alumni and alumna leave the podium to return to their seats. Bright illuminating smiles, eyes shiny with tears, unabashed joy melt away the cynicism which creeps in when one sees more closely the underbelly of the beast called university. My students know the price they have to pay as I stand right there to congratulate them and . . . to collect my exit hug. No more grumping about half a mark, no more bickering because they need an A to get into Medicine, the quality of their paper be darned, no more tears, frustrations and alarms that did not go off, sorry, Madame, can I take that test again? All is forgotten in that impulsive exchange celebrating the start of a new adventure for "my kids" who have – mostly – grown up.

Nothing but a small cog on an increasingly bigger, more impersonal campus. Nothing but a gesticulating ant on the scale of the Rockies and the prairies, nothing but a "naturalized citizen" trying to adapt while refusing to forget where she came from. Faculty Women's Club has nurtured the interstitial space where so many of us, arriving from elsewhere, can feel comfortable and contribute, in our own way. In turn, the space in which we evolve has allowed us to transform our inner landscape, to shape an "inscape" of memories, an inner community of friends, events, meaningful moments – an integral part of our life, with its peaks and valleys, much like the province in which we live, and in symbiosis with it.

A Modernistic Monogram

A Logo for the Faculty Women's Club

From the outset [in 1964], the Ball Committee wanted to do things right. As we thought our stationery should have a status insignia representative of the Faculty Women's Club, Mr. Robert Oldrich of Design Associates, Calgary, designed our present motif for $40.00. When viewed by the initiate, this modernistic monogram was described by its detractors as being either bird or bosom. However, it has won through as an elegant combination of our initials.

Norris, p. 10

Stories My Mother Told Me

Ilse Anysas-Salkauskas

51 cm w x 135 cm h x 46 cm d Leather

The title, "Stories My Mother Told Me," brings me visions of warmth, comfort, protection, and connection. The connection is to my past and my present, namely my grandmothers and now my two granddaughters. As a little girl my ninety-three-year-old mother, when in trouble, used to take refuge under her grandmother's multilayered petticoats and skirt. Times have changed and so have our clothing styles, but our needs are still the same. Now I am the grandmother and have two granddaughters who at times want my help.

This project has given me the opportunity to connect to my past through my mother's family stories. I am now telling these same stories to my daughters and granddaughters. Through this process I'm continuing to connect them to their past as well.

From my mother's stories I see that in every generation the young women start out their lives with similar dreams but life pulls and pushes them into many different directions. Things that all of the women of my family had and have in common are creativity, love of the land, and strong spiritual beliefs. I have created my sculptural artwork using colorful leather to show a family connection to the soil, and to our faith.

Looking back at the viewer from my sculpture is the face of tradition and the historic tension between functional and decorative art. On it, the three layers show aspects of the shared commitments and hopes of the women in my family. The unploughed landscape layers are there, showing the hope the young women had and have for their future. The stained glass windows represent the spiritual hope helping the women survive through good times and bad. The black layers are there because all of the women before my mother's generation wore black wedding dresses. Wearing them they also hoped for a great future. The fringes at the bottom stand for the many family stories that, for one reason or another, will never be told.

Reaching for the Stars

Ilse Anysas-Salkauskas

I was born December 14, 1942 in war torn Berlin, Germany, to Lithuanian refugee parents. After the war ended, my father worked for the United Nations Relief Organisation in Germany, managing two refugee hospitals. As refugees we were given food, clothing, and other household items to survive postwar living conditions in Germany. I have memories of my father coming home with some interesting and colorful items. One day he came home with a set of cobalt blue dishes for our family of four. The color was so brilliant that I still remember the dishes today. Whenever one of the dishes broke I played with the shards hoping not to lose the memory of the beautiful color.

Another time he came home with a bag full of US Army surplus khaki green and scratchy woollen men's scarves that the other refugees did not want. My creative mother promptly washed them and as a five-year-old I helped her unravel the thin wool. That was the beginning of a beautiful green and white sweater for my mother. This was my introduction to creative recycling. Inspired by my mother's work, I also wanted to knit and soon my rag doll had a green and white triangle shaped scarf made from my mother's leftovers. After seeing how well accepted his gift had been by his wife, my father promptly brought home a few more bags of unwanted scarves. When I saw my father come home with them, I was worried. Those were very itchy scarves to hold and I didn't want to have to help my mother unravel those new arrivals as well. To my delight, my mother traded them with the other village ladies for needed goods and soon there were other green and white sweaters worn in the village.

My father occasionally came home with brightly colored hard candies that my mother only let me eat as a special Sunday treat. After all those years I still remember the colors of my youth and how important they were to me.

Children's toys were hard to find after the war but my mother kept me busy doing simple embroidery and crochet work. In this way I learned to develop a love for handicrafts and continued my family's creative artistic traditions. My mother's mother had been a weaver, my father's mother a knitter, and my mother had been taught to not only knit and sew but to also work with a variety of other craft materials.

At the age of seven I designed a little table runner for my grandfather and gave it to him as a farewell gift before the family emigrated to North America.

After a very stormy two week winter crossing of the Atlantic, where the Liberty ship, the General Sturgis, almost sank, my overjoyed family landed on Manhattan Island on January 17, 1951. The train ride from Manhattan to Chicago kept me awake most of the night looking at the many brightly lit cities flashing by. Two days later we arrived in Chicago to start a new life. I remember being very impressed by the many bright neon lights that lit up the city that evening. I was so impressed that I didn't look where I was going and fell flat on my face.

Having lived in war ravaged Europe, the US seemed like a very bright and colorful country. To my delight, the children around me wore bright clothes and, loving color, I wanted a red sweater of my very own. My mother, after a few weeks of working in a jewellery factory, had saved up enough money to buy red wool. She drew a pattern for a sweater on sheets of newspaper and a half a year later, with some help from my mother, I completed my sweater.

The local Salvation Army store was a great place to shop for the family. My parents not only bought their beds, table, and chairs there, but eventually also a Singer treadle sewing machine for my mother. At first I learned to sew simple clothes for my dolls, but eventually I made my own school clothes on the same machine.

The first few years in the Chicago school system were difficult ones for me. I couldn't speak English and the one boy that could speak both English and Lithuanian was very unfriendly to me. At first the only subjects I received top grades in were Arts, Crafts, and Phys Ed classes. In Grade 4, every time the seasons changed, I was asked to create all the decorations for the classroom.

As a fourteen-year-old, I won a scholarship to attend children's art classes at the Chicago Art Institute School of Fine Arts. Even though the arts (attending art galleries, museums, plays, and concerts) played an important role in my family's life, I was not allowed to take the scholarship, and in its place, was signed up for church organ lessons. I was very disappointed with my parents' decision and hoped to study art sometime in the future. As a teenager, I attended a private high school in the suburbs of Chicago and upon graduation was accepted by the University of Illinois where I studied Biology.

In the summer of 1962, I married my Canadian boyfriend, Kestutis Salkauskas, and we moved to Waterloo, Ontario. There I continued my studies until the summer of 1963, when our first daughter, Audrone, was born. My studies were then set aside and motherhood became my passion. After my husband finished his PhD in mathematics and our second daughter, Anita, was born in 1966, we moved out west to Calgary, Alberta, where three years later our son, Arunas, was born. To my delight, Calgary had an art college and when our three children were small, I was able to attend several years of evening classes throwing clay around on a wheel.

Dornacilla Peck, who was also a faculty wife at the time (her husband was the Head of the Math Department in the early 60s), invited me to take an off loom weaving course with her and I loved it. I thought that's what I am going to do – go into weaving. I decided I was going to study fibre arts.

In 1976, once our third child was in school, I took the Alberta College of Art entrance exam and was accepted as a full time student. There I majored in fibre art, minored in printmaking, and graduated in 1980.

As a fourth-year student I was one of the organizers of the successful "FIBRE '80 – ACA" student textile travelling exhibition. The show was open to the college's entire student body and was juried by Less Graff, Katie Ohe, and Derek Whyte. Once juried, the art work travelled for a year across Alberta, British Columbia, and the Northwest Territories. For all my hard work in organizing this exhibition, I received a Students' Association Service Award from the Southern Alberta Institute of Technology (ACAD was still part of SAIT at that time).

After graduating, I taught for the Calgary Board of Education Continuing Education Department from 1981 to 2002, and children's and adult courses at the Alberta College of Art and Design, in the Continuing Education Department from 1986 to 2006.

Liv Pedersen, Pat Strakowski and I met at the Alberta College of Art and Design as mature students. We've known each other since 1978 and in 2004 made the decision to show our work at different venues around Alberta as the Three Muses. Liv has a university connection through her faculty husband and Pat's husband taught at the Southern Alberta Institute of Technology. As mothers, we nurture and guide our families. As teachers, we share our knowledge and encourage students to follow their dreams. As artists, we encourage people to see the world in a different way. My training in biology has probably influenced my way of looking at the Alberta prairie scenery and interpreting it in my work. I think I chose biology when I couldn't study art because it involved nature more directly and closely.

I was juried into the Alberta Society of Artists (ASA) in 1983 and have been an active member of the group, showing my tapestries in many of their juried exhibitions and organizing the jurying of new members for the southern part of the province from 2002 to 2005. I am also an active member of the Alberta Craft Council (ACC). In 2008 I was juried into the American quilting arts organization called Studio Art Quilt Associates, (SAQA) as a Professional Artist Member.

In 1985 our daughter was making horseback riding chaps and had a large collection of leather scraps piling up in our basement. I, not wanting to waste the leather, started experimenting and creating leather wall tapestries with her leftovers.

As my daughters were getting older and growing out of their clothes, they wanted me to save their favorite outfits and not give them away. After they left home I had several boxes of clothes sitting in my basement and not wanting to throw them out, I used them to create my first colorful quilt. I loved the quilting process and this was the start of a new artistic direction for me. I started investigating and exploring quilting techniques by reading quilting magazines, attending quilting classes, and participating in retreats with the Pincher Creek, Lebel House Quilters Guild.

I often can't find the fabric colors I need for my art work and solve this problem by hand-dying the needed fabrics myself. I prefer using white washed cotton which I scrunch up and dip into the color vat. This process produces a color combination of lights and darks. From these fabrics I cut out the needed colors. Next I sew these colorful fabrics together, cut, sew, re-cut and re-sew them several times until the desired colorful effects are achieved. The final colorful embellishment touches are added with one or all three of my sewing machines – a Bernina, a Kenmore, or an industrial Bernina. My sewing machine needles and threads have become my paint brushes. Whether working with leather and tying endless knots or sewing many miles of threads on fabrics, I find myself creating complex, multilayered, labor intensive constructions.

I have shown my Fibre Art in Western and Eastern Canada, the US, Japan, and Korea. My leather and fabric tapestries are in private collections in Canada, the US, and in the public collections of the Alberta Foundation for the Arts, Edmonton, Alberta and The Gallery and Library in Cambridge, Ontario.

Retiring from a successful teaching career in 2006, I have been creating my art work full time. I've lived in many places, but I wouldn't live anywhere else but Alberta. I really do love it here.

In the brochure describing the Alberta Craft Council's exhibition "All About Alberta," one finds:

> Ilse Anysas-Salkauskas is one of the leaders of an Alberta revival and "contemporization" of fibre arts. She is known for a series of projects using unconventional materials and techniques to comment on issues of landscape, land use, and environmental preservation.

Singing the Blues

Ilse Anysas-Salkauskas

74 cm w x 139 cm h Cotton fabrics and thread

An event in my family's past gave rise to this story quilt. In the fall of 1914, at the beginning of WWI, Russia occupied Lithuania while it was at war with Germany. The war was not going well for the Russians along the Lithuanian-German border, so the Czar sent his horseback riding Cossacks there to control the farmers that lived and flourished there. The Cossacks were looking for someone who would point a finger at his German speaking neighbors on the Lithuanian side of the border and accuse them of being spies. This would be sufficient to justify eliminating them.

They found a Lithuanian farmer willing to implicate twenty of his German speaking neighbors. The Cossacks told them that they were only being taken away for an interrogation, but the farmers knew better. One farmer made so much noise as the Cossacks dragged him away, that his older son came running to help him and the Cossacks hauled them both off. They could not find two of the farmers and took their wives instead. Another farmer had two small children and his wife was eight months pregnant; he was also taken away. So it continued from farm to farm. These farmers not only spoke Lithuanian and German, but the majority of them could also speak Russian. They had either learned Russian in school or while serving in the Russian army. Their pleas of innocence fell on deaf ears. By evening, twenty-one innocent people, nineteen men and two women, had been hanged and buried near the hanging tree. Their jackets and coats were left hanging helter-skelter all over the tree and the Cossacks moved on.

Of the twenty-one people hanged, nineteen were related to both of my grandparents in one way or another – their cousins, uncles, etc. The blue and white leaves attached to the border on the left and top of the artwork represent my nineteen hanged relatives. The twenty-one leaves loosely attached to the centre tree represent the coats left hanging on the tree for all to see. The large and small glass beads represent the many tears shed by the family members of the dead.

My grandparents lived approximately thirty-five kilometres away from the German border and my grandfather was not included in this horrible event. However, a few weeks later the Russian army came and gave him and his German speaking relatives a free train ride to Siberia instead. I felt that I had to create my story quilt to both honor the dead and remind the future generations of their past.

Memories of an ESL Teacher

Dorothy Krueger

During the eighties, I volunteered to teach English as a Second Language to immigrant women, who are often marginalized and have little opportunity to learn English because they are expected to stay in the home. Some brought children who were cared for by a lovely Estonian woman who enjoyed her little United Nations. It was great to see these preschoolers of every language and color playing together happily. There were five classes for women under the Calgary Board of Education who rented rooms for us in various parts of the city.

Although I had taught high school English, this was quite different, except that, to me, teaching of any kind requires empathy, enthusiasm, and dedication. We attended workshops, shared ideas with each other, and while we had a curriculum, we tried to engage the students in learning conversational English – making a doctor's appointment, turning off an eager telemarketer, attending parents' nights at school, shopping, homemaking – endless ideas! Great scope for our imaginations! The challenge was to meet their needs, build bridges with each other, and most of all, enable them to have a pleasant experience while learning basic English.

In the following narratives the names of the women have been altered to protect their identity.

Maria

A January day, the stinging wind with snow pellets sifted across the parking lot as two women in saris hustled into the church where the classes were held. By way of introduction, I began the conversation class by lining up all the words that refer to cold weather – freezing, bitter, frigid, icy, chilly (Inez from South America giggled at that one – she was from Chile!). I tried to empathize with their plight for they had come from lands of summer heat, brilliant flowers, and soft breezes. Then I asked if Canadians complained a lot about the weather, little smiles appeared on faces in agreement! But at the far end of the table, Maria, a little lady from Guatemala, quietly said, "Not war!" Indeed! Not war! No bombs on our heads! Snow and ice can be dealt with! How much I learned from those wonderful women!

Many times since, I have told this story to a young carryout boy at the Calgary Co-op; it takes just about the time required to get to my car and as I close the trunk invariably he agrees – NOT WAR! It restores one's perspective on disagreeable Calgary weather!

Eva

It was quite apparent that she had come to Canada from Europe in the company of a rough hewn, leather faced, stingy man! She had seized the opportunity to get out of Russia at any cost. But on every registration day she experienced great humiliation as he argued with us teachers about the twenty dollar registration fee for the biweekly twelve week course in English as a Second Language. He complained about the cost of educating "this woman" as he called her. We countered his objections by explaining that we were all volunteers and that the money received helped to pay the rent for the facilities and to buy textbooks.

She was a good student, shy, beaten down at first, but eventually became more comfortable and ventured answers even at the risk of being incorrect. One afternoon I endeavored to familiarize them with the intricacies of shopping in Canada. Terms such as "For Sale," "On Sale," or "Sale" needed explanation, as well as conditions such as "final sale" were very important. The ease with which, in most stores, one could return an object or a garment which had been purchased, as long as the original tags were in place, was considered a rare privilege by these women. With a couple of my jackets we played the shopping game. Soon it was Eva's turn. Gingerly she approached "the store," and was greeted by, "May I help you?" She stammered a reply and pointed to a white jacket. Now we had recently dealt with pronouns – he, him, his – although not too successfully. Eva reached for the white jacket which, as suggested, she tried on. To the amusement of the class she showed it off before a pretend mirror (the blackboard!); "I like; I have?" she requested. But I had carefully warned the class about the possibility of the need to return it, should it not be acceptable at home, and therefore it was important to enquire before the sale was finalized. Desperately Eva searched for the vocabulary, then, with some coaching from the class, ventured: "If my husband no like – can I bring *him* back?" A great laugh rose from the group, only too aware that it would likely be a welcome possibility! Her little smile when we explained it to her attested that she, too, agreed!

Rosa

When teaching ESL students I learned early the importance of having students laugh – at themselves, at a situation, or at me! Many had come from regimented if not cruel school situations; one who came from Ecuador trembled visibly when she approached me – the TEACHER! Fear of making a mistake restricted her ability to learn. Gradually, however, she relaxed and even laughed with us at humorous situations. Many of the women were anxious to get jobs; the only opportunity with limited English was cleaning houses. But that, too, required a reasonable vocabulary.

Rather than have the women be the potential housecleaners, I decided to reverse the role. In the supply cupboard down the hall I found a mop, broom, pail, sponge, and detergent – all requiring identification! After the class was assembled behind the closed door, I knocked on it and when a student answered I announced, "I'm here to clean your house!" Great hilarity resulted as I was wearing an old shirt and was armed with my cleaning tools which they proceeded to identify! Then I asked, "What do you want me to do first?" Rosa suggested, "Vash the floor," to which I countered, "Now?" Another said, "Vash the valls!" "O.K.," I agreed. Then, "Vash the stove," came the order! "No, clean the stove" is how to say it. "Vash the roof," said another. "You mean the ceiling," and so it went on! What a time we had!

We received complaints from a nearby classroom that we were having too much fun! I'm sure those women would agree that it was a great way to relieve the tension of a "school" situation and learn English.

Dalan

Although it was a program for immigrant women from all over the world, common threads seemed to bring us together, one being the desire to look attractive and in fashion. One mature lady sat by my elbow but never said a word until I asked the question, "What do you do for exercise?" (Note the complex word order in that one!) At once Dalan offered, "Yoga." "You do yoga," I asked eagerly. "Can you show me how to do the triangle?" At once she stood up and assumed the position expertly. I decided she was not nearly as old as she appeared to be. Her drab, grey clothing, sallow complexion, and tired eyes belied a much younger woman.

The very next day she appeared at the classroom early, then after some time in the bathroom came to class attired in a colorful plaid shirt, denim vest, designer jeans, with her hair swept back from her face which was expertly made up with lipstick and eye liner – the works! Needless to say, she was received with great admiration by the others, and having made her mark, she joined in the lesson eagerly. But on leaving the class she headed for the bathroom only to emerge carrying a plastic bag and wearing her drab attire of previous days. It all reminded me of teenagers who play this game with their parents! This behavior continued for several weeks, until one day, just as the class was starting, heavy footsteps came down the long hall, and stopped at my classroom door with loud, assertive knocking. I opened the door a crack, holding my foot against it, to be met by a young professional looking man who loudly enquired, "Is my mother in there?" I stalled, saying that he was interrupting my class and that there were twelve women here to learn English. He pushed his way past me, caught sight of Dalan beside me, gave a loud shout, turned on his heel, and stomped off! Ironically, I recognized the man as her intern doctor son whom I had encountered in a recent medical interview!

The next day she appeared in her drab grey outfit, cleared of makeup, dowdy and old, with the light gone from her eyes and with no interest in participating in the lesson. And that day I saw how another part of the world regards its women, be they mother, sister, or daughter.

Entertaining Faculty, Staff, Children, and the City
Program of Events: 1964-1965

Executive

Honorary President	Mrs. H. S. Armstrong
President	Elizabeth Challice
Past President	Marjorie Norris
Vice President	Marjory Holland
Recording Secretary	Vera Simony
Corresponding Secretary	Lorna Wright

Regular Meetings

October 21	Dr. Herbert S. Armstrong, UAC President
November 18	Madame Valda, Calgary Ballet School
January 20	Prof. Alban D. Winspear, UAC Department of Classics
February 17	Mr. Walter G. Coombs Canadian Mental Health Association
March 17	Guest Night
April 21	Annual General Meeting

Special Events

October 3	Faculty Welcoming Party, Calgary Allied Arts Centre
December 5	Staff Christmas Party
December 12	Children's Christmas Party, UAC Cafeteria Children aged 3 to 9 – of members only
February 6	University Ball, Palliser Hotel

A Warm Welcome
Pamela Harris

When we first came to Calgary in 1969, the FWC was one of the University's organizations which really made me feel at home, since we knew hardly anyone here. The welcoming party, with babysitting provided, was just great, and of course the Babysitting Swap gave me a chance to meet other FWC mothers and to have 'time out.' The Club has been a way of making close friends for many of us and a source of support and comfort for those who have needed it. Our young and vigorous leadership with new ideas have revitalized the club. Long may it continue.

A Letter in Nairobi
Joan Wing

We were packing up and leaving the University of East Africa to start a new life in Canada when a very helpful letter reached us in Nairobi, from the Faculty Women's Club in Calgary. This described life in Calgary and what we could expect to find there and contained suggestions of hotels and motels to use on arrival. This proved invaluable and made my joining FWC a top priority.

The University Hiking Club, which I joined in March 1972, introduced me to the mountains and I learned the joys of hiking from it and made lots of new friends. This Club more than compensated for the wonderful climate and scenery that we had enjoyed in Kenya. What I learnt from the Hikers I was able to pass on to my younger daughter who also learnt to love to hike, to backpack, to downhill ski and to cross country ski.

Written for the FWC's Millennium Tea, February 2000

Memories are Made of This . . .
Carol Reader

A letter of invitation from the Faculty Women's Club awaited me on my arrival in Calgary in July 1988. As I recall it was for a "welcome of potential new members" by the Executive Committee, led at that time by Elizabeth Challice. Memory tells me that it was scheduled for a lunchtime in September, fairly early in the Fall term. I was the only 'new woman' to respond to the invitation and I was disappointed for the FWC ladies who had turned out to welcome newcomers that there were not more, but I was nonetheless warmly welcomed by a group of strangers eager to see where I "fitted" into the University of Calgary and to introduce me to the benefits of FWC membership. It reminded me a little of my time in the British Navy when one was invited for the first time to some official function at the Admiral's house and there was the feeling of "having to pass the inspection!" However, pass the inspection I did, and there followed twelve years of wonderful comradeship.

During my first year in Calgary I did not work outside the home and so was able to enjoy a range of activities with the Faculty Women's Club: Quilting with Barbara Laurenson, the Out to Lunch Bunch, and Bridge. I never plucked up courage to go hiking with the stalwarts who made up that group – although I did enjoy looking at their photographs and hearing of their adventures. It was nice that there was frequently an overlap of groups and so whilst there would be some familiar faces there were nearly always new people to discover. I recall one hilarious Out to Lunch at the Cafe Royale (I hope I've got the name right) – service was very slow and the portions very small and a wonderfully outrageous Australian (no, not Amelia Kentfield!) went round taking buns off the other tables because she was still so hungry at the end of the meal! The rest of us were in various stages of hysterics at her antics.

I joined the Bridge group with some trepidation since I had not really played "in public" but rather studied books myself and then practiced my play with three teddy bears, one as partner and two as opponents. The feedback was rather limited! The Bridge afternoons were held in rotation at the houses of the ladies playing – a great deal of my pleasure was in visiting other houses to see design, etc., the Canadian houses being such a novelty to me after the cramped quarters we had left behind in England. I remember being at Vi Doucette's house and she served tea in a magnificent silver Russian samovar with an assortment of beautiful china tea cups collected during her travels. It was from her that I got the idea to start my own collection of demitasse cups which give me so much pleasure to this day, and to which collection my family makes the occasional contribution at Christmas or birthday. Sarah Glockner, Edith Zwirner, Joan Wing, Vi, and others (I wish I had a better memory because I really hate to forget names when the members were so kind to me) patiently partnered me through rounds of Bridge and tolerated my unfamiliarity with their "rules of bridge" as I labored to remember all the rules of bidding according to the number of points one had, the number of aces, kings, etc. held, and the benefits of Three No Trumps over being forced to go high in Clubs or Diamonds. Sadly, once I started work full time during my second year in Calgary my bridge playing days faded to memory and now I struggle to remember the point value of the picture cards.

The Quilting group was a chatty, pleasantly gossipy group, with one of us definitely there for the company and conversation rather than the patience to really learn the true art of quilting. The best I managed were two quilted panels for my mother which I then made into very successful cushion covers. My attempt at patchwork quilting still lies in a blue plastic bag, but reminds me of those "oh, so enjoyable" afternoons. However, these afternoons did at least give me a true insight into the huge amount of work which goes into quilting and I still gaze in awe at bed quilts and the beautiful pictures and patterns some individuals and groups manage to create. Barbara Laurenson was the group's teacher who came across as an endlessly patient, tranquil lady with an excellent sense of humor and a wonderful laugh and whose company I really enjoyed. She also taught Yoga which is where I always imagined she must have "learned" her aura of peace. Fellow quilters who gathered to sew were Ann Walker, Elizabeth Challice, Margaret Markotic, Vreni Gretener (excellent cook and author of the 'I'm Hungry' cookbook which I still use!), Ruth Armstrong, and again others whose names elude me and to them I apologize most sincerely. Ann Walker was a particularly good friend – in fact it was her husband's fault that we were in Calgary in the first place, Joe having nominated Graham for the Head's position in Mechanical Engineering! Despite a current distance of 4 000 miles we do manage to keep in touch with the Walkers at Christmas.

The Faculty Women's Club really made my transition from England to Canada a happy and successful one and I will always be extremely grateful to those women. Having spent a couple of years looking after the FWC newsletter and membership I was particularly delighted when recruitment of new and younger faculty meant increased numbers in the Club and I think all the "old" hands were pleased to see the Babysitting Swap appear once again after a gap of a number of years. It was as though things had gone full cycle and were starting afresh. I want to wish all in the Club much joy, friendship, and continued success from an Alumna now living in Windsor, Ontario – where it's warmer, but no Faculty Women's Club!

Liver Swiss Style
Vreni Gretener

1 lb	calf or baby beef liver (cut in thin strips)
4 Tbsp	butter
1	onion, minced
2 Tbsp	flour
½ cup	bouillon or white wine or half and half
¼ cup	heavy cream

Melt butter in frying pan. Add onions and fry until light brown. Add the liver and quickly turn until all the blood color has disappeared. Sprinkle flour over, add salt and pepper. Turn once more. Add wine or bouillon, add cream and serve. Do not overcook. Make this dish when everything else is ready for the meal.

Faculty Women's Club Favourite Recipes (1969). (2)1, p. 11

Where Have I Landed?
Martha Laflamme

July 1992: We moved to Calgary with our three daughters who were one, three, and five years old. It was new city for me, with a lot of new things to learn and a lot of adjustments to make, but it was fun, with exciting discoveries every day.

Fast forward a bit to August 1992: Swimming lessons at the Silver Springs outdoor pool for the two older children. Simple enough, only a two minute walk from home on adult legs, but something closer to an expedition with kids at that age, at the best of times. I just never expected that we'd wake up to a substantial snowfall! And so it was that I found myself bundling my kids into snowsuits to walk to their swimming lessons, with one thought going through my mind as we made our way there. . . . "Where have I land-ed?!"

But the water was generously heated, the lessons were a success, and of course, August snow melts quickly, right?!

A friend later commented that you can tell a Calgarian by looking in their front closet . . . jackets for all seasons remain there year round . . . too true.

A few months further to October 1992: I received an invitation to a cof-fee morning for the Faculty Women's Club, but along with the card in the mail, came a phone call from Louise Guy, a long standing member who introduced herself and offered to drive me to this get together. Some hesitation on my part that morning was quickly dispelled by her punctual arrival and generous patience while waiting for me to organize myself and my two-year-old.

Yes, it could be said that the warmth of the reception that morning con-trasted sharply with the snowfall surprise in August. Friendships were started that day that have remained strong over sixteen years later. Our children grew up with the children of some of these families, who they now happily refer to as their "pseudo-cousins."

So, "where I landed" is a place that was once only strange, but is now home, and it's the generosity of spirit of the people that we've come to know here that made that transformation possible for me.

A Hoosier in Calgary

Amy Friedman

Just like the refrain of a fellow Hoosier's song, I was "born in a small town" in Indiana, and I've ended up back in Indiana after moving several times. The most dramatic of these moves was from Columbia, South Carolina to Calgary, Alberta. Suffering from weather shock (and more subtly, culture shock) I was saved from lonely days longing for humidity and the familiar phrase "y'all" by the University of Calgary Faculty Women's Club. I was also spared the isolation of being an "at home mum" with two young children. We had the great fortune of finding a house in Silver Springs close to the home of none other than Kate Bentley and family! The first new member tea I attended was at Kate's and that was the beginning of a wonderful friendship and my happy association with Faculty Women's Club.

I have particularly fond memories of the Revolving Pot Luck Lunches. The conversations and the food were always interesting and of excellent quality. When I first joined FWC, several of us in the lunch group would have young children in tow for these lunches. By the time I left Calgary, these get togethers were for the most part sans kids as they were all at school. (Although once, Polly forgot hers were going home early and she wasn't there – a testament to how absorbed we all were in our FWC fun!) Now these children will soon be venturing out into the world on their own – or have done so already, and I believe they will carry with them an understanding of how a true community can be built by organizations like FWC, no matter how far from home they may go.

Sabbatical at -37°C

Linda Crouch

A six month sabbatical in Calgary! We had done our homework, and knew that it could be very cold. We borrowed coats for everyone before we left, and hoped that a "Chinook" would blow in until we could get boots, hats, and gloves. No such luck!!! The pilot on the plane announced that it was -37 degrees Celsius with the windchill, and blowing a gale! My husband and I bundled three children, ten suitcases, one stroller, seven pieces of hand luggage and ourselves into two taxis as quickly as we could, and headed for our new home for the next six months. As we drove up Shaganappi Trail, I wondered why they had removed all the trees off Nose Hill Park! In the next week we had to travel by bus everywhere, buy groceries, buy boots, hats, and gloves, and by the time we had bought a car, a chinook had blown in! We loved our six months sabbatical so much, we came back to live a year later.

This time we arrived in the summer, enrolled the girls into school in Edgemont, and my son in Campus Preschool, where I met Polly, which led me to Faculty Women's Club. This group welcomed me with open arms, I made many friends, and I really felt part of the community. With family so far away in Australia, Faculty Women's Club became my family. I served as Vice President for one year, and President for the following year. I never missed the Christmas luncheon, I participated in the Christmas Hamper program for students of the university, the Quilting group, the Walking group, Out to Lunch Bunch, the Christmas Cookie Swap, and, I learned a lot. We spent a total of six years in Calgary, making some great friends, and taking back to Australia three children who, to this day (now ten years later), still proudly speak with a Canadian accent.

Petit Bouquet – *Linda Crouch*
First Prize in Small or Wall Quilt (Amateur) and
Award for Excellence in Amateur Hand Quilting;
Sydney Quilt Show, Australia 2007

The Network of Women Staff Quilt and
Other Moments to Remember
Regina Shedd

We arrived in Calgary in 1968; my husband was about to start his first year of teaching in the Economics department at the University of Calgary. We had come a long way from home to a new country and a new life. It was a lonely time, away from family and friends, yet also a time of change, leaving the world of students for that of professors: we were full of excitement and had "great expectations."

Winter started almost immediately and with a vengeance. The warm, caring welcome extended by the University and the department made up for the freezing temperatures outside. There was ample opportunity for social interaction, parties, hikes, and we soon made new friends. As I started my journey on campus, it was the Faculty Women's Club that provided a bridge in my existence – a lifeline. I met many women who were to become lifelong friends. I was told immediately about the Babysitting Swap . . . but had to wait to become a mother before I could join! Without any family nearby to help with the demands of a young family, the Babysitting Swap members became my friends, companions, and my mentors. They helped form my attitudes towards childrearing and responsibility. I am forever grateful for the many friendships forged during these early years, and for the help I received along the way.

I must admit that my children had gained the reputation of being a bit of a handful among the Swap members. I was therefore understandably anxious whenever I was leaving them with a new, unsuspecting parent. Once, when a young father arrived to sit for the first time, I went into my "what to do in case of emergency" routine. I explained about our whereabouts and handed him the neighborhood contacts. He informed me that he was a father – i.e., relax, lady, I know what to do. Yet, I continued my nervous litany, explaining about doctors and hospital telephone numbers. He then said, "It's OK, I am a doctor." By then, my husband was anxious to leave but I continued to replay the same information like a learned parrot. Actually, by now any parrot would have sounded more intelligent than I. . . .

The now-exasperated sitter announced that he was a pediatrician . . . which only served to remind me of additional details to provide a first time babysitter. Finally, to cut short any more outbursts of information, he proclaimed decisively, "I am Head of the department!" At which point, my husband thankfully dragged me from the house. Needless to say, he never sat for us again. I always blamed the boys. . . .

This first foray into one of the various interest groups facilitated by the Faculty Women's Club offered opportunities to volunteer and led to my active involvement, first with the Swap and from there, as the next obvious step, with the Campus Preschool Co-operative (Co-op) which had been started earlier by University of Calgary faculty parents. Whether I was teaching English to new immigrants, school or hospital volunteering, teaching Spanish or organizing a social event, my contacts and constant companions were almost always another faculty wife.

Network of Women Staff Quilt

In 1995, then President, Murray Fraser announced he would be retiring from the University of Calgary in 1996, before the end of his second term as President. Professor Fraser, or Murray as he was mostly known, had brought to the university community, particularly to the support staff, a warm and welcoming sense of belonging that had not been witnessed before. He knew and acknowledged everyone on campus on a first name basis, whether they were faculty members, administrative assistants, clerks, ground workers, or caretakers. He was equally anxious to promote staff and women's issues. It was in this environment that NeWS – the Network of Women Staff – was started by members of the U of C women support staff. As Heather Travers once wrote, "Its primary goals are to create a collective voice for women staff, to bring concerns of women staff to the attention of appropriate bodies, to be a catalyst for change to benefit women staff on campus, to provide opportunities for networking and socializing, to enhance the sense of community among women staff, and to provide opportunities for growth and personal development."

It has been my privilege, then, to belong to two women's groups that promoted a sense of community. In either setting, I was able to weave my life with those of friends and colleagues with, at the centre, like a constant thread, the university community. In 1995, I attended a going away party for a friend retiring from the library. A colleague presented her with a beautiful quilt signed by many of her library coworkers. I was so impressed by the idea that I immediately thought it would make a fitting tribute to acknowledge President Fraser's contribution to the university community: I simply needed to think the same idea on a larger scale. I took the idea of a signature quilt to the NeWS executive for a decision and a plan. Myrna Haglund, NeWS Chair, convened what was to be the first of many meetings to organize the "NeWS Quilt Committee" project. The plan was an easy sell being, as it was, to celebrate the Frasers' contributions; we had no idea the project would mushroom the way it did. By word of mouth, friends of friends became involved and Val Pella, an experienced quilter from the Calgary community was designated my co-chair for the project which would eventually be best described as "if you build it, he — or they — will come." We were working on our own "Field of Dreams" right here on campus.

Our committee was formed of Myrna Haglund (Anthropology), Heather Travers (Faculty of Fine Arts), Val Cunningham (Student Employment), Marlene Robertson (Dean of Science Office), Susan Farmer (Drama), Hilma Baisch (Physical Plant), Judy Gayford (Faculty of Medicine), Judy Loosmore (Com / Media), Sharin Auchstaetter (Physical Plant), Carol McMillan (Senate Office), Val Pella (Calgary) and me, from the Gallagher Library. Ellie Silverman (General Studies, Advisor to the President on Women's Issues and History Department faculty wife) was our honorary faculty member. As we had no money, we needed to raise funds to purchase supplies. This is where the administrative staff proved very useful: we received donations from several deans and eventually from many U of C administrative units. We actually did not require much, we were richly provided with untapped talent and tremendous enthusiasm. Val Pella and I were the only members who had ever quilted . . .

We decided that the quilt design had to be fairly basic and leave enough room for signatures from the university community. Carol helped me buy quilting fabric at Freckles in Kensington and thanks to her whimsical eye, we came back from our shopping spree with great colors: cobalt blue with tiny brass stars and white doves. The accent pieces were to be a corn yellow fabric with tiny primroses. Carol was so excited that she pushed me right into a snowdrift during one of our most hilarious moments. Luckily the fabric was well protected! Val Pella, our quilt advisor, became indispensable because of her knowledge of quilting. Members would organize locations and advertise our meetings during the week. Fairly early, we made arrangements to cut the material on campus because of its ever growing size: What had originally been planned as a single bed cover had now become this enormous king size quilt. The news had spread throughout campus and anticipation arose in the university community.

The theme for the quilt was "thanks for the memories," from a song I had paraphrased for the retirement of one of President Fraser's favorite dance partners, Mary Nowakowski. We scheduled the distribution of the muslin signature squares for January 22, 1996, and when we went to the Bookstore to buy the necessary – and expensive pens – Phyllis Nivens, on learning their purpose, donated the pens for the cause. Armed with the new pens, women from across campus made themselves available to circulate the squares that would make up the quilt, and allow members of the university community to sign them. We would eventually collect more than 2 200 signatures. This showed how appreciated the Frasers were on campus and how the community pulled together around us to celebrate two of their own. One of our members from Printing Services arranged for the university logo to be embroidered on the centre square and she made the templates for the lettering on the quilt. Undaunted by the task we had set up for ourselves, we chose March 20, 1996 as our presentation date for the finished project. We had only to assemble the material, add the lettering and hand quilt the bedspread . . . in less than two months.

Needless to say, as for many women the world over, all our members were already juggling full time jobs, family obligations, and responsibilities, not to mention household chores . . . which meant we could only work at night. We agreed to meet every Wednesday after work, at my house because of its proximity to the university. Members brought desserts or salads, and I cooked the meals. The quilting square was set up in the basement and "my girls" went for it. Val Pella made our quilt design come to life and we actually began to believe "it" would happen. This is when we discovered that only two of us could sew a straight seam. Luckily for us, some could sew beautifully, Val taught us everything she knew; Heather brought her sewing lamp and sewing machine; Susan regaled us with feminist and union songs. We quilted to stories of past times spent together, Hilma's work with women in need, and Judy's bicycle trips. Heather told us how, years before, she, Ellie, and a friend had started the Calgary Birth Control Association. Marlene's infectious laughter kept us in the mood and we enjoyed Ellie's unending support and spirit. We quilted, talked, laughed, joked, panicked, and planned for the presentation date. Each woman did her bit; one stitch at a time, we built a circle of friendship. The same faithful three always helped with the clean up.

Since we were planning a Tea on campus to present the quilt to Anne and Murray Fraser, we requested, and obtained, the support of Food Services to be able to bring food on campus. Then Head George Thomson provided tablecloths, plates, napkins, and a coffee and tea service for 600 guests. All we had to do was pay for 300 cups of coffee. Buoyed by such a generous deal, we booked the Nickle Arts Museum as a venue for the event. The staff, especially Anne Davis and Don Sucha, were of enormous help with the hanging of the huge quilt on the wall. Bill Lindsay from Furnishings took care of our furniture needs and provided assistance with our NeWS banner, a donation from

Calgary Flagworks the previous year. A request for goodies was sent across campus; we would receive more than sixty donations of homemade delights. A suggestion to hold a raffle to guess how many signatures were on the quilt, at 25¢ per ticket, helped defray costs. Some of us sold tickets, some helped receive the food and set up the tables, Carol took care of flowers, Marlene handled the publicity, and Val worked on posters to acknowledge our many special donors and volunteers. We created books of memories that visitors could sign and that would be given to Anne and Murray Fraser. Heather Travers, Ellie Silverman, and I agreed to speak at the presentation and we arranged for Mary Nowakowski, our honorary NeWS member, to emcee on D Day. So far, we had given up many lunch hours, but I must acknowledge the strong support from all our respective departments.

The day was fast approaching. A special invitation was created for President Fraser and his wife: a color replica of the quilt was printed by Debbie Angus. The announcement for the Tea was sent to the campus community through AOSS and email, and the *Campus Gazette*, which had supported our project throughout with ongoing announcements and pictures, was involved at this point as well. The last detail was also the most important: we had to finish the quilt on time . . . I am still in awe at how we managed to accomplish this task. The night before the event, my true diehard sewers, Judy Gayford, Hilma Baisch, and I spent the evening fixing some of the quilting boo boos. As a final touch, we hand embroidered the NeWS name and the date on the back of the quilt. This has to have been my favorite evening. I had already arranged to have the quilt registered with the Alberta Heritage Quilt Society and had sewn mini quilt nametags from leftover material for each of our committee members.

On the day of the Tea and presentation, everything went like clockwork. The project had come together with the support and guidance of our committee members, but its ramifications went far beyond our little group: countless individuals and groups throughout the university community rallied to our cause and helped create a tangible memorial to the power of collaborative work. We were generously rewarded by the gracious acceptance by Murray and Anne Fraser of our "labor of love." President Fraser made us proud to be members of the University of Calgary support staff and brought us joy and dignity from the deep sense of belonging he created for us. We tried not to notice our tears.

Our committee worked very hard and yet we had a lot of fun. The friendships we made are alive today, even though we are dispersed around the world. I will always be grateful for the joy we shared on the NeWS Quilt Committee Project, and I would be remiss if I did not acknowledge my husband Stan's constant support during this, and my many other endeavors. When President Fraser died suddenly the following year, it was a very sad time for the university community. Anne had lost her beloved companion and we had lost our friend. When Anne Fraser asked us to act as ushers at his memorial service, we did so proudly. And for a last time, thanked him for the memories – memories still inscribed in each stitch of the quilt.

Two Countries, Two Loves
Michelle Caird

My story is one about dual citizenships, and at the same time, about mothers and daughters. My mother was born and raised in Manitoba; I was born and raised in Wyoming. My daughter was born in Minnesota and is being raised in Alberta. I can go even farther back to my mother's mother who was born and raised in Ireland and immigrated to Canada. Here are the stories and here is how they converge. . . .

My great-grandmother hopped a ship to Canada so she could be married to my great-grandfather – he was Protestant, she was Catholic. It was the only choice they had if they wanted to be together. They came from Limerick, Ireland and settled in Brandon, Manitoba. My grandmother was born and raised there and lived there all of her life so she really had nothing to do in the chain of immigration that I am writing about. However she did cheer Canada on every chance she got and when I was about to move here, she was extremely happy telling me it was "the best country in the world!"

After growing up and having a nice childhood in Brandon, my mother decided to become a nurse and moved to Thunder Bay, Ontario to pursue her degree. Once she became a registered nurse, she had her first experience in the United States. She went to St. Mary's Hospital in Rochester, Minnesota to further her knowledge in the area of surgical nursing. There, at the Mayo Clinic, she was able to learn a lot. I think it was while there, as well, that she decided to seek out opportunities in America. She had two choices: Duke University Hospital in North Carolina, or Cheyenne, Wyoming. She chose Cheyenne where she took on the challenge of being operating room supervisor at Memorial Hospital. I am glad that she chose Cheyenne because that is where she met my dad. They were married in 1960 and I was born a year later. Although my dad died four years later, my mother did not return to Brandon as I think I would have done. She liked Cheyenne, she had a strong support group with my dad's family and I think she was becoming American even then!

I had a nice childhood despite the loss of my dad and had really never planned to leave a place I loved. But, I met someone I loved more than my hometown and off I went, first to many places in the USA as Jeff pursued graduate degrees. Then we got our big chance to move to another country when Jeff was offered his very first professorship at the University of Calgary – Canada here we come! I didn't think I would have such a hard time with the move because I had spent every summer of my childhood in Brandon and I was used to it. In a way, I felt like I was closing the gap that my mother had made when she left so long ago. I did not realize how different Canada was than the USA and I was about to find out!

It was tough at first. We suffered the Klein-era wage rollbacks and getting used to the Canadian economy was hard. What was missing was the "American Spirit" that we had grown up with. The idea that anything is possible and that with a little competition, change can happen. We were disappointed to find that things didn't quite work the same here in Canada. It was hard to adjust to this new way of being. We often fought it. I remember often thinking at this time, "Now I know why my mother left Canada!" However, what we did find out is that there is a tremendous "Canadian Spirit," the amazing compassion and acceptance held for all peoples of the world. The true thirst for peace and the extreme pride that comes from being a peaceful nation kindled the first flames of our love for Canada.

The first year we were living in Calgary, we went to Wyoming for Christmas. I will never forget flying back into Calgary after being away for three weeks. I was very surprised to find myself excited to return. It was then that I realized that somehow, even though I was trying to fight it, Calgary, and indeed Canada, had lodged in my spirit and was now a part of me. More than just being the Canada of my mother's homeland and the place where my grandparents and aunts and uncles and cousins lived, it was now an intrinsic part of me: my story was being weaved into the history of this place and, in return, it was having an effect on my life. I remember smiling and embracing my new home. I felt pride and contentment.

I often reflected, during in our early years here, on how I had grown up in Wyoming calling a butt a bum, a hat a toque, a couch a chesterfield, and a napkin a serviette – among many other pronunciation differences. I was raised by a Canadian mother in America . . . and here I now was, raising my daughter the American way in Canada. Most kids called their moms, "Mum," like I did when I was little. Hannah calls me, "Mom," like my American peers called their moms when I was a kid. It was a very interesting perspective.

This is not to say, though, that since we have lived here in Calgary that I haven't wanted to return to the USA at times. I have met many a dual citizen who is completely happy with being here and would never leave. They have turned their backs on America so to speak. I have also met many other American expatriates who were here for a few years and went back to life with Uncle Sam. They couldn't take Canada's high taxes. We definitely lie somewhere in between. Personally, I can't imagine my life without living in Canada and I can't imagine my life without ever returning to live in the USA. Basically it is like having two lovers. I am intimately connected to both and can't imagine life without either one of them! I know – and love – both of them so well.

Back to my mother . . . as I was busy getting my Canadian citizenship in order, she was busy getting her American citizenship taken care of. For years, when I was growing up, I pestered my mom to obtain her American citizenship so she could vote. I lectured her on the American pride that we were taught in school. I taught her the Pledge of Allegiance and Stars and Stripes. Finally, she was going to be an American citizen! She did it the Canadian way – in time, when it felt right and after giving it a lot of thought. I obtained my Canadian citizenship the American way – as soon as I could so that I could vote in the upcoming elections, with lots of pride and fanfare. She would never consider returning to Canada. I, as I said before, could go either way. I love both countries and that is the way it should be as a dual citizen. As for my daughter, Hannah . . . time will tell. She has a broad range of choices, thanks to those women who have come before her.

The Gift of Community Within a Community
Evelyn Braun

It was the fall of 1974. We had just arrived in Calgary. I was busy unpacking, getting our four children settled in the various schools. Meanwhile, my husband was getting acquainted with his new position at the university. As for me, would I find a job like the one I had left behind in Winnipeg? How would I go about discovering a new circle of friends? While I was musing over these concerns, Mary Huber, a neighbor who was an avid supporter of the Faculty Women's Club, invited me to the first meeting of the year. The reception at the meeting was very warm, and that meeting marked the beginning of my involvement with the group.

Attending these gatherings was a pleasant experience. The meetings were interesting, and I found getting to know the women who came from different parts of the globe very exciting. Conversations around experiences during a sabbatical year in some faraway land always delighted me. I, too, would experience the excitement firsthand. The Faculty Women's Club also provided the venue where women from different faculties could meet and discuss what was happening in the various areas of the university, adding another interesting aspect to the meetings.

Because of the diverse interests and experiences of the women, many felt a need to form smaller groups to pursue particular interests and passions. The range of topics encompassed in these "Special Interest Groups" catered for the diversity of needs and interests represented in the membership. When the Bible Study group was formed with the most delightful and knowledgeable resource leader, Cathie Nicoll, I joined with enthusiasm. My interest has been sustained over the thirty-three years since I joined the group. The format of this study group provided a forum in which Christians from wide rang-ing perspectives could share their faith in a nonthreatening atmosphere. We soon discovered that while we attended churches of different denominations, we shared common basic beliefs. The participants in the group have become very close friends, and through the years we've discovered the gifts of support that members of the group would offer in the most natural, selfless ways.

Another "Special Interest Group" which I have enjoyed for many years is the Yoga group. I can't remember when Barbara Laurenson asked for women in the club to join her for Yoga in her home basement, though I responded with enthusiasm. The interest in Yoga grew so rapidly that we outgrew the basement and moved to a church basement. Not only was Barbara precise in the Yoga positions she taught, but also as a former physiotherapist she was able to pinpoint which muscles were involved in the varying positions. I'm sure that many of us credit our health in large measure to Barbara's expertise and commitment to the cause of exercise.

One never knows what influences our actions and aspirations, but it seems highly probable that my involvement with women of a wide range of interests, commitment, and perspectives brought about my involvement in an organization that offers support for women in developing countries, "Ten Thousand Villages." This organization has established shops across North America to market beautiful crafts of women from many countries. The income realized through our sales empowers these women in many ways: improving their lives and the lives of their children through increased opportunities for education, and it enables at least some girls to postpone marriage, enabling them to achieve some measure of independence. Often our support has enabled women to achieve some level of solidarity, enough to demand improvements in their lives and for their families. From a very modest beginning on Crowchild Trail twenty-three years ago, we realized sales of over a million dollars in 2006 – thanks to the belief of a growing number of Calgarians who subscribe to purchasing gifts that "give twice."

My sincere thanks to many women, especially, Mary Huber, Ainslie Thomas, Dorothy Krueger, and Barbara Laurenson who mentored me into a vibrant group of interesting and caring folks – a kind of community within a community. My thanks to people like Polly Knowlton Cockett, Kate Bentley, Lynn Williams, and others who sustain the club's energies and always push boundaries and new perspectives.

Snapshots from Our Family Album:
From Winterpeg to Cowtown
Winn Braun

Drivin' in a Chevy Vega

My older brother and I finally made it from Winnipeg to Calgary into Varsity Estates in our trusty little Vega where we circled around houses where driveways featured Porsches, caddies, and trans ams. Our arrival at our new house in Calgary was emphatically punctuated by the sound of the persistent backfiring of the car engine, announcing that the Clampetts had arrived. Dad had accepted a position in the Faculty of Education at the University of Calgary. We were leaving scores of cousins and friends in the Gateway to the West to come to a cowtown, a veritable cultural desert, on the cusp of an economic boom. The house in Varsity Estates with its triple garage, large yard backing onto a golf course was an indication that Calgary was on the brink of growing up. I didn't care. I was fourteen and was sure that the world had ended.

Sir Winston Churchill High School

I survived my three years at Sir Winston Churchill High School, a school with a student body more than three times that of the school I would have attended in Winnipeg. I hadn't lived in Winnipeg all of my life, but Grade 3 to Grade 9 was long enough to develop some very close friendships. Now as I watch my son Tyler and his friends wandering the streets on warm summer evenings (of which there are many more in Winnipeg than in Calgary) followed by a gaggle of girls on cellphones, I think that perhaps my parents had the right idea. Time to shake things up.

LacLu

I lived for the summers when we'd return to Winnipeg, or more accurately the family cottage on LacLu just across the Ontario border near Kenora that had been purchased two years before we moved. Keeping it had been a negotiated concession made by my parents to appease their oldest two children. Those first summers were times of reuniting with family and friends and enjoying the silky warm waters of a Canadian Shield lake.

The U of C

Entry into General Studies at the U of C was a tangible sign that Calgary had become home. I had contemplated going to the University of Manitoba, but new friends, the lure of downhill and cross country skiing in the mountains, and a young university within cycling distance of home weighed in favor of four years at Oxford on the Bow.

My somewhat passive approach to high school was replaced by a flurry of activity and involvement in the university community. The offerings were almost overwhelming. I never had any real doubt that I was going to be a teacher, but the course selection all but distracted me. I took Greek mythology, biology, calculus, political science, European and Russian history, English. . . . The final two years were only to be endured as I now had to fit in the not-so-stimulating compulsory Ed Admin, Ed Psych, and methodology courses along with a rigorous year of student teaching.

With my newfound friends, I filled time between classes playing racquetball, squash, and joined the recreational volleyball league. Regular jaunts to the mountains on weekends to hike and cross country or downhill ski, no matter how rainy or cold, ensured that my university years would be wonderfully memorable and that marks, at least during the first two years, would be less than stellar.

A Diversion, A Passion: The Cessna 150, Springbank

I'm not sure where I found time to study during the last two years of my degree because every moment I could I spent at a beat up hanger at the Springbank Airport, west of Calgary. Flying a small plane on a crisp, clear winter's day with the majestic snowcapped Rockies as the backdrop, has to be one of the most enchanting experiences imaginable. How Dad ever consented to me using his car to pursue my dream of flying, I don't know. He was the consummate worrier, a trait I'm trying not to succumb to now that I have teenage children.

To support my flying habit, I worked for professors, including Ted Giles, doing spelling research and Ed Psych research into biofeedback, early word processing/book publishing, and keypunching, which involved sending data to the mainframe computer in the basement of the sciences building and wondering whether it would turn up there (or somewhere else on campus). I also typed a few theses for MA students, which was a few years before the personal computer, so it meant retyping the entire document each time the student's advisor suggested changes. It was one of the less appealing jobs I had during my university years and definitely the least lucrative.

The Education Tower

Looking back, it almost seems that the university was my second home. Dad was the director of The Reading Clinic on the sixth floor of the Ed Tower for many years, and when the observation rooms were not being used I would study in one of them, after making a hot chocolate in the clinic library. I could usually get a few minutes of Dad's time, too, a gift since he was busy with his daytime and evening classes, Saturday clinic, and advising grad students.

The Education Block

It wasn't long into my teaching career that the U of C was once again a part of my life. I went back for graduate level education courses; this time the courses were in my interest area – literacy – and so much more motivating. These courses were offered by wonderful professors who challenged us to dig deep within ourselves and to embark on a life long journey to develop frameworks for thinking about literacy, about learners, and about our roles as effective mentor/coaches. The connections continued with several U of C students doing projects with me in the elementary classroom, literacy and ESL related.

The Teaching World and Summers

Summers during my first years of teaching were spent travelling, sometimes for pleasure and often in a voluntary capacity. Given the generous flow of money for education in the early eighties, inservice courses for teachers were many and the range of opportunities unbelievable, including sailing lessons. Along with several other teachers from my school, I signed up for sailing on the Glenmore Reservoir two consecutive springs. Each year I waited and watched anxiously for the ice to break up on the reservoir so that the lessons would go ahead. By the end of the second spring, I had successfully completed my level III White Sail, and had only capsized once and experienced firsthand how quickly hypothermia sets in on a cold and windy Calgary spring day. My White Sail III and my love of travel enabled me to work as a sailing instructor two summers – first on Cash Island at Manitoba Pioneer Camp and then at Atlantic Pioneer Camp on Prince Edward Island.

After five years of teaching in Calgary it was time to venture further afield. I almost accepted a teaching position which involved "driving the back hollows" of Kentucky, but an ancient junior high yen of mine to explore the Far East surfaced when the possibility to teach ESL in China was offered. I taught at two medical universities for two years and returned to Calgary to find that there was a growing ESL population and the need for ESL teachers was great, with or without a diploma. For me to feel a little more prepared for entering the elementary school world of ESL, I was once again destined for the U of C campus and a summer school course. It gave me the opportunity to meet other teachers interested in the same field and helped me to mesh some of my overseas experiences with the realities of elementary ESL teaching.

It would still be another year until I met my future husband, so I was a relatively free spirit. Teaching ESL had its challenges, but certainly was not as demanding as teaching classroom. So this time, I decided to pursue French language studies through the Faculty of Continuing Education. The professor was a wonderful French woman with the most enchanting voice and the patience to encourage a diverse group of mostly young adults to converse comfortably in French.

Campus Preschool

Any chance of becoming remotely bilingual was interrupted when I was swept off my cross country skis on Skogan Pass one Christmas Break by a teacher who had taught in Northern Manitoba, travelled through South Africa, and was visiting his sister and her young children in Calgary. . . . Two children later we had become established Parkdale residents with its wonderful access to long stretches of walking and biking pathways. I stayed home with Tyler and through an ESL colleague and friend Christine Laurell, whose son Mattias was a few weeks older than our son, was introduced to a walking group that was to weave in and out of our lives for years to come. Polly Lee Knowlton Cockett, Kerri Blair, and Patricia Etris and their children were regular walkers and we found ways to stay connected during the winter months. Somehow three of us had our second child around the same time, so that they, too, would have playmates when we got together for various activities. There was some coming and going of other women and their children, but our core group continued walking together regularly until our youngest children began their formal schooling.

The Brentwood Playgroup was founded by Patricia Etris during this time, and the walking group children and their mothers were active members of the group. By October of Tyler's year with the group, his new baby sister, Mikala, was brought in her bucket to each Tuesday morning session. Tyler was the protective big brother, supervising who would be permitted to have a Mikala viewing. It was also another regular opportunity for Tyler to play with his walking group buddies and for me to socialize with women who shared a similar view of the world and often discussed things beyond our comfortable and safe little community.

Preschool options soon became part of the conversations and since we had a cooperative preschool close to home, it seemed natural that Tyler would attend and become acquainted with more of the neighborhood children. It was within easy walking distance, an activity that has always held appeal. Tyler had a good three-year-old preschool, but the stories of Heidi and Campus Preschool and a chance to reconnect with the walking group children were excellent reasons to make a switch. And a great move it was! From Heidi's carefully chosen stories, to fun crafts and a wide variety of play centres, to her soft spoken approach dealing with the often times rambunctious four-year-old boys with strong opinions about who was in the right in any given situation, gave Tyler a rich preschool experience.

You would think that I would have gone with the known and undisputed excellence of Randie's three-year-old program at Campus Preschool, but for the same original reasons Tyler had gone to our community preschool, Mikala was registered. The difference, and it was huge, between Tyler's time and Mikala's was that the teacher had left and been replaced by a nice, but extremely incompetent person. Fortunately, since Mikala didn't turn three until October, I went with her to school. It wasn't long before I could see the negative impact the experience was having on my gregarious and happy little girl. The decision was soon made to withdraw her from the program, but unfortunately there was no room in Randie's class, but the moment registration opened for the following year, Mikala was on Heidi's class list. Mikala went happily with her friend Connor who lived around the corner from us and met up with Tenzin, one of her walking group buddies. She soon made friends with a number of the other children and couldn't wait to go to school every Tuesday and Thursday. Mikala remembers hatching ducklings, making ice cream, the little homemade stockings with a candy cane at Christmas, and going up into the "gym" to play her favorite game: Duck, Duck, Goose. Playing outside with "every toy imaginable" and running in and out of the bushes are other favorite memories. I also remember springtime and Tyler dressed in rain pants and boots, having the time of his life running and playing in the vast puddles left by the hockey rink and snow melt. Watching very serious four-year-olds take turns with the safety goggles and wielding hammers to pound nails into two large tree stumps was fascinating. If the activity was safe, there was no stopping a child from playing and exploring. It was always fun volunteering at the preschool and seeing the children having fun and learning about the world and how to get along with each other.

Back to Winnipeg

Despite the almost incredulous "Why?" when my husband and I announced that we were moving to Winnipeg in 2004, we arrived to find our house not ready for possession and one of the soggiest, coldest summers on record. There are similarities to my Mom's move from Winnipeg to Calgary thirty years before when she, too, left friends and family. Age forty something, four kids to my two, a new life. Not the easiest age to make new friends when you've left a place called "home," and left the work force to make a new home for your family. The Faculty Women's Club, and particularly some special members, enabled Mom to find outlets for her feelings and energies shortly after our arrival in Calgary. Significantly, the biweekly Bible study originally led by Cathie Nicoll very quickly became a focal point for enduring relationships and support. Indeed, many of these women became lifelong friends. In later years a group, under the gentle guidance of Barbara Laurenson would meet in a church basement for weekly Yoga classes. It would seem that the Faculty Women's group had become a significant force to ease an otherwise daunting transition. I would love to have found a similar group to make settling into life in Winnipeg easier.

Please Don't Grieve for Me
Dorothy Sharman

Scenic Acres, August 2003

Dear Richard and Philip and Jodey,

I hope when the end comes it comes quickly and in case it does, I want to tell you how much I love you all, and to thank you for being so wonderful, so kind, so patient and forgiving of my slowness and hard-of-hearing-ness. I feel so grateful and want you to know how much I appreciate all you have done.

Please don't grieve for me, I have had a long life and a happy one but I'm long past my "best before" date! I'm ready for the next stage and for being with Bernard again.

All my life I've been lucky. I had a very happy childhood and loved school. Then University life was marvellous (except Intro Physics when the weeks went from Thursday afternoon with its three-hour practical work to Thurs) and there I met and fell in love with Bernard. The war marred the last year at University of course, with its blackout and curtailment of social events (as President of Oxley Hall I would have been invited to all the other Halls of Residences' formal dances) but they were cancelled of course. Teaching wasn't all that great, nor the blitz on Sheffield but there again I was lucky – a stick of bombs fell on either side of the house I was in, and the third on the school where I was teaching, but I was O.K. I was in the Anderson Shelter in the next door garden and oddly enough I wasn't a bit worried about being blasted to bits but I was furious that I'd just bought a packet of 'A' envelopes (i.e., prestamped ones) and that they might be destroyed – a whole packet! Of 12, I think. And a 1½ penny stamp on each!

Even the illness that the doctors thought would prove fatal didn't worry me and wasn't painful though Bernard and my parents were worried stiff. Anyway I survived to everyone's surprise. (And to big injections every other day for the next two years and that was a nuisance.)

Then we were married – a wartime wedding was very simple of course. Rationing of food was in force and it was actually illegal to ice a wedding cake so we started off our married life by breaking the law! But my mother has scrounged and saved [rationing] coupons and she managed wonderfully. Clothes too were rationed but somehow one managed. A honeymoon was impossible but we had our tiny flat waiting for us in Leeds and after a tiresome train journey, with I think five changes, maybe more, from Builth Wells in Wales to Leeds, a journey of seven hours of so, we were glad to get to our new home. I still wasn't really well you see. It was two years before they removed my spleen but after that I never looked back.

Being married in wartime had one asset, food was so scarce Bernard was grateful for anything at all edible! Not that he was ever critical but always appreciative, bless him. During the war he was always hungry. We never starved like the poor folk in the Netherlands but Bernard was always hungry. He used to drink hot water from the tap to fill his tummy. Rationing – to a limited extent – was still in force when Richard was born. In fact bread wasn't rationed during the war, though so scarce, but when places in Europe were liberated we sent precious wheat to them so BUs or Bread Units were necessary to buy bread or cakes for a few years. Biscuits were always of course rationed. We had one of those big English prams of course, the sort you could turn into more of a push-chair as the child grew older, by putting up a back and letting down the front. So he sat up instead of lying down. One day I'd been to the shop and got the week's ration of eggs, one each for Bernard and me and two for Richard if I remember rightly, and put them in the pram behind the seat. Unfortunately Richard got excited (probably by a steam roller!!!) and put his hand back and smashed the week's eggs! So we had scrambled egg and that was that!

Fortunately by the time Philip was born rationing was a thing of the past. As newborns both boys were ill but thank God both survived and flourished. Richard was white as marble and spent his first few days in an oxygen tent in the nursery. Bernard thought it wasn't fair for him to see him before I did but I urged him to; so after a few days he did. Anxiously I awaited his reply to my question but imagine my dismay when he replied, "He looks just like a tadpole!" What a thing to tell a new mother! But the nurse had lifted Richard up with a blanket trailing down like a tail and a baby's head is always big in proportion, so later I forgave Bernard. Philip too spent his first days in the nursery having his blood transfusions, so I didn't see him for a bit either.

So I have been very fortunate, very blessed. During the years I have been very proud of them both and now I rejoice in having a wonderful daughter-in-law.

This started off as a "thank you" note with a "don't grieve" bit added, but it seems to have become a potted autobiography. Sorry.

I love you all. You're a wonderful family.

Mother – Dorothy

A letter to her children, read by her daughter-in-law at her Memorial Service on July 5, 2007

Poppies I Do Remember
Ilse Anysas-Salkauskas

97 cm w x 153 cm h   Leather

After a second trip to Europe, I created this leather tapestry. There I saw many poppies as we travelled from country to country. These red flowers reminded me of the freedom won in both world wars by Canada and its allies.

Chop Suey (Serves 5)

Penny Storey

2 cups	boiling water (approximately). Water from Chinese vegetables can be used.
2	bouillon cubes
3 Tbsp	soya sauce
2 cups	diced cooked pork (I use left over pork roast)
¼ cup	flour
1 tsp	salt
1 tsp	sugar
1 cup	sliced onions
2 cups	celery strips
Large can	Chinese vegetables

Pour water over cubes and soya sauce to make stock. Brown pork in shortening, stir in flour. Add stock slowly, stirring constantly. Add onions, celery, salt, sugar; cover and cook slowly 30 minutes, stirring frequently. Add vegetables 5 minutes before serving. Serve with rice.

Faculty Women's Club Favourite Recipes (1969). (2)1, p. 10

Madeleine "Penny" Storey was a Charter Member of the Faculty Women's Club.

Nurturing

A Special Legacy
Cookbooks as Collector's Items

We have a special legacy from the suppers of the mid sixties – the cookbooks. The idea of publishing the first one originated from the time when we displayed the recipe beside the special dish we had brought to the supper. Our members' requests for the recipes resulted in publication. Volumes Number One and Two of our *Faculty Women's Club Favourite Recipes* and the *Christmas Supplement of Holiday Cookery Samples* became permanent memorials to our varied cooking backgrounds. Penny Storey compiled Volume No. 1 in 1967 and its outstanding gourmet collection of international cuisine resulted in a second printing. Vera Simony prepared the second volume and now both are out of print. Collector's items!

Norris, p. 9

A Recipe for Friendship
Lorri Post

Five moves in four years! An exhausting time for spouses of university professors! To say nothing of finding new friends with each change of city.

I discovered a Faculty Women's Club when I arrived at the University of Wisconsin in 1987 with a one-year-old in tow. Frantically searching for some companionship, I contacted the Chamber of Commerce, who asked if I was somehow affiliated with the University. The result was a number of wonderful friendships with many other women in the same circumstances.

A few days after arriving in Calgary four years later, the current President had a welcome evening for new faculty. It was there that I met a wonderful

October 7, 1970

The Social Convener's Report was given by Elizabeth for Ruth.

A crisis had arisen when the new manager of the Dining Centre insisted we pay rental of the Blue and Gold Dining Room each meeting, and other expenses were involved if china cups were used and coffee made by catering staff. Room rental $60.00; Cups and coffee $20.00.

However, we do have written assurance that we may use the room free of charge.

This situation is to be investigated.

Authorization was sought and granted for buying either a new coffee urn, or, if available, replacing the missing components of one urn.

November 12, 1970

Coffee Convener's Report given by Burdette for Ruth.

A new coffee urn has been purchased.

Business arising from this report: Eileen asked if any decision had been made on the disposal of the old coffee urn. No arrangements had been made, so she asked to be allowed to buy it as her husband could use it. Her request was granted, and the price left to her discretion.

May 18, 1973

It was suggested by Berta that the Coffee Convener be a hostess at the general meetings.

July 3, 1974

Coffee Convener If the cost of cookies from the dining centre increases, the coffee convener will arrange for the membership to bring "goodies" to the meetings.

person named Kate. She asked if I had any children so that we might get together for coffee and playtime with the kids.

I arrived at Kate's house the next week, two children in tow (one now five and a six-month-old) and with fresh, homemade muffins. Our playdates continued, and each time I made a different type of muffin. We became great friends and the secret was never let out . . . the muffins were from a mix!

Years passed with Kate still convinced that I was a wonderful cook. Many potlucks, coffee mornings, and barbeque get togethers with other friends (Polly Lee, Martha, and Amy, to name a deluded few) all continued with the illusion that I was a great cook. It is amazing what you can make from a mix.

It wasn't until many years later that Kate discovered my secret. Still after nineteen years of friendship, I am known as "the box lady." However, those boxes helped to create a lasting friendship for which I will be forever grateful. Did you know wine comes in a box?

A Recipe for Friendship

A bit of time
A few children
A steaming cup of coffee
A huge helping of friendship

A holiday celebration
A late night phone to relieve a worry
A shoulder to cry on
A friend that offers unrelenting support

This is the recipe for a life long friendship!

Dear Friends

Beatriz Bland

When I think of the Faculty Women's Club the first person that comes to mind is Mrs. Elizabeth Challice. That is because when John first joined the Physics Department, Dr. Cyril Challice was the Head, and that meant you treated his wife with a certain awe. Years later, when John became Head, I would ask myself: What was all the fuss about? A few ladies from Physics, Sarah Mathews, the late Claire Sreenivasan, and others joined the FWC. This was great for me because I didn't know ANYBODY in Calgary and all our relatives were either in the UK or Bolivia. It was soon after that the Babysitting Swap was formed and . . . boy!, did that change my life, and, I am sure, that of many others FOREVER. I had three and a half-year-old Julie Anne and eight-month-old Henry when we first arrived from Italy (both kids were born there), and through the Babysitting Swap, they were able to make some new friends and so did I! Not only from Physics but from other departments, too. It is true that most lived in the northwest, so many were really close neighbors . . . even as near as across the back lane! That was Barbara Stevenson; up the road Pamela Harris, down the road Ilse Salkauskas; just a couple of blocks around the crescent Regina Shedd, past another house, Linda Heidemann, almost next door to her, Marlene Peattie, a block up the Green, Pamela Morrow, a few blocks down the road Jan Gregory, more to the west Ute Dilger, Sheena Rauk, and at least 10 others that have since moved away or left the country. If I am not mistaken, the Babysitting Swap's greatest organizer and founder was Ann Walker; her husband Jo was in Engineering, that much I remember.

But there were other FWC activities too, like the Town and Gown Balls. Outstanding amongst the organizers was my good friend Norma Oliva. She was the great artist, painter, and decorator and came out with impossible ideas (only she made them possible) like: a late February or early March 1972(?) she went to the river's edge and picked up armful upon armful of pussywillow branches that she placed in containers of water using as many undeveloped basements as possible (we were all starting our homes, remember!). The willows needed a warm, well ventilated environment for the next 4 to 6 weeks before they sprouted. Then with this glorious greenery all around, we were ready to enliven the largest ballroom at the University in what was the Dining Centre and had ourselves the greatest Spring Ball of the year.

Many moons have passed since; new faces have replaced old ones. I might remember a face but not the name or vice versa, yet, there remains that warm feeling that lingers within me when I think of the Faculty Women's Club.

Meningiomas

Kate Bentley

Why is writing so difficult? In essence we write everyday with our voices, but when it comes to putting it to paper many of us freeze. So where do I start this story that I want to write? Do I start many years ago in 1991 when we first moved to Calgary and within days met people associated with the university and Faculty Women's Club who are still really good friends or do I start a few Novembers ago?

Maybe I'll start in November 2006. Two things happened that November and although I cannot be sure of the order of events, I think the first one was to attend an interview at The Calgary Foundation. This was an effort to convince TCF to give FWC $10 000 to publish a book. I remember the day quite clearly: Polly and I both very nervous but knowing that we had our ducks lined up; we gave the best presentation we were capable of that day. Fortunately we were successful in our bid and our book is going to be published soon.

The next event I remember happening that November was meeting with a neurologist. He took one look at my gait, and told me I didn't have a lower back problem but had an upper motor neuron problem which could be MS, ALS, or any other nerve disease or even brain tumors. The tumors however, couldn't be malignant or I would be dead (subsequent to this meeting we have discovered that neurologists and neurosurgeons have strange senses of humor!!).

Fast forward to early January 2007 when I had an MRI of the upper body (finally) and then a further meeting with the neurologist in late January. The first thing he said was, "Well, the good news is that it's totally treatable." "What is?" both my husband and I asked. He responded, "The meningiomas." "What are meningiomas?" we both asked. His response, "Brain tumors which are usually benign, and by the way you have six of them." Believe it or not at this point I was euphoric, mainly because I had convinced myself that I had ALS or MS and I was so relieved that I didn't have either. He had also told us my condition was treatable. At that stage I certainly hadn't considered the ramifications of brain surgery. That frame of mind, however, did change.

So as mentioned, the meeting with The Calgary Foundation went well and we were given a grant for $10 000 which was to enable Faculty Women's Club to publish an anthology of women's stories – women who had stories to tell and were in some way or another affiliated with the University of Calgary. As we were celebrating the 50th anniversary of FWC it seemed a very apt time to get many of these stories on paper. Also it seemed an important time to commemorate some of the incredible works that have been accomplished by many of the women associated with U of C. So that included me and before the second tumultuous event happened in November 2006, I had no idea what I would write about. However, once "meningiomas" became an everyday word in my vocabulary, my story became as clear as daylight.

Both leading up to and during and after my surgery I have been surrounded by a community of loving, caring people who pretty much all in some way or another are affiliated with the University of Calgary. They are the people who came to see me during my time in hospital. They are the nurses and doctors who got their degrees at the University of Calgary, my family and my community of family who are mainly faculty women. We have all developed such a bond that our children now refer to each other as "surrogate cousins."

So let me write a synopsis of my journey. Not from the beginning. I started feeling not well so many years ago that I can't even remember when, but I can tell you that I had more MRIs, nerve conduction tests, x-rays, etc. than a person could ever wish for. However, had one of the specialists along the way ordered an upper body MRI my body's debilitation would not have gone on for so long. Having said that, the good news is that it hasn't done me any harm. Hallelujah. The other good news is that three of the tumors are gone and I only have three left, all of which are quite small and manageable.

So I will continue this tale on the morning of my surgery – March 15, 2007 – the Ides of March.

We had to be at the hospital by 6:30 a.m. for a 7:30 surgery, and it had been decided that Larry and Meghan would accompany me. Surprisingly I slept well, woke up with the alarm and trudged off to the bathroom. Even without surgery I was not in a good mood. Not being allowed a cup of tea to wake up with is never good in my book. So into the shower, where I had to prep my head for the surgery. I was given an antiseptic block, the kind of scrubbing brushes you see on the TV that all the hunky doctors use when scrubbing in. So I was scrubbing my head. I had to wash my head, coat it with this sponge stuff (coal tar soap smell), scrub it and leave it for five minutes and then rinse it off. To be honest I can't remember if I did all the things they told me to do. The morning of my surgery has kind of hidden itself in my mind somewhere and hopefully will never be fully retrieved.

So off we trot to the hospital. Larry dropped Meg and me off and we dutifully went to Admitting, and then were sent to the 4th floor. The 4th floor was full of people, all either waiting for surgery or the families of people waiting for surgery. You could only tell the people having surgery if they had already changed into their very attractive surgical suits. You all know the kind. So we checked in and were told to take seats. No sooner had we found seats than we were called into another room. At this point I became less Kate Bentley and more "a patient." The nurse gave me the surgical wear, green gown which does up at the back, pants, and very lovely green paper slippers. She also took all my health cards, drugs, etc. and in return gave me two more fashionable bracelets. I believe one was fuchsia pink which mentioned my allergies. Shrimp. The other was fluorescent green; this one had my name on it. I had a further one which was yellow and had all my blood information. These were to become my constant companions until I left the hospital.

So back out into the hall, more seats and then name calling. I then discovered that I was special because I had to go to the MRI Theatre. At this point Meg had to leave us. Apparently only one person was allowed to stay with the patient in the room next to the operating room. Larry and I head to where we're supposed to be going. At this point things become surreal. Larry and I were sitting in the anteroom outside the operating theatre. Nurses, doctors, orderlies, the tea lady for all I know were coming and going, semi-gowned, normal day on the job for them, right. For me my fear was absolute and I had no idea how they could be so NORMAL when I felt so TERRIFIED. Finally somebody notices us. The anesthetist comes in and introduces himself. Alas, alack, nobody had done a heart monitor test on me and he certainly wasn't going to knock me out for 8 hours plus without checking my heart. Brownie points to him. The heart monitor cart appears out of nowhere and guess what – my heart is fine – thank goodness for that. I then have to start signing all sorts of things. For example, did you know that my tumors are no longer mine – they belong to the tumor bank?

At this point I told Larry I was ready to do a bunk. I really didn't want to go through with this and I would like to leave right now. He wouldn't let me but I was ready, if he had looked the other way I would have been gone. Full green hospital gear including bracelets and green paper shoes. The image of a crazy women running down 29th Street still lingers in my mind from time to time. Eventually the surgeon wanders in. Asks me how I am doing – does my shaking not make it obvious. As he's asking me how I'm doing, he's coughing. I'm thinking, "Why is he coughing?" So when he walks away I say, "You have a bit of a cough." His response, "That's what happens when you live with a six-month-old." I'm thinking, "Why is this guy doing surgery on me when he's got a cough?" Sense prevailed; if we all stopped doing our jobs because of our children and what they can give us, I guess we would get nothing done. So the moment arrived and this very sweet, perky nurse from England (a trick to make you feel more comfortable – I am sure they match nurses with nationalities of people to make them less nervous) comes to get me. "Okay Kate, it's time to go now." Quick hug and kiss to Larry and he, poor soul, is left there to watch me walk into the operating room. Yes, I WALKED into the operating room – hey what is this? If you watch the TV, people are wheeled to their operating beds and they are lifted, "One, two, lift." No, not me. I had to climb up onto the operating table and scoot my bum down to the required line and then they strapped me in. They knew I was ready to do a bunk. They told me, "We don't want you to fall off." But I've got them sussed.

So then Ms. Perky, actually a very nice nurse, told me to relax and that they were going to do this and that. Face mask, drip for anesthetic, blah, blah, blah. I was totally wide awake, nobody had given me even the faintest touch of a drug to calm me. Then the mask comes over the mouth, trouble is it wasn't working. They couldn't get a complete lock so somebody else walks across and helps. That was it – I woke up with a very fat lip and my next conscious thought was many, many hours later. So in a sense I do feel cheated, not being wheeled into the operating room, no "One, two, lift", no counting backwards "10, 9, 8, 7, 6 . . .," none of that. However, the surgeon was correct. He told me I would sleep through the whole thing, so shouldn't worry. You know what, he was right.

As it turns out the surgery was textbook. They nabbed three tumors, all of which released themselves from my brain exactly as they should. As mentioned earlier, I will have to have more surgery eventually, but progress happens fast and they have already discussed using a robot next time.

My story could go on and on what with recovery, incisions getting infected, going back into hospital for another week and a second surgery. I won't bother since I know it happened and I came through it. I came through because of the love of family and friends. Apart from the constant flowers, cards, gifts, and visits when in hospital, I felt surrounded by love. My sister came from England for three weeks and waited on me hand and foot. She made me do my exercises, took me for walks around the block or initially just outside the house, and most importantly, cleansed my wound. After Judy left, a roster of meals was arranged that would appear every night so that all I had to do was eat. I could go on and on, but won't. All I know is that without the community I have, I would not have recovered as quickly or as well as I did. For that I am eternally grateful and am glad that I am finally able to put this on paper. Without friends, community, sense of place, and time, our lives would be nothing.

Companions in a Golden Bean Patch

Karen Gummo

A Certain Comfort

Audrey Andrews

It was while I was tidying up my filing cabinet recently that I began to think about our old coffee group. There were four of us, four women, who met weekly at the same coffee shop, for about fifteen years. At first, all of us were graduate students at the University of Calgary. We were preparing for second careers now that our children were old enough to be on their own during the day. We arrived at the coffee shop within minutes of each other and gathered around one of the small square tables. Sometimes our voices, our laughter, intruded briefly upon the conversation of other customers close to us, but we didn't worry about this. Neither did the people sitting near us, who were regulars too, and accustomed to the overlapping not just of voices, but of purses, briefcases, newspapers, coats, scarves. No one worried much about sorting things out until we were ready to leave, and we did it then without ceremony.

We almost never met in each other's homes; we did not include our husbands, if we had them, or other men or women, in these meetings; when an "outsider," a man or a woman, was invited as a guest, it was with the group's agreement, and an unspoken understanding that this was an isolated event. Over the years, the four of us spent a few weekends together at academic conferences and at Jennifer's cottage in the mountains, but even then, and perhaps then, in particular, we were, I thought we were, cosseted by the familiarity, the safety we felt in our relative isolation, but in each other's presence.

There was no beginning or end to our weekly conversations. We continued our discussions from one week to the next, picking up the thread as we remembered it or had elaborated upon it alone or with others since the previous week. Occasionally a question or objection arose in someone's mind during the week, and it might take precedence when we met next, but usually there was a quick and generally agreeable resolution. As the years went on and we were no longer students, we talked about our teaching at the University, about novels, stories, poems, literary criticism, our writing, about other books we read and ideas that were important to us. Our conversations were not really about what we did everyday. They were seldom about our domestic lives. But as Jennifer said once, we talked about what we think every day. I believe that women have always found, or wanted to find, groups of friends such as ours. I remember my mother belonging to such a group from the University of Alberta, for thirty years at least. They called themselves the Fidelis Club.

As I try to think how to describe the interrelationships among us as a group, I find myself remembering specific details of our days together in places other than the coffee shop. What I do remember about our weekly meetings was the urgency of our discussions. So my active engagement in the mental exercise of these moments must have taken precedence, in my memory, over other more subtle observations.

My memories of our days at Jennifer's cottage, particularly of one weekend, are quite specific: no music, no TV, no films on video, no deep analytical discussions or academic gossip. There was silence mostly: long walks; easy, political, environmental talk; general agreement; gentle conversation during dinners together; laughter; comfortable sharing of bathroom time; pleasure in an escape, a change, a rest, for everyone.

I remember that one afternoon I put on a sweater and a jacket to go out on the deck. It must have been May, after we had finished marking exams. Jennifer was there, her feet up on the ledge.

"You should lie down for a while, Emily." She took her feet down and curled up in her chair.

"I may. Did you see the blue heron on the beach this morning?"

"Yes. And you at the end of the dock with your coffee."

"The water was so clear, glassy. I could see right to the bottom – and all the fish!"

"In the summer during the day the boats stir it up, and the kids. They are in and out, swimming all the time. But when I get up it's clear."

We sat silently for several minutes looking out at the lake and the tree-covered hills, the almost mountains surrounding the lake, embracing it. The water was not glassy now and the cool spring wind was ruffling the surface. There were a few ducks near the dock, but no other birds in sight. The sun was bright, making me think that I should go for a walk, look for stones and the frogs that I knew gathered in the little inlet down the beach from the cottage.

Later, I went to the bedroom Louise and I were sharing that weekend, sleeping on the narrow cots there for children during their summer holiday months. I took hold of the door knob firmly, turned it silently, and opened the bedroom door. I expected to see Louise lying on her cot, either resting or sleeping, and I thought that I, too, would lie down. But Louise was not lying down. She was standing directly in front of the window, dressing. She had pulled down the cream-colored, old fashioned blind that did not darken the room, but, instead, gave it a soft, gold, hazy glow. I was looking directly at her profile and she had not heard me open the door. Louise had put on her panties and now was leaning forward slightly, allowing her full breasts to fall into the cups of her brassiere. She straightened, fastened the hooks at the back, lifted the straps on her shoulders, and ran her hands gently over her breasts as she reached for the band at the bottom of the brassiere to lift and smooth it comfortably over her midriff. Louise looked down at her body, as one does when one is alone. Her torso, her slender, straight legs, her feet, narrow, delicate, the feet of a younger woman. Louise's straight, auburn hair, cut expertly to the tips of her ears, fell forward, almost covering her face. I shut the door quickly, silently, wondering how long I had stood there, transfixed by this vision of Louise, and by my own accidental intrusion into her privacy.

I remember two occasions when I spent time alone with Margaret. One time we drove through the mountains together on our way to an academic meeting. Our conversation was easy, agreeable, but not particularly intimate. Margaret pointed out to me the wildlife we passed: deer, a bear, mountain goats. When we stopped for coffee a Steller's jay came onto the picnic table where we sat, boldly alert for a crumb of whatever he could take from us. I had never seen a Steller's jay and I was stunned by the brilliant blue of its sleek feathers.

Another memory that I have of Margaret is from a weekend at Jennifer's cottage. It was early evening, dark inside the cottage because of the foothills surrounding us. Margaret and I had offered to make the salad while the others went out for a walk in the last moments of daylight. The low kitchen light shone on and past the kitchen counter and over the long oak dining table that was set now for dinner. The rest of the large room adjacent to the kitchen, except for the fire in the grate, was dark. As we finished the salad, picking up individual leaves of lettuce to rub the oil gently into them, Margaret and I talked quietly about George Herbert's poetry and especially his spectacular list of metaphors in the sonnet, "Prayer 1." I don't remember much of our conversation, but I have thought many times of the pleasure of those moments with Margaret, of the domestic skills that have become second nature to our lives as wives and mothers and professional women.

I believe that Margaret is, of the four women, the pure academic. The papers she has published are perfect, faultless. For years I have seen Margaret as the coolest of us all, and the most knowing and observant of human behavior. Margaret is the only one of us who embraces an orthodox religion and she rarely, almost never, spoke of it. She must have listened many times to comments from the rest of us that offended her. She barely reacted when such incidents occurred, keeping her thoughts to herself and thus unnoticed. But, finally, she began to speak quite frankly about certain events or public figures, films, novels, leaving us nonplussed. We looked at each other, acknowledging silently that here was an aspect of Margaret we did not know, that we did not know at all. I was surprised to realize, as I was sure the others do as well, that we do not know each other perfectly, despite the intimacy we have shared for years.

Our group does not meet weekly anymore. Some of us do not live, still, in Calgary. But when we meet together, two or three of us, there is a certain comfort in our having known each other for so long, in our being together.

One time, only a few minutes after we all arrived at Jennifer's cottage, I said, as much to my surprise as that of the others probably, that I was so glad I had come and that I felt perfectly safe there and in their company. This was a rather strange thing to say, actually to say. Although we knew each other well and relied on each other in many ways, we were not given to overt expressions of our acceptance of and dependence upon each other, or the affection we felt for each other. Later, alone in the bathtub, I thought about my remark, my sudden candor. But as I slid down into the water to rinse the suds off my back and shoulders and then stepped out of the tub, I thought only of the pleasure we would share during the next few days.

Cream of Tomato Soup
Dornacilla Peck

4 Tbsp	margarine
1 cup	sliced onion
1	diced apple
1 20 oz can stewed tomatoes	
½ - 1 tsp whole pickling slices	
2 tsp	sugar
½ tsp	salt
1/8 tsp	pepper
1/8 tsp	paprika
2 Tbsp	butter
2 Tbsp	flour
1 tsp	salt
2 cups	milk

Melt butter, add onion and apple. Cook slowly. Add tomatoes, spice, sugar, ¼ tsp. salt, pepper, paprika. Bring to a boil. Simmer 5-8 minutes.

Rub mixture through sieve (about 2 cups). Melt 2 Tbs. butter, blend flour, salt. Slowly add milk. Cook until smooth and thick. Remove from heat and combine with tomato puree.

Beat with beater and reheat in double boiler.

Faculty Women's Club Favourite Recipes (1969). (2)1, p. 42

Creative Caring Practices of Nurses

Carole-Lynne Le Navenec

Introduction

I began my career in the Faculty of Nursing at the University of Calgary in 1981 after working as a public health nurse associated with a large psychiatric hospital near Toronto. It was likely this past work experience that influenced me to explore the research literature to identify approaches that might be effective both in promoting health prior to any illness condition, or as a mode of *creating health* in situations or contexts of chronic illness (which in that particular case involved individuals with a serious mental illness). Furthermore, I came to value the use of the creative arts in health care through my doctoral study of families caring at home for a relative with Alzheimer's disease or a related dementia. As outlined in the book about these findings (see Le Navenec & Vonhof, 1996), many of the older people and their families used music or singing to help manage the stress they experienced. The findings of members of our Creative Arts/Integrative Therapies in Health Care Research Group (the CAIT group: www.cait.fr.nf) will show how these approaches helped to promote health and well-being for individuals and their families in both health and chronic illness contexts.

Music, Reminiscence and Humor

As we noted in our article entitled, "Laughter can be the best medicine" (Le Navenec & Slaughter, 2001), caring practices that include the use of music, reminiscence and humor have been found by many researchers to create a healing environment:

- they strengthen the whole person (Le Navenec & Vonhof, 1996)

- the people involved find them meaningful (Dossey, 1998)

- they foster an environmental tone characterized by [what some people refer to as the big 3] hope, happiness (for example, a sense of inner joy, peace, security, or comfort) and humor (Bruce & Cumming, 1997; Forbes, 1994; Herth, 1993). [downloaded May 3, 2006 from www.nursingtimes.net/nav?page=nt.print&resource=213246]

In her discussion entitled, "Unleashing the positive through music" (see Le Navenec & Bridges, 2005, pp. 136-166), CAIT member Jennifer Buchanan, a Calgary-based music therapist, has indicated examples of how music therapy has helped people of all ages address "personal goals such as creativity, self-exploration, enhanced quality of life, memory performance, stress reduction, motivation, accessing feelings, empowerment, and communication" (p. 165). She concurs with George Eliot's perspective of the power of music for promoting health and well-being, which she expressed this way: "I think I should have no other mortal wants, if I could always have plenty of music. It seems to infuse strength into my limbs and ideas into my brain. Life seems to go on without effort, when I am filled with music" (p. 165).

In that spirit, in addition to collaborating on the book chapter mentioned above, and working on presentations and projects together, Le Navenec and Buchanan, along with help of two colleagues (Dr. Marcia Epstein and the late music therapist, Gaile Hayes), developed a senior level undergraduate course entitled, "Nursing 511: An Introduction to Music and Sound for the Helping Professions" in 1996 (see Le Navenec, McEachern, & Epstein, 2003). Similarly, Buchanan was one of the two music therapists involved in Le Navenec's (2002) research project entitled, "The Responses of Older People with Dementia to Small Group Music Therapy Sessions." The findings of that six-week study, involving thirty-minute group sessions held three times a week in two different nursing homes, were not statistically significant. However, qualitative analyses revealed that both alertness and smiling were more frequent over that time span, which may indicate the participants' greater sense of well-being and connectedness with others.

Reminiscence and Humor

Two other commonly used creative caring practices include the use of reminiscence and humor. Le Navenec and Slaughter view reminiscence as a process and/or practice of thinking about and/or telling past experiences (2001). Contrary to the societal notion that reminiscence is a classic sign of "old age," Snyder (cited in Le Navenec and Slaughter, 2001) has emphasized that it "begins at about age ten and continues throughout life" (p. 43). In many reminiscence group sessions, the group leader(s) assist the participants in discussing memorable events of the past, such as one's school years, how holidays were spent, and so on. As Gillies and James (cited in Le Navenec & Slaughter, 2001) have indicated, "older people have a wealth of memories but few friends left to share with them" (p. 43). Hence, it is important that the relatives of older people, and/or the staff of long term care centres in which they live, listen to their stories. Past research has indicated that reminiscence can have a number of positive outcomes for an individual including: (1) an enhanced ability to cope with or adapt to change, (2) increased opportunities for integration by offering participants a chance "to be given voice (to be heard)" and/or to have their stories acknowledged positively by others, and (3) enhanced knowledge of one's "lived experience" with both relatives and/or staff of long-term care centres. In turn, the latter may help better understand the participant's beliefs, values, or practices which may influence current behavior (Le Navenec & Vonhof, 1993).

According to McCloskey and Bulechek (cited in Le Navenec & Slaughter, 2001), humor refers to being able to perceive, appreciate, and express what is funny, amazing or ludicrous in order to establish relationships, relieve tension, release anger, facilitate learning or cope with painful feelings (p. 43). The following statement illustrates those types of positive outcomes – in this case, the relief of tension and coping mechanisms: "If I could not have these good laughs, I would spend my time crying." Staff and families wanting to increase their use of humor with others must first determine the other person's typical responses to humor, what is or is not culturally acceptable, and what time of the day he or she is most perceptive to humor. To evaluate another person's response to humor, you might observe for increase in smiles, laughter, as well as verbal reports of "feeling good after such a good laugh." Once that assessment information has been compiled, one can assemble what some of us call *a humor first aid kit*. Such a kit might contain humorous games, jokes, cartoons, and any number of DVDs. One might also use a formal evaluation tool, such as Snyder's *Situational Humor Response Questionnaire* (cited in Le Navenec & Slaughter, 2001, p. 43).

Other Creative Arts Approaches to Create Connections or Rapport with People

Contributors of the recently completed book edited by Le Navenec and Bridges (2005), entitled *Creating Connections between Nursing Care and the Creative Arts Therapies,* include professionals with various backgrounds such as nursing, (social) psychology-sociology, social work, music and art therapy, therapeutic recreation, music psychology, education, and dance/movement therapy and hailing from Canada, United States, England, and Ireland. With two exceptions (Allan Brisk and Jon Parr Vijinsky), they are all women, intent on providing clinical and research evidence of the various ways such art forms can help create harmony, happiness, and enhanced quality of life in both health and illness contexts, using the entire life-span for their case study (newborns to persons who are at the end-of-life), as well as persons who are both in good health (e.g., mothers during childbirth) and/or experiencing an illness condition (e.g., childhood cancer, dementia, depression, abuse and/or self-harm, traumatic brain injury). The use of the following art forms: visual art, crafts, music and sound, creative writing, dance and movement, and drama (or what some refer to as performance creation), yielded outcomes similar to the findings of Jonas-Simpson (2001), a nurse-researcher in Toronto. She used the title, "Feeling Understood: A Melody of Human Becoming," to convey the positive outcomes associated with the creation of a musical expression of feeling understood among a group of women experiencing an enduring condition.

As a founding member and Director of the CAIT research group, I am pleased to realize that during my twenty-six years as a university professor here at the University of Calgary, an increasing number of women are using these creative caring practices, in both their clinical practice, and in their research programs. And perhaps more importantly, they are using one or more of these modes (especially humor and reminiscence, as well as music) with their colleagues at work, in order to create a caring community in the workplace; that is, they are contributing to the creation of another Fifty Golden Years of Women Creating Community at our University.

References

Bruce, H., & Cummings, B. (1997). Worklife: Surely you jest; Bringing humor to the workplace. *Canadian Nurse, 93*(7), 51-52.

Dossey, B.M. (1998), Holistic modalities and healing moments. *American Journal of Nursing, 98*(6), 44-47.

Forbes, S.B. (1994). Hope: An essential human need in the elderly. *Journal of Gerontological Nursing, 20*(6), 5-10.

Herth, K.A. (1993). Humour and the older adult. *Applied Nursing Research, 6*(4), 146-153.

Jonas-Simpson, C.M. (2001). Feeling understood: A melody of human becoming. *Nursing Science Quarterly, 14*(3), 222-230.

Le Navenec, C., & Bridges, L. (2005). *Creating connections between nursing care and the creative arts therapies*. Springfield, IL: Charles C Thomas.

Le Navenec, C., McEachern, O., & Epstein, M. (2003). An introduction to music and sound approaches for health professionals: Overview of an undergraduate web-based nursing course. *Australian Journal of Holistic Nursing, 10*(2), 19-24.

Le Navenec, C., & Slaughter, S. (2001). Laughter is the best medicine: Music, reminiscence, and humour enhance the care of nursing home residents. *Nursing Times, 97*(30), 42-43.

Le Navenec, C., & Vonhof, T. (1996). *One day at a time: How families manage the experience of dementia*. Westport, CO: Greenwood Publishing Group-Auburn House.

The Keepers of the Stories
Monica Paul

In Retrospect

I had not been involved with a community of women since my years on the volleyball teams. Even my choir experiences were male-centred as I was a tenor, so my sectionals were with men as were most of my notes. Therefore, I was not sure what to expect as I had recently become a "Faculty Wife" who was considering membership in the Faculty Women's Club at the University of Calgary.

Our two-year-old Janay, our new home, and our second child due in December seemed to be keeping me busy. Did I have time to exchange recipes, become more literary, roll bandages, complain about husbands, or volunteer time to some charity – that's what women's groups did, didn't they?

Well yes, it turns out they did to some degree, but this particular group of women had so much to offer so many of us.

There were women who were the keepers of the history, the keepers of the events, the keepers of the interest groups, the keepers of the service opportunities, the keepers of the communications and most importantly, the keepers of the stories. Many members will share varied personal and public experiences spanning the fifty year history of the Faculty Women's Club. We will smile as we recognize ourselves, someone we know, a familiar experience, and the wit and wisdom that created a caring community. A women's group – who would have thought . . .

In the Beginning

I was rather impressed and intimidated by my first meetings of the FWC. Anne Fraser's welcome was always warm in her beautiful home but she was, after all, the wife of the University President. I was always grateful that she did not immediately recognize me as the wife of the new young professor in the Education Faculty who left her welcome get together with his hands full of beautiful petit fours for his small daughter who would "just love them – thank you so much."

Our meetings always seemed "so continental," including the food which was a fine icebreaker as far as anyone was concerned. The compliments were issued in Southern drawls, Australian nuances, German directness, Brazilian staccato, Irish brogues, British precision, Asian subtleties, and a host of other pleasant accents from people who had been born or lived in far more exotic places than Alberta. In fact, I rather enjoyed celebrity status as my husband and I had both been born and raised in this province; we had lived here all our lives. How it was that we were the only ones with accents, I never understood!

So many of the women who were soon to become my friends had such interesting faculty and immigration experiences that each meeting with them brought new stories about their adventures as faculty wives. It was the misadventures that found the most input from everyone in the conversation! I soon realized that as a member of the Faculty Babysitting Swap and the Newcomers Group, I could offer some tips and stories of my own about life in Alberta, which my new friends had yet to experience. As for misadventures, it didn't take long for me to have my own at the expense of some veteran members of the Faculty Women's Club but that's another story . . .

The only time I really wished I was an American citizen was the weekend of Polly's American Thanksgiving Celebration. It always sounded like such a great time for adults and children alike.

Third Wednesday of the Month
Program of Events: 1975-1976

Executive

Honorary President	Mrs. W.A. Cochrane
President	Louise Guy
Past President	Betty Schofield
Vice President	Judy Heintz
Recording Secretary	Loraine Seastone
Corresponding Secretary	Daphne Lester
Treasurer	Susan Soule
Special Events Chairman	Wendy McDougall
Social Convener	Jennifer Abouna
Membership Convener	Angela Rokne

Regular Meetings	8:00 p.m. Third Wednesday Blue and Gold Dining Room
September 17	Social hour and presentation of interest groups
October 15	J. Brooks Joyner, Curator U. of C. Art Gallery "The Female Image Past and Present" (with illustrations)
November 19	Barbara Scott – Alderman "Problems in City Government" Husbands are cordially invited
January 21	"Recent Sabbatical Experiences" A Panel discussion with members of the University community
February 18	Dr. Lorna P. Cammaert "Can Women Be Independent and Married"
March 17	Dr. H. Brody, Dr. Marsha Hanen, Gunilla Mungan, Sheila Ross "Abortion and Alternatives"
April 21	Annual General Meeting and Election

Special Events	
December 7	Children's Christmas Party – Calgary Hall Sandra Nichols and Peggy Watson
February 14	Buffet Dinner – Faculty Club Regina Shedd

Three Old Pals
Ilse Anysas-Salkauskas

96.5 cm w x 67.5 cm h Cotton fabrics, cotton and synthetic threads

Abandoned buildings similar to "Three Old Pals" can be found on the prairies from Manitoba to Alberta. These old, abandoned, and weather beaten granaries have seen many things in their lifetime. They seem like real characters, somewhat like three pensioners sitting in the field waiting for the neighborhood's animals and birds to visit and entertain them.

Circles of Courage
Monica Paul

We do not think the article written for our Class Act on June 12, 2008, "These kids refuse to give up," accurately represents Alternative High School, nor does it do the school justice. The one thing Alternative High School's graduating class has in common is well-earned success. They have a well-developed understanding of democracy and the values of the Circle of Courage, which include Belonging, Generosity, Mastery, and Independence. Each graduate feels they are part of a family of learners that include parents, teachers, support staff, and alumni. They have been generous not only with each other in countless ways, but in the larger community as fundraisers for Right to Play, the Crohn's and Colitis Foundation, and the Big Brother Foundation. These graduating students have achieved mastery in their academics, receiving honors marks, scholarships, and recognition for their various contributions in many areas. They have shown independence by choosing a small high school where individuality is honored and celebrated. Students have been accepted to programs at SAIT, ACAD, Mount Royal College, Trent University, and the University of Calgary. Alternative High School Students have initiated opportunities for success and they have achieved success. There is a strong sense of passion and love in this school, and there is also a desire to share it.

Monica Paul is a Calgary Board of Education Teacher at Alternative High School. Her Letter to the Editor, above, was published in The Calgary Herald *on June 18, 2008, on page A19.*

Reflections on Forty Years: 1967-2007
Faculty Babysitting Swap

Established in 1967, with Ann Walker as the first President, a post which she held until 1971, the "Swap" carried on for forty more years. The final meeting was held on May 11, 2007, with outgoing President Debbie Hall and her second generation Swap family, her spouse having been one of those cared for many years before.

In between, the Swap boasted more than thirty active families and a waiting list in the 1970s, for swapping childcare time, day or night, rather than money – with extra points charged after midnight or on New Year's Eve. Many a Swap Member jumped up in alarm around 11:30 p.m. on a Saturday night, crying out as they charged out their host's door, "Is that the time? We must go: it's Double Points after midnight!"

There were family barbeques (which even included bringing your own BBQ to Bowness Park as there was no budget for booking a site), playground meets, and semiannual sales of children's clothing and outdoor equipment. There were monthly newsletters from rotating Secretaries who kept track of everyone's points on multi-paged hand ruled spread sheets for producing the regular Auditor's Reports. The newsletters were sometimes handwritten, or typed on thin typewriter paper, or maybe run off on a Gestetner. Sometimes, after finishing a month as secretary, there was the long afternoon hand delivering the newsletters all over northwest Calgary, rather than entrusting them to campus mail lest they never get out of the professors' inboxes. By the time email arrived and simplified all the paperwork, the Swap was diminishing in membership.

There were grievance committees to deal with all and sundry concerns on behalf of beloved children, and rules to ensure equity, respect, and safety. When Monica Paul was President in the 1990s, the 1971 Rules and Information were transformed into communal Agreements, influenced by her experiences teaching at Alternative High School.

Having the fathers go out to do the sitting were rare and special opportunities for them get some insight into children beyond their own families; they might come home either relieved or worried about their own children in comparison. Rex Westbrook used to take video recordings of recent soccer matches to watch after getting the kids to bed, but was sometimes disappointed when the other person's home didn't have a VCR. Many women used to take their sewing or reading or even ironing when they went out to sit of an evening, things they might not have had time to get to at home.

Outgoing comments from sadly resigning members when their children grew "too old" were always like the following: "We have enjoyed the opportunities for friendship, both for ourselves and our children, gained by Swap membership," and "It has always given us great peace of mind to know that our children were in very caring and capable hands when we were out."

By the 1980s, membership began to decline. In 1984, in an effort to increase a potential catchment, "Faculty" was redefined as anyone working at the University. In 1990 when the Swap was down to twenty families, Shawna Edworthy and Pam Bradley suggested merging with a neighborhood swap near the U of C that they also belonged to. In 2000, Michelle Caird suggested reviving an old connection by opening membership to Campus Preschool families as well.

Once upon a time, the reference was the job on campus. But in the new millennium, with FOIP, three required letters of reference, and police checks being the norm, not to mention changing situations for women in the home and kids busier than ever with extracurricular activities, a humble cooperative such as the Swap could no longer sustain itself. For the final few years, it tried expanding into swapping other sitting duties while families travelled – caring for pets, and plants, and gardens, too.

In summer 2007, the Swap Agreements and sample Registration Packages were lodged with the Women's Resource Centre on campus, as a potential resource for a future incarnation. All of the Swap's ideas are still valid, and there will always be a need for childcare. On July 16, 2008, U of C News and Events announced the University had just signed a new partnership that would guarantee the availability of child and elder care for all employees.

And so, on that lovely May evening in 2007, the final three swap families – Hall, Hurly/Yarranton, and Knowlton/Cockett, along with the alumni Bentley family and four guests – declared all points null and void. Glasses were raised for the grand success it was for so many years.

> We are sad to hear that the Babysitting Swap is folding. It was one of the best arrangements for us when the kids were little.
>
> - *Blanka Kuhnel and Frans van der Hoorn*
>
> Congratulations to all for their efforts in building and sustaining that forty year tradition, and for being there for us and for each other when you were needed.
>
> - *Ted Horbulyk and Katie Johnson*

The Swap Brought New Life to the Family
Marie Collins

I am writing this to express how much the Babysitting Swap meant to my family, me as a young mother, my husband John, our five-year-old daughter, Rachel, and our eighteen-month-old son, Alan.

We moved to Calgary in 1976 and were immediately invited to share a dinner with Linda and Gene Warren. From them we learned where to shop, where to find a dentist and doctor. The very best news we heard that evening was the description that there was a very organized and experienced group of University women who had a Babysitting Swap. It was a Swap that was not only running but running smoothly. Hurray! I knew it would be the best chance I would have to meet new people. That is exactly what happened.

We moved into a rented house in Brentwood and found out that there were several "Swap" families who lived only a few blocks away. We met the Izzo family (Luisa, Herb, Sylvia, and Daniel), the James family (Marie, Don, Neil, Tanis, and Gina), the Fishers (David, Kyra, Petra, and Adrian). Each of us were looking for a sense of neighborhood, a sense of community. I particularly found emigrating to a new country difficult and I was feeling very alone.

As our children played together, we discovered that our neighborhood Swap families were becoming an extended family. As young mothers we struggled with how to be good mothers, supportive wives, and still allow a space and time for ourselves. We observed and modeled for each other. We faced challenges together. We sang, we camped, and cleaned together. We expressed, consoled, and helped each other in not only the joys and challenges of child raising but through the joys and challenges of life itself. We experienced all of life and we did it together: first words, toilet training, first day of school, music lessons, Time Out, carpooling, cats, rabbits, snakes and spiders, overnights, weekends away, teenage angst, school plays, graduation. Together we faced life, death, depression, divorces, and marriages.

The Swap brought me a life full of love and caring. It gave me what I needed. By sharing and living life together, we discovered that our efforts to support each other developed a life lasting bond. We became family.

Still Up and Wide Awake
Joanne Wyvill

The Faculty Babysitting Swap: all of us who belonged to it, fondly remember how invaluable it was – providing child friendly, reliable, and free babysitting services. Being the "sitter" could also be quite entertaining. My then husband Brian, once spent an evening sitting for the Clearys, and became so engrossed in a game of Dark Star with James that he was surprised by the return (quite late at night) of Dot and John – none too pleased to find their offspring still up and wide awake.

We (Brian and I) firstly used the swap as a couple; then I was even more grateful for it after we separated and divorced. As an impecunious single parent, struggling to juggle kids and an education degree, followed by the early years of teaching; being able to leave my kids with other mothers (or sometimes fathers), all of them known and trusted, was an absolute godsend.

Escaping the Usual Chores
Sue Stodart

Since many of our friends also belonged to the Babysitting Swap, whenever we had a general social occasion calling for babysitting, there would be a big demand for babysitters. I remember that the Secretary would groan if she found out that there was a Computer Science Department evening event, because half the Swap would be looking for sitters.

I have fond memories of babysitting. It was a great opportunity to do knitting and sewing and artwork, without having to do the usual chores that would intervene if you spent the evening at home. It was always nice to chat to other kids. Sometimes kids told very funny stories which could not be repeated, on the strict understanding that our own kids were giving away our secrets to other members when they babysat for us.

On being the Secretary, making those points add up . . . aaarrgh!

A Win-Win for us All!
Marion Krause

The Faculty Babysitting Swap at the University of Calgary was a great resource to families with young children. As immigrants to Canada we did not have extended family close at hand, and having other parents mind our children provided an extra measure of comfort. In the mid 80s, when we joined the Swap, I was still an at home mother, so both Fed and I had the time to use the Swap actively. It was a win-win for us all!

Macaroni and Ham Salad
Ainslie Thomas

8 oz	shell macaroni
2 cups	diced ham
¼ cup	cubed cheddar cheese
¼ cup	chopped sweet pickle
2 Tbsp	minced onion
1/3 cup	chopped green pepper or celery
½ cup	salad dressing
2 tsp	prepared mustard
¼ tsp	salt

Cook macaroni in boiling salted water until tender; drain, cool. Combine with remaining ingredients and chill.

Faculty Women's Club Favourite Recipes (1969). (2)1, p. 41

A Proposed Program for Preschool Children June 3, 1964
Barbara Wilson and Lorna Wright

It has been suggested that a Program for Preschool Children be started in September 1964 for the convenience of mothers in Calgary who wish to continue studies at the University and at the same time provide their children with opportunities for creative and intellectual development in a group situation.

- The program would also be available to the children of all employees of the University and to children of graduates and undergraduates.
- Hours should be geared to suit the University timetable so that fathers could provide transportation.
- Location should be as close to campus as possible with ample place for loading and unloading cars.
- The program would operate during the academic year.
- Children of all ages up to six should be eligible. Babies under two could be cared for for shorter periods (only for mothers in classes) corresponding to the academic timetables. It is not intended at this time to offer day care for full time working mothers.
- The project needs to begin with a qualified paid person to teach and to supervise the untrained assistants.
- Education, Psychology and Sociology students would be employed as assistants.
- Mothers would help on a co-operative basis and in lieu of helping, contribute to the employment of a substitute student helper. In general, children seem to behave better when mothers are kept out of sight.

- An emergency baby-sitter service should be available to help at home when for reasons of sickness, etc., it is impossible for the mother to bring children to the University. Perhaps a file of domestic help could be attempted.
- The project should be administered by a board of directors composed of representative persons.

The main departments to be looked after are: 1) Accommodation, 2) Personnel, 3) Capital Equipment, 4) Treasury, 5) Correspondence, 6) Materials, 7) Books for a Library, 8) Art Gallery, 9) Survey of Local Nurseries, 10) Music, 11) Legal Problems, 12) Health.

It should be understood that the project is separate from the Kindergarten plans of the Faculty of Education which would be established in the Demonstration School. It is hoped however, that the idea of a Playschool on or near campus may be useful to eager research students at the University. We welcome the assistance of the faculty in making this a successful effort which could stimulate some new ideas in improving nursery school programs elsewhere.

We note that there is a pressing need for improved day care centres for working mothers.

Comments please!   Barbara Wilson & Lorna Wright

University of Calgary Archives 86.022.03.05

Memories of Campus Preschool Co-op 1965-1974

Dorothy Krueger

Among my souvenirs are black and white snapshots of the preschool days of our three children. Our oldest, Kathryn, was fortunate to be in the first class of the Campus Childcare Co-op (original name) in September, 1965. It was initiated by Barbara Wilson and her committee; the class that year was held in the basement of Kananaskis Hall with fifteen students under the excellent teaching of Sylvia Dixon. She had newly arrived in Calgary, having graduated from Queen's University and the Ontario Preschool Education program. Thus it was a new experience not only for the children but the parents and teacher as well!

At that time there were few opportunities for preschool education in Alberta, the general mindset being that children should remain home with their mothers until starting Grade 1 at the age of six. News of European children beginning education at the age of four appalled many! Not only was the early start a benefit to the children but as the feminist views of Betty Friedan and Gloria Steinem seeped into Alberta, some wives of faculty and graduate students were ready to seize the opportunity to complete their own education while their children were in school.

As a new teacher, Sylvia soon realized that her task also involved educating the parents of her charges, for some of them expressed disappointment by October that their child had not yet learned to read! Carefully she stemmed the criticism by explaining the necessity of preparation for learning, development of social skills, and responsibility for personal effects while enjoying the whole process of learning with and from others. Sylvia was careful to see that each child was attaining his/her own development level (according to individual age), rather than treating the whole class the same, since a differential of several months in a child's age made a significant difference in his/her development. That is, the child born in November would not be expected to be at the same development level as those born in May in the same calendar year.

Thus we learned a lot about our preschoolers, their development, and their delight in socializing and learning. Once in October, Mrs. Dixon asked me if there was anything different or changed in our home recently. After a moment's thought, I responded that my husband was out of town at a conference for a few days. "Ah," she said, "That's it! I could tell Kathy wasn't herself, a bit uneasy, not her merry, funny self!" I was greatly impressed by her perception and skill.

Later that autumn, Kathy required corrective eye surgery to restore her binocular vision; she was required to wear a patch over her "good" eye for six weeks to enable the "lazy" eye to reach its potential prior to the surgery. To the parent, it seemed an insurmountable challenge and cruelty to the five-year-old child. But we were inspired to draw a picture on the outside of the patch, a picture of something familiar; for example, on the first day, when people asked her, "What happened to your eye?" she replied, "I've got an apple in it!" So it continued – bunny, birthday cake, dog, rainbow, etc., forty-two of them, while we were challenged to think of objects easy to draw and recognizable! It became a game, both for Kathryn and her school friends; some of them wanted a patch on their eyes too! We made a "patch book" in which, at the end of the day when the patch was removed, it was pressed into the book where she had marked off the dates. Since Sylvia's husband was completing his ophthalmology studies in Calgary, she was most complimentary of our creativity to get through a hard time. People at the Children's Hospital whose children were experiencing the same problem called to inquire about our idea.

But the surgery experience in the Children's Hospital was not so pleasant. Just as Kathryn was emerging from the anesthetic, all visiting parents were "kicked out" of the hospital. When we brought her home the next morning she described the harsh treatment of these little postoperative children – not allowed to go to the bathroom, now disoriented because the operated eye was patched, and in strange surroundings. Breakfast for the post tonsillectomies was ice cream but for the eye surgeries it was whole, stone-in prunes! When she whimpered to the attending "nurse" she was told, "Shut up and eat your prunes!" What a contrast to Sylvia's kindly consideration for her "little people" as she called them. In protest, I wrote a stiff letter to the Children's Hospital Board, which eventually revised their rules and their treatment of young children, relieving the unnecessary trauma for both child and parent.

A significant feature of the Campus Preschool Co-op was the requisite volunteer service in the classroom. About twice a month the volunteer parent assisted with clean up, coat zippers, boots, and a snack time. This, too, was a good learning experience as one observed how the teacher handled difficult situations while keeping her "cool," as well as demonstrating the nature of the program and the reasons for it. Because it was a cooperative, without any grant funding, the budget for the next year was set by the Board, taking into consideration any deficit or surplus from the preceding year. Fees were adjusted accordingly and parents provided a set of postdated cheques for the entire school year, to provide some feeling of solvency. This whole venture was only possible because Board members in the early years provided such excellent leadership, and the involved parents were determined to make it work.

Another exercise in togetherness was the carpool experience. Fortunately our group lived close by – Jenny Toews, Graeme Armstrong, Rod Magee, and of course, Kathryn and her younger sister Vivian as well as Graeme's sister Maureen; these younger siblings were thus able to sample life at the Co-op while aspiring to become participants in the next year or so.

For the year following our sabbatical (1967-68) a lovely English girl, Christine Drury, who had been Vivian's teacher in the four-year-old program in Ottawa, came to Calgary. She was eager to see "the West," explore the mountains, and teach in the Co-op. Our carpool that year included Maureen Armstrong, Oliver Betz, Susan Fryer, and Vivian. One of the many songs Miss Drury taught them was, "Bow, Bow, Bow, Belinda," which, with her English accent, was pronounced "Belinder." We tried to correct Vivian's rendition to no avail; the teacher is always right!

Perhaps the greatest test of the value of the Campus Preschool experience came with our son, Jonathan (1972-74), a very active little boy, very social and eager for playmates. The teacher then was Helen Milone, a calm, mature woman who often began her responses to our questions with "studies show … !" After observing Jonathan in the Tuesday/Thursday program, she suggested that he should have three consecutive mornings. I protested, saying I would feel guilty as he was not yet three, but Helen believed that the progression of days would help him to "settle down." How right she was! He soon showed great progress in listening and learning.

At that time "brinkmanship" was a term applied to political matters, but Jonathan had his own application of the word. At the Parkdale church, where the preschool was now held, the bathrooms were down a long, dark hall, then up six steps and down another long hall, turning left to the bathroom at last! Because he was so interactive with other children – well, you've guessed the problem! But Helen proceeded to lecture me on how to handle the embarrassment and not to make too big a deal over it! I was still learning and will always be grateful to her for her wisdom.

Thus, Campus Preschool was of inestimable value for our children. Not only were they well prepared for school, but we as parents learned so much about parenting our own children.

A Carpooling Cooperative: Campus Preschoolers at Kananaskis Hall, 1965. Left to right: Rod Magee, Jenny Toews, Graeme Armstrong, Vivian Krueger, Kathryn Krueger

Editors' Notes: When Campus Preschool first opened its doors as Campus Child Care Co-Operative in April 1965 in the basement of Kananaskis Hall at the then University of Alberta at Calgary, Randie Lind was a student in residence in the same building. Little did she realize she would later go on to teach at Campus Preschool for twenty-eight years, including through its moves from Brentwood schools to Capitol Hill Community Hall, its home since 1988. When Campus Preschool celebrated forty years since its formal registration along with Randie's retirement in June 2006, all the teachers who had served with Randie attended, and together with several parents, some from each decade, each spoke eloquently about Campus Preschool's innovative Kids on Camera and Parent Education programs, its development of a library with high quality materials, its dedication to nature-based field trips for the children, its community outreach and social activism such as lobbying for a provincial seatbelt law in 1983, and its enduring commitment to professional development for its teachers. Attendees included parents, children, and even grandchildren who spanned the entire forty-one years to date, including Ruth Armstrong and Dorothy Krueger, whose children were in the original 1965 class.

Campus Preschool Association of Calgary
Notes from the Archives: 1964-1986

Established in 1965, Campus Preschool is the longest running preschool in the city that is operated as a parent cooperative.

Notes from the University of Calgary Archives

June 3, 1964 – Letter of Intent to Establish Program

April 13, 1965 – Date of Commencement of Operations

Summer 1965:

> We're looking for a teacher whose emotional maturity, training and physical stamina will enable her to coordinate the Cooperative nursery school program. A cooperative pre-school is set up to provide an educational experience for both parents and children who can benefit from the experience. Every parent, therefore, will want to assist the teacher, in keeping with our minimum requirement, at least one hour per month. Our summer school pilot project has given us some insight into some of the difficulties that can arise and therefore has been a very educational experience for all of us.

1965-1966 – First year on campus, in Kananaskis Hall

February 8, 1966 – Date of Formal Registration

February 9, 1966 – Letter to the Calgary Board of Education asking for help in purchasing supplies through their supplier

August 1966 – Letter from Chair to members, acknowledging successful completion of first year. Ready for Year 2, 1966-1967, at Parkdale United Church

University of Calgary Archives 86.022.03.05

Notes from the Glenbow Museum Archives

June 1973 – Board meeting minutes

- Mrs. Challice and the Music Program [usually spelled Challis in the minutes]: Mrs. Park further advised she had contacted Mrs. Challice with regards to the coming year. Mrs. Challice stated that she was happy with the honorarium but dissatisfied with her program. She advised she and a friend of hers would be setting up a much better program for the next year and she would be very happy to return.

- Mrs. Pearce's Accident [Mrs. Cathy Pearce – Teacher-Director] The Board was advised that a freak accident in the play yard had chipped one of Mrs. Pearce's teeth when she was hit in the chin by one of the children, causing severe pain and extensive dental work. The Campus Pre-School does not have Medical and Accidental Insurance and Mrs. Pearce was going to contact Blue Cross to see if all or a portion of the cost could be realized through them. Morgan Molberg and Ches Loov second that we pay any portion of Mrs. Pearce's expenses not covered by Blue Cross, or all expenses should none be paid by Blue Cross. Carried. Mrs. Pearce's Dentist estimated the cost between $160.00 and $200.00.

- The Gestetner is running out of ink and needs servicing.
- Names of Note: Heidi and Wayne Price, Susan Stone, Regina Shedd
- Helen Milone, teacher, was sent to conferences

January 1974 – Board meeting minutes

- Duplicating machine problems. Our present machine makes only 35 copies per stensil. When anything else is needed in bulk Sandy often needs to make several stensils. Morgan suggested Sandy price more adequate machines. Board moved and passed a motion to purchase a better duplicating machine.

June 1974 – Board meeting minutes

- Remuneration for Mrs. Challice: Regina Shedd reported that she met with Mrs. Challice in May and asked her to submit conditions, pay, etc. needed as per discussion at the previous board meeting. Mrs. Challice submitted a letter read by Regina: Mrs. Challice will come 4 mornings and 2 afternoons per week. She suggested $50.00 per month remuneration and would like to discuss her program with the new teacher-director.

September 1974 – Board meeting minutes

- Dorothy Krueger had suggested French be taught at the CPC and that Sheana Rauk was suggested as a teacher.

March 1975 – Board meeting minutes

- Our large hamster cage is for sale for $5.00. We need new hamster cages as the animals keep getting out.
- Names of Note: Marjorie Boorman, Rossanne Moore, Judy Hall, Madeleine Oldershaw, Linda Heidemann

January 1978 – Board meeting minutes

- Rossanne, as Chairman of the Board, had to write a letter to a parent who continued to bring other children with her on her parent help day, despite a firm policy otherwise.
- Rossanne stressed the importance of books.

February 1979 – Board meeting minutes

- Randie Lind Freeman, teacher of the three year old class was introduced to parents.

May 1979 – Board meeting minutes

- Gestetner: Marilyn reported on alternative duplicating machines, and types of Gestetners available for possible purchase in addition to typewriters available. Moved/seconded to authorize purchase of a reconditioned IBM Selectric. MOVED that our gift to Chief Crowfoot this year be $50.00 for a Gestetner.

June 1979 – Board meeting minutes

- Gestetner: Bob's contact did not have the necessary information and Bob will pursue further.
- Typewriter: Mona has back ordered a new IBM Selectric as this model is not available as a reconditioned typewriter, and we will receive it perhaps by September.
- Names of Note: Gillian Kydd, Fran Davies, Pam Witten

September 1979 – Board meeting minutes

- Bob is still waiting to interview the Gestetner representative. Bob will provide any reproduction required until a decision is made concerning the purchase of duplicating equipment.

October 1979 – Board meeting minutes

- Gestetner: Bob purchased an electric model Gestetner for $3000, which has been delivered. Lettraset won't work on a Gestetner.

November 1980 – Board meeting minutes

- Photocopier: Marilyn has decided that she does not want a photocopier. Photocopying may be done inexpensively at the University.

April 1981 – Board meeting minutes

- Randie accepts Teacher-Director position

May 1981 – Board meeting minutes

- Chair of Committees confirms position of who will run the Gestetner for the year, and be part of the Collating Committee.
- The newsletter was late due to reproduction problems

October 1981 – Board meeting minutes

- Parent Education Committee has arranged for Dr. Dick Hirabayashi head of U of C Early Childhood Services Program, to speak at the October General Meeting about toys and parent expectations.
- Names of Note: Diana Kary, Meghan Sired, Bernie Andrusky, Liz Westbrook

February 1986 – General Meeting Minutes

- Simon Fraser JHS Band members will be coming once/week for about 4 weeks to entertain pupils and answer questions about instruments, etc.
- Names of Note: Becky Trussell, Barbara Kennard, Dorothy Cleary
- Randie wants to take course in Early Childhood Administration – granted permission to take class and have substitute for this.

June 1986 – Board meeting minutes

- The Gestetner needs cleaning. It will cost approximately $62.00 not including parts. Randie moved that the Gestetner be cleaned up to a limit of $100.00.
- Buddy the Clown was too loud and performed for too long, and Randie wasn't sure whether she wanted him to come again.
- Name of Note: Carol Barwick/Wardell – who volunteered as a Gestetner operator.

September 1986 – Board meeting minutes

- The principal of Brentwood Elementary [where the Preschool was then located] has said we may use their paper towels free of charge.

October 1986 – Board meeting minutes

- Duplicating. The equipment committee, with Judy and Randie will research the relative cost and convenience of leasing a photocopier for the school or using a Printing House for our duplicating, instead of the Gestetner, as this is very inconvenient to use.
- The Gestetner Company will make a stencil for our Logo at a cost of $8.

Glenbow Museum Archives M.8220

Randie in Oz
A Play on Learning Through Play

Written, Produced, Performed, and Directed by the Preschool Group of Seven: Lisa Brattland (Parent Helper), Michelle Caird (Child #1), Patricia Etris (Board Member), Polly Knowlton Cockett (Randie), Jane MacTaggart (Child #2), Diane Poole (Child #3), & Jocelyn Samson (Committee Member), with Heidi Dick, as herself

Excerpts from Play written in honor of Randie Lind's 20 years of service as Teacher and Director of Campus Preschool Association of Calgary – May 1999.

INTRODUCTION:
Narrator: One day, Randie was once again riding her bicycle, Rosebud, to work at Campus Preschool.

PART I: Riding to Campus Preschool
Randie: (Riding bicycle mounted on trainer frame, and talking/listening to Billy the stuffed dog, who sits in the handlebar basket. Patting Billy, Randie begins monologue.)
Well, here we are, Billy, off to Campus Preschool again.
Yes, it is a beautiful day. Look at that blue sky.
What's that? Yes, blue would be a good color to put in the water table today?
Maybe we'll put in the mermaids, too. A few sharks as well?

Hmm, yes, Billy it does seem to be clouding over. There go some Canada geese flying by.
What's that? Yes, we could play 'Duck, Duck, Goose' in the gym.
Hmm, did I bring my key to the gym? Yes. I wonder if my key will work today.

Yes, Billy, that did feel like a raindrop. Lots of raindrops, actually. Oh, well.
I wonder if the children will have their rain boots.
What's that? Yes, that last batch of playdough was a bit sticky.
I wonder if the playdough committee has made up a new batch of playdough yet.

Hmm, it does seem to be turning to sleet, Billy.
I wonder if the children will have their hats and mitts in their back-packs.
What's that? Yes, last week's notices might still be in their backpacks.

Yes, Billy, it is snowing now. In fact, it's getting rather deep.
It's a good thing you've got snow tires on, Rosebud.
The camping ought to be good this weekend.
What's that? Yes, it is too bad we don't have a snow shoveling commit-tee anymore.

Hmm, yes, it does look a bit like a tornado coming this way.
What's that? I'm getting hungry, too, Billy. I hope the parent helper brings a good snack today, and hopefully not Rice Krispie squares again.
Yes, there is a board meeting tonight. There better be snacks there, too.

What's that? You wish Lou the cat was here? Why? To chase the mouse?
The MOUSE!!!!!!
(Randie 'faints' off bicycle, twirls to the ground; loses sandals, helmet; grabs Billy.)
Stage Crew: (Sign on easel changes to '?.' Streamers; mystical noises and wind chimes; Put out flowers and palm tree; bicycle disappears; sounds dissipate, and Randie slowly awakens.)

PART II: Enroute to Oz
Scene 1: Preschool Children
Randie: Where are we, Billy? There's no school, no playground, no field, no big red happy face. I wonder where Heidi is.
Oh, Billy, I have a feeling we're not at Campus anymore.
Hmm. What's that? (Randie notices slippers.) Yes, they do seem to be Ruby slippers.
(Randie holds up Ruby Birkenstock sandals.)

Click Three Times
Ruby Birkenstocks

You think I should try them on? All right. (Randie puts on sandals, and admires them.)

Yes, I could wear these to the Folk Festival.

Children: (Enter in unruly, squabbling confusion. Then they see Randie.)

Who are you?

Randie: My name is Randie. I'm a Preschool Teacher, and I was just riding my bike to Campus Preschool, and I saw a mouse, and something happened.

And now I don't know where I am.

Who are you children?

Child #1: I'm Ann, and I'm three.

Child #2: I'm Mark, and I'm four.

Child #3: I'm Libby, and I'm five.

Randie: What's the matter?

Children: We're looking for a preschool.

Child #1: I'm looking for somewhere to play where I can learn important social skills such as cooperation, conflict resolution, and problem solving.

Child #2: And I'm looking for a preschool where the teachers are patient and kind, and make the children feel loved and respected as people.

Child #3: A place where the teachers have university degrees in early childhood education and attend annual workshops.

Children: And Peanut Free!

Randie: I know just the place: Campus Preschool. But how do we get there?

We can't go the way I came.

Child #1: It's always best to start at the beginning.

Child #2: All we need to do is...

Child #3: Follow the YELLOW BIKE PATH.

Child #2: Follow the YELLOW BIKE PATH.

Child #1: Follow the YELLOW BIKE PATH.

Children: Hooray, we're off to Campus Preschool!

Randie and Children: (Singing, and following the Yellow Bike Path around the audience while scene changes on the stage, ready to meet first parent. Randie's yellow chair from the classroom is used for the meeting of each of the three parents.)

Follow the Yellow Bike Path.

Follow the Yellow Bike Path.

Follow, follow, follow, follow,

Follow the Yellow Bike Path.

We're off to Campus Preschool,

The wonderful Preschool of Campus.

We hear it is a wonderful place

If ever a wonderful place there was.

If ever, oh ever a place there was,

Then Campus is the place because,

Because, because, because, because, because,

Because of the wonderful things it does.

Scene 2: Board Member with Brains
Randie and Children: (Arrive to first parent, the Board Member, who has lots of binders, a computer, cell phone, and other office paraphernalia. She also has a modern suitcase with wheels and a pull handle.)
Randie: Who are you?
Board Member: (Sighing, a little bored.)
I'm a parent.
Randie: What's the matter?
Board Member: Well, you see, I have all this neat stuff. I've got these great binders. Yellow, and green and blue. And this great computer; want to see? And a stapler, and a hole punch so I can put things in the binder. And look at all of these paper clips! Look, I even have a cell phone, and it really works. Listen! (Push button on phone.) But I need something to do with them. What I really want is to be the chair of a Board of Directors for a not-for-profit, cooperative, parent-run organization.
Randie: Don't you have a brain?
Board Member: Yes! And I want to use it. Do you know where I could use it?
Randie: Well, why don't you come along with us to Campus Preschool. We always need volunteers for the Board of Directors there.
Board Member: Okay! But how do we get there?
Child #3: Follow the YELLOW BIKE PATH....
Children: Hooray, we're off to Campus Preschool!
Randie: How about we play a game along the way. How about 'Fast and Slow and Backwards?'
(Randie explains rules of game. She has her big drum and stick. A slow beat means walk; fast means run; tapping on the side means backwards.)
Randie, Children, and Board Member: (With Randie in lead, and parent following, everyone sets off on YBP, playing game while scene changes to meet the second parent.)

Scene 3: Committee Member with Heart
Randie, Children, and Board Member: (Arrive to second parent, the Committee Member, who is wearing a tool belt, fixing an old vacuum cleaner, and has lots of interesting items related to the preschool surrounding her.)
Randie: Who are you?
Committee Member: (Sighing; a bit wistful.)
I'm a parent.
Randie: Well, what's the matter?
Committee Member: Oh, well, you see . . . I have all these things I love to do . . . Would you like to see them?
Randie: All right.
Committee Member: Well, let's see. I love to fix vacuum cleaners.
Randie: It looks as if that one needs fixing.
Committee Member: Yes. And what else, oh yes . . . I love to fix things like toy sheds. You see, I have a hammer. And playdough; I love to make playdough. All different colors: red, yellow, green, blue. And

painting; I love to paint things like tables and chairs. And toys; I love to clean toys for children to play with. And fundraising; I love to raise money. (Shows Monopoly money.) And shovelling; I love to shovel snow so that people can walk on nice cleared paths. And children's books; I love to take children's books out of the library for children to read. And laundry; I love to wash dirty paint shirts and mend dress-up clothes.

Randie: Wow, it sounds as if you have a lot of heart.

Committee Member: I do. I have a lot of heart! I just need someone to do all these things for.

Randie: Well, I think I know just the place for you: Campus Preschool. We're always looking for parents to be Committee Members and to do all the things you love to do.

Committee Member: Really?

Randie: Yes. Why don't you come along with us? We're going there now.

Committee Member: Okay. I'd love to. But how do we get there?

Child #2: Follow the YELLOW BIKE PATH….

Children: Hooray, we're off to Campus Preschool!

Committee Member: All right. May I bring my vacuum?

Randie: Of course. You'll need it there. Now wait, let's see how many are here. (Counting of children and parents. Patting heads.) One, two, three, four, five. Is anyone   missing?

Children: Not today.

Randie: We could sing a song along the way.

Children: Okay!

Randie: How about "There was a teacher, had a dog, and Billy was his name-o?"

Children: Yes!

Randie, Children, Board and Committee Members: (Singing, and traveling the YBP again, while scene changes to meet the third parent. Tune is 'Bingo.')

There was a teacher, had a dog, and Billy was his name-o.

B-I-L-L-Y. B-I-L-L-Y. B-I-L-L-Y.

And Billy was his name-o.

(Twice through.)

Scene 4: Parent Helper with Courage

Randie, Children, and Board and Committee Members: (Arrive to third parent, the Parent Helper, who is surrounded by bins and bags of stuff for parent helping.)

Randie: Who are you?

Parent Helper: I'm a parent.

Randie: What's the matter?

Parent Helper: Well, I feel like I need a new challenge in my life. I love being with kids and I love helping them learn through play.

I have all this stuff with me.

I have snacks!

Randie: Mmm. What kind of snacks?

Parent Helper: Nutritious ones. I also have juice for kids, and you know when kids spill their juice at snack time - everyday - I think they must be learning something, and Imust be too... So basically I do it all! I have Kleenex to wipe noses, and I do dishes.
I sweep and I vacuum.
(To Committee Member) Hey, could I use that vacuum? Thanks!
I even have snowsuits and I like to help kids put on snowsuits when it is cold out.
Randie: Wow, it sounds like you have a lot of courage.
Parent Helper: I do have a lot of courage. I just need somewhere to use it.
Randie: Well, you could come along with us to Campus Preschool. We always need Parent Helpers at Campus Preschool.
Parent Helper: Sure I would love to be a parent helper at Campus Preschool.
(It begins to snow, and the kids get cold.)
Child #1: What's happening?
Child #2: What is it?
Child #3: It's snowing!
Child #2: No, it isn't!
Child #3: Yes, it is!
Children: We need our snowsuits!!!
Parent Helper: I could start helping right now by putting snowsuits on these kids.
(Chaotic scene as all parents and Randie help kids into snowsuits.)
Parent Helper: But how do we get to Campus Preschool?
Child #1: Follow the YELLOW BIKE PATH….
Children: Hooray, we're off to Campus Preschool!
Randie: Just remember, though, you parents: one parent's a helper. Two parents are half a helper, and three are a party.
Children: Yay!
Randie, Children, Board and Committee Members, and Parent Helper: (Singing 'Follow the YBP,' and traveling the YBP again, while scene changes to arrival in Oz. The sign says 'Oz,' but there is nothing on stage.)

Scene 5: Arrive and Depart Oz
Randie, Children, Board and Committee Members, and Parent Helper: (Arrive to empty stage; end of YBP.)
Randie: Hmm, now what? We've come to the end of the path, and this still isn't Campus Preschool. What do we do now? Hmm, the sign says 'OZ.' (Pacing, listening to Billy.)
Yes, Billy, that does remind me of a story. I wonder if these Ruby Slippers are magic. Does everyone have their magic with them? In your pocket, or in your sock, under your hat perhaps? Get out your magic. (Everyone gets out their imaginary magic.)
Okay, everyone, gather around, and hold hands. Are you ready now? Close your eyes, and tap your heels together three times.
(Pause, and then heel clicking while saying:)
Randie: There's no place like Campus.

Everyone: There's no place like Campus. There's no place like Campus
. . .
(Randie faints. Everyone else removes snowsuits, puts away gear, and
is wearing Campus Preschool T-shirts by the end of the scene change.)
Stage Crew: (Sign on easel changes to 'Campus Preschool.'
Streamers; mystical noises and wind chimes; Remove flowers and palm
tree; sounds dissipate, and Randie slowly awakens. Other characters
are busy doing ordinary preschool activities.)

PART III: At Campus Preschool
Heidi: (Enter with ducklings hatched from eggs from Mink Hollow
Farms in Cochrane.)
Wake up, Randie. Randie, it's Heidi.
Randie: Oh, it's you, Heidi! I see the ducklings have hatched. Where
am I?
Heidi: You're at Campus Preschool.
Randie: What happened?
Heidi: Well, I don't know. We found you by your bike. Were you nap-
ping?
Randie: Hmm, I was riding to preschool. Then there was a mouse . . .
and I . . . fell off my bike.
Well, then I left you, and tried to get back. It wasn't a dream, it was a
real place.
There were three children who really wanted a good preschool. So I
asked them to come with me, and they knew the way along the yellow
bike path. They looked like you, and you, and you . . .
And then there was a parent with lots of brains that wanted to be on
the Board of Directors. And another parent with lots of heart fixing a
vacuum cleaner, and she wanted to be on a committee. And then it
started snowing, and another parent was there just when we needed
snowsuits, and she had a lot of courage, and some good snacks, too.
They all came with us to Campus Preschool. Yes, you, and you . . . and
you were all there.
(Pause. Randie looks confused.)
Randie: How long have I been here?
Heidi: Oh, about twenty years!
Randie: Hmm. There's no place like Campus!
Everyone: 'There's no place like Campus!'

Freely adapted from L. Frank Baum's The Wonderful Wizard of Oz

CAMPUS COOPERATIVE PRESCHOOL

Preschool as Community
Randie Lind

When I began teaching at Campus Preschool, my older son was just starting kindergarten, my younger not yet born; when I retired, twenty-eight years later, my first grandchild was one year old. Most of the major events of my life happened against the Preschool background, and the Preschool was in many ways my intentional community.

Campus Preschool was a wonderful place to teach for many reasons: its philosophy of learning through play fit well with mine; there was a great deal of personal autonomy; parents and teachers alike were committed and dedicated to the school's well being, and the involvement of whole families meant that a real sense of community was fostered.

As a result, children, parents, and teachers were able to find meaningful relationships at Campus Preschool and many long term friendships were developed. Often, when I spoke to "old" parents in the grocery store, I would be told that friends from preschool days were still close ten or fifteen years later. I met two of my closest friends through the school, one as a teaching partner and the other as a parent; when I helped to found the local chapter of the Jane Austen Society, three of the first members were former Preschool parents; when I decided it was time to find a church community [at the Unitarian Church], several parents from the Preschool were already involved; this September my granddaughter will begin her first year at Campus Preschool. The links just keep happening, and I feel blessed to have been involved for so many years with this "village" within the context of the "big city."

Anecdotes

For many years when I lived close to the Preschool, a favorite field trip was a city bus ride to my house. The children were given a guided tour of my home and were enchanted to find that I actually had a bed and a kitchen just like they did! After the tour, we played in my backyard, "painted" the fence with water, and enjoyed an outdoor snack. One particularly hot June, I had the wading pool set up, and as the children took off their socks and shoes I ran in to get a few towels. Imagine my astonishment when I returned to find sixteen naked and semi-naked children cavorting in the pool and around the garden! I took a deep breath, and decided it was one of those times when the best solution was just to go with the flow!!

Each class at Campus Preschool includes a gym time with movement sessions, games, and free play with equipment. We teachers would usually take the equipment needed up to the gym as part of the setup routine before class started. One day, I took up the large bag containing twenty big pink balls and left it on the gym floor. An hour later when I came up with the children and parent helper, I dumped out the bag and was greatly surprised to see a mouse tumble out along with the balls. The mother and I just stood there in shock; the mouse darted about in all directions and finally disappeared under a closet door, but strangest of all the children were all so focused on finding a ball that not one of them even noticed the mouse!

For many years I have had my hair cut at the same salon, and I was pleased when I noticed my hair dresser's small son was on the class list for the fall session. He was a very active little boy and quite a character. When the children washed their hands before snack each day, they took it in turn to stand on a set of stairs in order to reach the sink; I would pop back and forth between the two sinks to make sure all was going smoothly. Donovan had waited until the end of the line and stood at the sink, his hair richly lathered up with suds and a big smile on his face as he watched himself in the mirror. I helped him with the rinsing, and fetched a towel; it seemed the least I could do after all the shampoos his mom had given me!

Teacher Credentials Have Seen Dramatic Changes
Early Childhood Development

There was a time, as recently as the 1970s, when nursery school teachers had to possess only one qualification.

They had to be at least 16 years of age.

Early childhood education has changed considerably since then. Not only has society shunned the infantile word "nursery" and adopted the more sophisticated term "preschool", teachers are now required to take post-secondary education.

Heidi Dick, teacher of the four-year-old classes at Campus Preschool, has a Bachelor of Arts degree in early childhood development and education from Pacific Oaks College in Pasadena, Calif. She grew up in the U. S., and says the original intent of nursery schools was to be a learning lab for education students at colleges and universities. From that sprung early childhood development courses and training for pre-elementary school teachers.

When Dick and her husband moved to Lethbridge in 1979, she started a parent co-op preschool and also taught early childhood education at Lethbridge Community College. Mary Aubie, teacher of the three-year-old class at Campus, received her diploma in early childhood education from Mount Royal College in 1985 and has many years of related experience.

Dick says the difference between training to be an elementary school teacher and a preschool teacher is the study of child development.

Photo by Leah Hennel, *Calgary Herald*

Pre-school teacher Heidi Dick, who has also taught early childhood education classes at Lethbridge College, reads to some of her students (from left) Jasper Coles Liland, 4, Jacob Olsen, 5, Rowan Griffith, 4, and his sister Juniper Griffith, 3, at the Campus Preschool.

"You're learning about the child and studying them as they develop," says Dick.

"You still need training to teach, but that's the biggest difference."

Preschool teachers are regulated by the same licensing body as day-care centres in our province.

"We're licensed by social services and are inspected," says Dick. "But it's really evolved and they realize we're different. The requirements have really changed over the years." All teachers are required to recertify their CPR annually, and, while not a requirement, most stay in touch with the latest research and teaching information by taking professional development days.

"We go to conferences and things like that. It's something we believe in and something our parent board supports," says Dick.

While it's important to consider the credentials of the teachers at a prospective preschool, mom Robin Galey says the recommendations of friends bears equal weight in deciding where to place her children.

"Some teachers have 25 or more years of experience, but does that make them a good teacher?" says Galey, who has two of her four children in preschool.

"Those things count, of course. But how to direct children in a non-confrontational style and how to manage children in a group situation are important components as well. You want to know how they teach, not just that they're qualified to teach."

Galey, a work-from-home mom, urges parents to look at preschools carefully and to not just take the nearest and easiest options.

"Go meet the teachers," she says. "Listen to what your friends have to say, too."

Article and image reprinted with generous permission from The Calgary Herald, Stephen, C. (February 19, 2009). Neighbours Preschool, p. N16.

Campus Preschool: A Wonderful Decision
Lynn Moore

Campus Preschool was a marvelous blend of optimism in the promise of children, kindness, calmness, and professionalism. It was a special "home" for parents, teachers, and students. I am sure I am not the only one whose personal life and the lives of my children were so enriched by our sojourn with Randie, Heidi, and Frances. I hope my children and I returned in some small way to the fullness of their lives, too.

All children are a miracle, and the teachers recognized and nurtured the gifts of each individual child. Professionally, they also recognized some gifts that were a bit "hidden" in each child and worked hard to help the students to develop those.

Heidi, Randie, and Frances were always striving to improve their practice. I remember them coming back enthused from a professional development day that emphasized the use of cooking in preschool curriculum. In a few days little plastic cutting boards, plastic knives, and making fruit salad and other tasty treats became part of the daily fun.

The time the students spent at the preschool was professionally structured to help them develop the many interests, needs, and skills kids have – fine and large motor skills, art, science, drama, music, reading, writing, manners, outdoors, and social interactions. Of course the kids never noticed that they were very skillfully being exposed to all the things they needed to develop into wonderful people. They just had a great time.

As a scientist, I totally appreciated the science that was offered all the time at Campus Preschool. Frances, Heidi, and Randie understood well that science is just loving all aspects of life, but wanting to know "why?" or teaching people to be interested enough to ask all the "whys!"

As a parent I appreciated the exceptional learning and developmental environment provided at the school. I also appreciated the wonderful adult models the teachers were; since we were thousands of miles from our families, the teachers were very important adult models in my children's lives. I couldn't have asked for better models. I know the wonderful values of the teachers are part of my kids' very fibres! And mine, too. I was so impressed with the preschool I kept both my children in the school for an extra year before enrolling them in kindergarten. A wonderful decision for all of us.

Thank you Randie, Heidi, and Frances.

From Lynn, Rich, Christopher, and Erica Moore

Curious Minds and Imagination
Gillian Kydd

When we arrived in Calgary in 1971, I was enveloped in a community of women connected to the Faculty Women's Club, and we were thus given a foundation for a long and rich chapter in our lives. This group has been integral to the development of community within Calgary and deserves that recognition. Here is one story:

Each morning the group of four-year-olds would rush into the classroom, knowing that something interesting would happen that day. The room held an eclectic collection of things that appealed to children. The teachers, Marilyn and Randie, would often be out of sight, down at child level, working on something that was sure to be fascinating. They loved it when someone brought in a project from home or wanted to talk about what had happened the day before.

Campus Preschool Co-op was a special place for our children and for us in the 1970s. My husband, Ron Kydd, was a faculty member in the Chemistry Department and our friends encouraged us to enrol our children there. We took turns volunteering and being on committees. What I didn't realize then was that I was learning too. I had completed a BEd degree the previous year at the University but it was observing the daily life at Campus Co-op that helped me to understand what real learning was all about. Children were valued and treated as individuals. Flexibility and imaginative play were key. Both our children flourished in that atmosphere and I'm sure that those experiences had an impact on their lives. Today both are independent creative thinkers, one in medicine, the other in the arts.

But I too was affected. When our children got older, I began to teach in the school system and loved the curious minds and imagination of young children. My background was in science and I built my philosophy of science education upon what I had witnessed at Campus Co-op. My students, as young as six, were using microscopes, making electrical circuits and generally "messing about." Later I was fortunate to be able to teach at University Elementary School with another faculty spouse, Sue Chivers: we were the first job sharing pair in the Calgary Board of Education. I then became a science consultant helping teachers to understand how important it was to teach science in a hands on way. Experiential learning is nothing new, even if it has become a buzz word nowadays!

As a science consultant in 1993, I began to work with the Calgary Zoo and spearheaded a project that gave teachers the opportunity to move their classroom to the Zoo for an entire week. Angela Rokne, a gifted teacher (and a faculty spouse), developed the first pilot week of Zoo School which she used as a catalyst for an exciting in depth study for her Grade 3 class. Angela's children did research, wrote poetry, and learned to draw with incredible detail. After the pilot classes that followed, Don Harvie, a Calgary philanthropist and head of the Devonian Foundation, laid the financial groundwork that allowed the Calgary Zoo to begin Zoo School in 1994 with an experienced educator as the Coordinator. The program grew steadily and we added the Glenbow Museum School the next year, and then the Science Centre School. There are now 11 sites in Calgary including University School Week, Petro-Canada Bird School, Canada Olympic Park School, City Hall School, Stampede School, Talisman Centre School, Aero Space Museum School, and the Cross Conservation Area School. More than 6000 students, mainly at the elementary level, participate each year in Calgary. Funding comes from corporate and community partners such as The Calgary Foundation and The City of Calgary. Four of the sites are funded by Chevron Canada and that part of the program is called Open Minds. The other sites, grouped under the name Campus Calgary, have other funders.

The teachers are in "the driver's seat" and they develop a long term study that integrates many subject areas. They are assisted in their planning by the education coordinator from the Calgary Board of Education and the coordinator at the site they are attending. Each week is tailor made for the needs of the teacher and her students. There may be sessions, for example with an architect at City Hall, a curator at Glenbow, or the astronomer at the Science Centre. The students learn how to slow down, to observe carefully, and to write and draw in journals. Research has demonstrated that writing skills improve dramatically because the students have interesting things to write about and they are given guidance by their teachers.

Teacher practice is enhanced because participating teachers are encouraged to think about learning in new ways and they receive a great deal of support. This important outcome of the program was the focus for the research for my doctorate which I completed in the Faculty of Education at U of C in 2003. I was able to tell the story of one teacher over a five year period as she wove the experiences with Open Minds/Campus Calgary into her daily teaching life.

The concept for the program has spread to other cities in Canada, the United States, and in Singapore, with a further 6000 students each year immersed in a week of learning at such diverse settings as the Legislature in Edmonton, the Vancouver Aquarium, the East Lansing Zoo in Michigan, and a wetlands reserve in Singapore. All of these programs help to connect children to their communities in deeper, more meaningful ways. Schools are sterile environments that remove children from daily life and the natural world: that needs to change.

When I look back on all those threads that wove in and out of University life, so many involved the friendship and support of others. My husband and I are now both retired to the Sunshine Coast of BC and our network has expanded to groups such as Eldercollege, the University Women's Club, and my breast cancer dragon boat team.

The Faculty Women's Club, with all its facets, has been important for us, but it has done much for the City of Calgary.

How to Preserve Children
Anni Adams

1 large grassy field
½ dozen children
2 or 3 small dogs
1 pinch of babbling brook
A few pebbles

Mix children and dogs well together and put them in the field, stirring constantly. Pour the brook over the pebbles, sprinkle the field with flowers. Spread all ingredients under a deep blue sky and bake in the hot sun. When thoroughly brown, remove and set aside to cool in a bath tub.

Glenbow Museum Archives M.8220: Campus Preschool Newsletter, October 1983

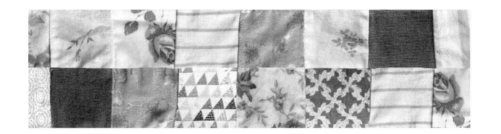

Journeying

Fringe Benefits
Calgary Local Council of Women

One of the reasons why our Club has remained happily durable is the sensitivity executives have shown in adapting regular meeting format to our changing interests. A [later] detailed description of our Constitution and its subsequent revisions indicates that the organization, principles, and laws by which our Club would be governed were matters of great concern to us. Being one of our charter members, I can attest to the hours spent putting forth motions, debating them, amending them, and enforcing Robert's Rules of Order to guide us through voting on an amendment to an amendment! Guest speakers languished in the wings while we 'finished the business part of our meeting'; janitors prowled the hallways waiting for us to finally disperse. I am certain that on many occasions they sorely wished that we had written a closure clause into the by-laws because that would have necessitated only one month of waiting!

One of the fringe benefits of all that debating was that we were well prepared for leadership in other Calgary organizations. Mary Winspear persuaded our Faculty Women's Club to affiliate with the Calgary Local Council of Women [in February 1964]. We have given them three presidents: Mary Winspear, Joni Chorny and me.

Norris, p. 22-23

Editors' Notes: As recently as the Annual General Meeting in April 2003, Dorothy Groves spoke on behalf of the National Council of Women in Canada, an organization whose mission is to empower women through regional and national representation. Dorothy suggested that the President of the Faculty Women's Club could attend a Calgary meeting of the National Council with a view to the permanent representation of the Faculty Women's Club. FWC President Sally Goddard said she would be willing to attend the meeting and

June 22, 1976
Budget, Special notations:
Pam will arrange to have the broken coffee urn repaired. One urn will be offered to the Faculty Club for storage and its use unless we need it. Anyone may rent the urn for $1.

September 8, 1976
Business:
Rental of coffee urn, a sum of $1 per week is to be charged.

September 1976
Newsletter item: 75-cup coffee urn available to rent for $1.

September 14, 1977
Coffee Urns – FWC owns two coffee urns and Carol Irons offered to look after one. Regina moved and Isobel seconded that the FWC will rent these out at $1.00 for 3 days then $1.00 for every day thereafter. Carried.
The other urn is at the Faculty Club.

October 11, 1978
The coffee urn is now defunct so is not available for hire.

a decision could then be made. At an Executive Meeting held on Sunday, June 1, 2003, Sally reported on her attendance at the organizational meeting for reopening a local chapter. It was decided that this was not within the mandate of our group at this time but we would follow the progress of the Chapter. Over the years, the FWC has given approximately $300 to the Local Council of Women, along with uncounted hours of volunteer efforts.

An Historic Event, and Other FWC Anecdotes
Ute Dilger

This is not another anecdote but a legal victory for the women of Canada and the members of the Faculty Women's Club helped to achieve it. Many of these women who acted at the time and worked so hard are no longer with us. We honor their memory and take courage from the example they set for us. Of course no woman could achieve this victory alone. A great undertaking like this needs the support of many, who might now be forgotten and unnamed. You know and remember how you personally helped in your role within the Faculty Women's Club, your church, or your organization. Bless you all.

Flashback to 1968, and try to remember the law case *Murdoch vs. Murdoch* and how it unfolded. Irene Murdoch, the wife of an Alberta farmer, found herself locked out of her home. After twenty-five years of marriage her husband had taken in a new woman. Irene Murdoch was homeless and destitute. Women helped her financially during this hard time. Divorce proceedings were started and Irene sued for maintenance and her share of the farm. Together, Irene and her husband had built up the farm with backbreaking work. She also had contributed money – a loan from her mother – to buy the land in the beginning. They later paid back this loan. She worked alongside her husband and did a farmer's work, doing the same tasks he did. Every year, she ran the farm for five months on her own while her husband worked elsewhere. During all these years she did the housework, the garden, and bore and raised their son.

Despite all this the Alberta Courts denied her a share of the property on the grounds that her contribution was "no more than that of any other wife and that this routine work did not justify a share in the property." In 1973, the Supreme Court of Canada heard her appeal but to no avail. She was even ordered to pay a portion of her husband's legal fees. After the courts granted her a divorce in 1974, she petitioned for maintenance and won. At last, Irene Murdoch was paid the lump sum of $65 000, a fraction of what the property was worth. No additional payments were to be made.

The Supreme Court decision outraged Canadian women and triggered an intensive round of lobbying across Canada for law reform. Women from coast to coast organized to support a resolution that would provide women with rights comparable to those granted to men. In 1980, a major reform of Family Law was established: the principle of spousal equality in marriage. This change, however, came too late for Irene Murdoch.

Now we come to a new chapter. The Prime Minister of the time, Pierre Elliott Trudeau, planned to patriate the Constitution. When he made this announcement, Doris Anderson was president of the Canadian Council on the Status of Women, a government appointed body. In 1978, Trudeau gave power of divorce to the provinces. But women realized the relevance of the constitutional issues that might arise with the new Charter of Rights. At Anderson's instigation, the Advisory Council published a primer on "Women and the Constitution" just as the debate on patriation of the constitution started. In October 1980, Anderson and Parti Quebecois Vice President Louise Harel led a seminar on the constitutional change proposed by Trudeau. Women across Canada were alarmed. The new Charter of Rights and Freedoms seemed to jeopardize women's legal rights. A conference was planned on the Status of Women.

Lloyd Axworthy, the Minister for the Status of Women, cancelled this conference organized by the Advisory Council of Women. After this cancellation, Anderson resigned as President of the Advisory Council. An explosion of support followed. The press put the story on the front pages of all Canadian newspapers and it was in the headlines for weeks. Anderson, with the help of women from many organizations, spontaneously called a new conference in Ottawa.

The women came to Parliament Hill from all provinces. They paid their own way or were supported by their organizations. They were billeted in private homes. Meeting places were hastily arranged. Hurrah for the power of these women! There was a lot of dissent at first among these women's groups. How could it be otherwise? It was challenging to reach consensus among 1300 women with different values, but it was done. On St. Valentine's Day, February 14, 1981, women met in various locations on Parliament Hill, wherever they could find room including offices and conference rooms. Private women and women of different organizations financed this conference. They were also supported by women Ministers and administrators and by representatives of the political parties. Many women worked tirelessly to help mobilize the conference. On the advice of capable lawyers, it was agreed upon to insert the very important word "Notwithstanding" at the beginning of Section 28, so it could be used in litigation.

Section 28 of the *Charter of Rights and Freedoms* States: "NOTWITHSTANDING anything in this Charter, all the Rights and Freedoms in it are guaranteed equally to male and female persons."

Dorothy Groves (an FWC member in 1966 and later President of the Faculty Women's Club, Alberta President on the Advisory Council of Women, and President of many other organizations), was chosen to go to Ottawa as representative of the Faculty Women's Club and the Local Council of Women.

That is our place in history; we helped to make it come true. No woman can be wronged like Irene Murdoch or her work dismissed. Thanks to all the women of the Faculty Women's Club who worked so hard for equality and thanks to all the countless women like the Famous Five who tirelessly fought for Women's Rights.

This report is an accumulation of various articles, excerpts from the book, *Ten Thousand Roses* by Judy Rebich, which was loaned to me by my sister Raging Granny O.J. Zawalsky, who had personally experienced divorce. Without the help of many friends I could not have written this report. Thanks to Berta Fisher, Marjorie Norris, Dorothy Groves' daughter, my neighbor Jan Hansen, and my two daughters.

Nothing good is ever easily achieved but the effort is worthwhile. Canadian Women, good for you!

The Festive Dinner

My memory plays tricks, I cannot remember when this dinner took place, nor do I know anymore what the occasion was; nevermind. Who was there and still has a great memory?

The Festive Dinner was planned to be in the Blue and Gold Dining Rooms. The committees discussed it very thoroughly and every detail was thought out: the date, the decorations, the guest list, the special nametags, and of course the menu. What to serve, what to serve?! The Food Services of the University were consulted. This sounds easy enough but with all the many guests from different nations, it was not. Some could not have beef, some could not have pork, some were vegetarian. With patience and much to and fro, the menu got set.

The evening came, how festive it was! Everybody arrived in "dress up clothes" as was the case in the sixties. The decorations were wonderful, handmade stars were hanging from the ceiling, swaying softly in the breeze. We mingled with friends until everybody got hungry and ready for the buffet. No sign of food, no cooks or servers showed up. Finally, some took action and learned that the Food Services had forgotten and forsaken us.

What to do, what to eat? Well we ordered Colonel Sanders to the rescue. The big buckets arrived with all kinds of edibles. Festive? Not! At least we ate and afterwards we had a very good time – as always when the Faculty Women's Club held a "Festive Dinner."

Ceremonial Unveiling of the University of Calgary Crest

All eyes were up front looking with suspense on the new crest high up above the stage where all the dignitaries were seated. There it was, the big red crest; you know it, have seen it many times. Madge Aikenhead and her husband Doug, a Professor in the Faculty of Education, had brought me along. Bless them, good friend and neighbors. Suddenly Doug groaned and said, "The Engineers have done it again. The Red Bull, do they have no respect at all? A pub sign? What next!" It is true that the Engineers had been up to more tricks than usual that year. This once, however, they were blameless. The Crest was authentic, the Angus Bull.

We had a good laugh later and a little grin every time we saw the magnificent Bull shown.

Dear Friends

If you move to a different country, maybe for a sabbatical, it helps if you are pregnant. Everyone is very helpful and patient.

In the fall of 1966, my husband Walter joined the Engineering Department and we came to Calgary with three small children and one on the way – despite my parents' warning and the good advice of many. We brought four suitcases and a bedroll. We did not intend to stay long. In my purse was also a "Spatzles Brett " – ask a German housewife about this.

Now it is time to praise and thank all the Calgary people who helped us when we arrived. The pioneer spirit to help newcomers was alive. Peter Glockner, a Professor from the Engineering Department, met us at the airport. We were all exhausted after the move and sixteen hours travel. Thank you, Peter. Our children still talk about you and your wonderful car. The new neighbors close to our rented house were kind and helpful. They came over to greet us, gave advice, asked us to dinner, and had us over for Christmas and New Year's. How good of them. I was so terribly homesick and not well at all. It helped a lot. In fact, everyone was so considerate when they saw my increased shape. Men who probably would not have done so otherwise brought chairs, cups of tea, and put their hands under my elbow. Their wives gave helpful advice and offered baby stuff. Thanks, Gail Trofimenkoff.

My first outing was to the Faculty Women's Club. Mary Neville, the Dean's wife, picked me up. How fascinating to meet all the Ladies there from so many countries. My school English, mostly forgotten, never held me back. I was happy to talk to the other women, sometimes to the embarrassment of Walter. Soon I was caught up in various activities with the Club: dinners, dances, balls, decorating, planning, and visiting other couples. Some weekends we went to three events. We were young and had a very good time. Everyone was new at the university and that formed a bond between us.

Over the years we moved a few times, always further west. We now have lived for over thirty years in our present home – with a "Mountain View," my condition to stay in Calgary. How I love to see them. We and our five children are proud Canadian Citizens.

After our children finished University and moved out one by one, taking with them all the telephone calls and their many friends, the house seemed deserted. No more volunteering at kindergarten and school. That was the time I started volunteering at the Alberta Children's Hospital.

One day a week, for the last fifteen years, I go there to help: holding and feeding, changing and bathing the smallest and sickest babies, cuddling, rocking, and singing. I give thanks for my healthy children and eleven grandchildren. Volunteering there is very rewarding, even when I often cry on the way home.

When the "Raging Grannies," a group of activists, formed in Calgary, I joined them. I never wanted to be one of "the silent majority." The Raging Grannies are a Canadian "invention," formed in BC. Now there are eighty-seven "Gaggles" in Canada and the USA, some in Europe and Australia. The Raging Grannies write new lyrics to well known melodies and I am glad that I now can do this. We Grannies march and sing at peace rallies, against homelessness, at nurses' and teachers' strikes. We demonstrate for universal health care, the environment, women, children, and seniors' issues.

Here I must interrupt myself for an unsolicited and unpaid commercial: "Ladies, we need you! If you like to sing, dress up in silly flower hats and shawls to support worthy causes, please call me. No qualifications necessary." As Raging Grannies we meet interesting people, Paul Martin, Ralph Klein, David Suzuki, and many more. It is fun.

On certain days every week I take care of our smallest grandchildren so the mothers can have part time positions in their professions. It gives me the chance to be close to our grandchildren and to love them well. One of my other activities is to take care of the playground by our house as a "park volunteer." I am involved in many causes as an activist, not as a "do-gooder," mind. Thanks to my husband, Walter, I am able to do this. Not to be active anymore with the Faculty Women's Club I regret. It always makes me happy to see you from time to time. My thoughts return often to our first years in Calgary and I remember with love the good friends no longer with us.

Here is to the next fifty years of the FWC. Best wishes and good luck for the future.

Spatzle (drop noodles) for Chicken
Sarah Glockner

4   eggs
2 ½ cups flour
3 tsp   salt
¼ cup   melted butter or margarine

Bring to boil in 3-4 qt saucepan: 2 qts water and 2 tsp salt.

Meanwhile, sift together and set aside 2 ½ cups flour and 1 tsp salt.

Combine in a bowl and mix together: 4 eggs slightly beaten, ¾ cup water.

Gradually add flour mixture to egg mixture, stirring until smooth. (Batter should be very thick and break from spoon instead of pouring in a continuous steam). Spoon batter into boiling water by ½ tsp, dipping spoon into water each time. Cook only one layer of noodles at a time, do not crowd. After noodles rise to surface, boil gently 5-8 minutes, or until soft when pressed against side of pan with spoon.

Remove from water with slotted spoon, draining over water for a second, and place into warm bowl. Toss noodles lightly with ¼ cup melted butter or margarine.

Serve on plate with chicken paprika. Garnish with parsley.

Faculty Women's Club Favourite Recipes (1969). (2)1, p. 24

An Academic, Maternal, Political Skip through Fifty Years
Susan Stratton

1956

I'm in Grade 8 in Tokyo, where my US military father is on a three year tour of duty. As a US Army brat, I moved from my birthplace in Wisconsin to brief stays in Kentucky, Kansas, Virginia, North Carolina, Germany (first Mannheim, then Heidelberg), Pennsylvania, and California before what was to me a thrilling and romantic ocean liner trip to Japan. My mother may have thought otherwise, focused on keeping her four daughters, aged three to thirteen, from washing overboard, as she travelled alone with us to join our father in Japan. We lived a year in downtown Tokyo, waiting for accommodation on the Army base. Our home there was supported by two maids and a houseboy. The latter, Ishikawa-san, was a law student at the University of Tokyo, on whom I had something of a crush. The maids wore shoes of about size 1, while my own were size 8. In this society, I felt large and gawky and awkward, though the Japanese people were unfailingly polite, and quite interested in blond, blue-eyed foreigners. I rode the trains with anxiety, because I couldn't read the signs identifying train stations, so I had to stay alert enough to count the right number of stops from where I started to where I got off. I learned to ride horseback, including jumping, at the Emperor's Palace. Once we moved onto the US Army base, my life became as "normal" as possible: not only attending an American school, but hanging out at the base teenage club, listening to Elvis Presley and becoming adept at shooting pool. There were opportunities to experience Japanese culture, but recreating "normal" American life as far as possible was the objective. In another year, we'll be back to the States, and I'll be in high school.

1966

My husband, Mike Stone, and I are in graduate school at the University of Colorado in Boulder, he in Math, I in English. We met in 1959 in Carlisle, Pennsylvania, just before I left for my first year at Lawrence College in Appleton, Wisconsin and he for his last year at Wesleyan University in Connecticut. Both Army brats; my family moved the next summer to Fort Sam Houston, Texas, so Mike and I spent four years briefly visiting over Christmases and summers and then married the day after I graduated from college. This created no strong basis for a relationship, though we are well matched in every way that's supposed to matter, including being well loved by each other's families.

Mike opted for three years as a volunteer Army officer to avoid being drafted as an enlisted man. We spent a few months at Fort Detrick, Maryland, a few in Oklahoma (where my most vivid memory is the day that JFK was assassinated), and then, just when we thought he was doomed to a tour in Vietnam, Mike was posted instead to 18 months in Fort Richardson in Anchorage, Alaska, a delightful adventure. After his time was up, we headed for grad school at the University of Colorado. Despite (or perhaps because of) my life path moving frequently from one school district to another, meaning I was challenged by disjunctions between every planned curriculum, I am a natural scholar: curious, interested in a wide range of things, rewarded with good grades (excepting an F in Grade 10 French that resulted from a gap between my French experience in Tokyo and the subsequent experience in Pennsylvania) and strong references from my college profs. Given free rein by my parents in the matter of choosing a college, I made a lucky choice in Lawrence College, a small liberal arts school in Wisconsin, where I was born and some of my mother's relatives still lived. Overwhelmed by the breadth of choice, and not knowing where my family might move next, I simply chose the school my mother went to, and it turned out to be a very fine place to acquire a real education, in small classes taught by excellent professors who encouraged creative enquiry. Despite my academic success, my priority was, then and is now, marriage and children (I did grow up in the '50s). However, Mike is adamant there will be no children until his PhD is within reach, so I might as well pursue a PhD myself in the meantime. Maybe I'll teach part time in a junior college while focusing on family. We hike in the Rockies, enjoy the camaraderie of other grad school couples.

1976

I'm a professor at the University of Calgary, as is Mike. We have explained repeatedly that we did not come to Canada so Mike could dodge the draft. Rather, he loved the mountains and applied up and down the Rockies. The University of Calgary was expanding furiously and hiring vigorously at a time when the US market for professors was limited, so to Canada we came, I having completed all of my PhD except the dissertation. Even more to my satisfaction, I had given birth to a darling little boy in 1968, on whom both parents doted as did two sets of grandparents whose first grandchild he was. Blake was a year old when we moved to Calgary, at a time when the first big cracks in the marriage were being felt.

I completed my PhD a year later and taught a couple of courses at Mount Royal College. When Blake was three, I started teaching full time in the English Department at U of C and Blake entered a preschool strongly recommended by European colleagues of Mike's. In March, Blake reported that his teacher had taped a child's mouth shut. Even though I thought it must surely have been a threat rather than actuality, I went to talk with the head of the school. Far from sharing my dismay, she backed the teacher, explaining that the children must be prepared for the rigors of elementary school: learning to follow directions was of the utmost importance. Torn between my wish to rescue Blake on the spot from educational hell and my dismay at the prospect of no child care for the remaining month of university classes, I gritted my teeth in favor of keeping him there for just one more month. But Blake came home the next day with a note that said, "Since you are not satisfied with the school, this will be Blake's last day." Great! My educational ideals got my three-year-old kicked out of school! I no longer remember how we survived the month; Mike and I probably passed him back and forth between classes and occasionally treated him to a lecture on calculus or T.S. Eliot.

We got better advice on preschool, and Blake enjoyed the privilege of Campus Preschool for two years. It was designed in part as a parent co-op, and early in the process of living up to what one of my grad school profs called my "natural leadership," I was President of the Preschool Board during his second year. Blake moved on to University Elementary, and now spends the second half of Grade 2 in Boulder, Colorado, back where we were in grad school, and where Mike has gone to reconnect with his old profs for a sabbatical project. I've taken an unpaid term off teaching at U of C to join him in the hope of saving our marriage with some time away from the demands of two careers. It's no good. By summer, after years of working to maintain an obviously imperfect marriage, I've decided it's over.

I'm a more successful academic than a marriage partner. I love the teaching; I like my colleagues; I'm getting into the administrative ("service") side of the profession; I'm publishing articles on George Bernard Shaw's plays (the subject of my PhD dissertation), and I'm planning a bigger research project that suits me and seems important for my time and place: a book on Robertson Davies' work as a playwright. I specialized in drama as a graduate student but I came to Canada knowing nothing of Canadian drama. I found that generally speaking, my Canadian colleagues didn't either; Canadian drama was not taught in Canadian literature courses, and in the early seventies, even much better known Canadian poetry and fiction were struggling to emerge from a colonial sense of inferiority. Davies is the only English Canadian playwright with a substantial body of published plays that well deserved a book length study. I'll be making a contribution to my new country. Probably I'm working harder to compensate for my sense of failure as a wife, but the academic side of life is very satisfying.

1986

I'm Associate Dean of Humanities; my book on Robertson Davies has finally been published; I'm promoted to Full Professor this year. Again, I'm experiencing more success on the professional than the marital side of my life. I married again in 1977, had two children in 1979 and 1980, and that marriage to Bill Blackburn, another English professor, (ill considered, though I initially thought of it as adventurous), broke down in 1983. I did want more children than the one Mike had decided was enough, but I hadn't really planned to become a single mother of two preschoolers. Blake was old enough to be helpful in theory, but as a teenager, he was largely absorbed in his own world, which consisted mostly of computing. By the end of Grade 6 at University Elementary, he'd already made his mark as an emerging computer programmer. In junior high, he was enjoying programming competitions and science fairs and was the subject of a full page spread in *The Calgary Herald*. (The angle was something like "Boy genius has ordinary messy bedroom.") Now he's in high school, challenging his mother, who always worked for good grades in everything on principle, by ignoring what he's not interested in and excelling only in what he is interested in. I feel a grudging admiration for this approach. He's doing research in the university library to keep abreast of the rapidly developing field of computing; so what if some of his grades are just

average. He's a geek, but an extroverted one, happily maintaining a friendship circle of other geeks.

I've shifted my research field to science fiction, an interest since my
youth that feels now increasingly important. When I was a new young professor, science fiction was a secret vice, but now it's an established course in
many universities, and I've been teaching it for some time. The students think
they're taking the course just for fun, but I tell them it may be the most
important course they take in university. The world is changing so fast, we all
need the ability that science fiction offers to imagine possible future paths, for
better or worse. We need to know that the way we live now is not the only
way, not necessary or inevitable, and that we are responsible for choices we
make that will lead to one future or another.

My little ones, Alan and Lynn, now seven and six, are beautiful and funny
and challenging. Just nineteen months apart and always close buddies,
they're in French Immersion at Banff Elementary School. Alan's class is two-
thirds boys, the terror of every teacher in the school as they make their way
through one grade after another. He tells me he's one of the challenges,
explaining that all the boys in his class except three are bad, and all the girls
except one are good. Ah, gender roles! I admired that one girl. Lynn's class is
the opposite: two-thirds girls – a relief to the teachers the year after they've
dealt with Alan's class, no doubt. She discovers that her particular group of
girlfriends is of interest for their varying skin tones; they call themselves the
Rainbow Club. I love this feature of Calgary, which I see mostly in the university and the nearby schools; the mix of races and cultures is quite marked.
Alan's enthusiasm for soccer provides my chief entertainment. Though I wondered at first how I'd find time to be a soccer Mom, I value the leisure of chatting with the other parents while we watch our kids chase a ball around the
field. I miss my own mom, who died after a stroke in 1984. My parents have
lived in San Antonio since 1960, so they have not been very close to my own
kids, but my mother's steadfast interest and pride in everything I did, including my children, was always a welcome support. My three sisters, far flung in
the US, supply some of the same support, even at a distance.

1996

A formative role as the University's first Advisor to the President on
Women's Issues is behind me (1989-91). That appointment to a position created by Murray Fraser, the best university president ever, transformed my
teaching, my research, and my work in administration, because gender roles
touch everything in our lives. After my appointment, I spent several months
researching women in universities, which taught me how my own experience,
a relatively easy ride through life to the position of university professor, dif-
fered from almost all other women's experience. Feminists weren't just making mountains out of molehills, as I had been inclined to think! I stopped say-

ing, "I'm not really a feminist, but . . ." I was a feminist! In the first year of my role as Advisor, I researched and wrote "Women in the Nineties," a report on the status of women at the University. In my second year, the Status of Women Committee, which I chaired, produced 123 recommendations, ranked by importance, based on that report, designed to improve the status of women at the University. One of those recommendations was to create an Academic Women's Association, so as one of my last acts before I left the position for a sabbatical in 1991, I called a meeting of women who were interested, and the Academic Women's Association was born.

That feminist conversion also propelled me into a role as public speaker. Feminism infused everything I did, after the shock of dealing with the effect on the University of the 1989 Montreal Massacre at L'École Polytechnique. I was astonished at how it quickly polarized the University community into those who thought the murderer (who proclaimed a hatred of feminists, apparently a category into which women at an Engineering school automatically fit) was an extreme end, but part of a spectrum of sexist behavior, and those who thought feminists were just using a freak happening to advance their agenda. I set out to teach the world more about the subtleties and hazards of perceiving women generally as the subordinate and men as the dominant sex. I spoke at universities and conferences in Vancouver, Edmonton, Saskatchewan, Ottawa, and my own, as well as accepting invitations from organizations in Calgary, the first and scariest of which was the Knights of Columbus. I learned that when I had something I really wanted to say, I was no longer afraid to speak out.

Now I'm Associate Dean of Graduate Studies, overseeing half the graduate programs at the University, a development that recognized the success of my work as Advisor on Women's Issues and which offers opportunities to follow up on some of the 123 recommendations in the Women in the Nineties report. I'm amused to be using my own advice as a rationale for innovations in the Faculty of Graduate Studies.

A growing interest in environmentalism is following on my immersion in feminism, a recognition of a relationship between dominance of men over women and humans' dominance of other species. I'm developing a new course in Literature and the Environment, the first in the English Department to focus on environmental issues. My studies in science fiction, now extended to utopian fiction, highlight the shift from atomic warfare as the chief threat to civilization in midcentury writing to environmental degradation as the greater concern in more recent fiction. I want to teach about environmental issues, and the wonderful thing about literature courses is their versatility; really, one can teach just about anything through literature.

1996 is a red letter year for romance. After thirteen years as a single parent professional – not the easiest combination of roles – Bernie Amell entered my life. Our shared interest in environmental issues, our shared background as single parents, our shared sense of failure in two marriages and cautious hope for better, our shared interest in reading, politics, and intellectual life, and in the Unitarian Church where we met, all of this supports what is primarily an emotional leap into close relationship. Spring sees the emergence of romance, to the surprise of both of us. At the end of October, we join households, his eighteen-year-old and my sixteen and seventeen-year-olds merging cautiously. Each of us had grown one child up and out – his daughter Jessie, who is at the University of Victoria finishing a degree in French and working toward certification as a teacher, and my son Blake, who dropped out of the U of C after a year and is blazing his successful path in the world of computer programming.

Lynn's been giving me grief since she was fourteen, after an early lifetime of being the ideal daughter. She'd make sure her older brothers didn't forget my birthday, she'd help around the house, she was a sweet tempered, beautiful delight. I worried that she might turn out to be one of those women who still live with their mothers at forty. At fourteen, she made sure that I could stop worrying about that! No more Mother's darling, she was bent on being her own person, if only she could figure out who that was. Over the next couple of years, she took to wearing black with chains and bizarre hairdos, getting the odd tattoo (mercifully, fairly subtle and not particularly grotesque); worst of all, she'd stay out all night without telling me where she was or ever giving me a clue what she was up to. Booted out of school for nonattendance near the end of Grade 10, she's moved to the Alternative High School, which, to my relief and hers, suits her perfectly.

In contrast, Alan, who'd been giving me some degree of grief over most of his early life, with no break from determined self assertion between his terrible twos and his early teenage brushes with police, has become the good kid, seizing on the opening Lynn provided. He's made the choice to withdraw from his peer group, which brings an end to his risky behavior. He does well in school with no apparent effort. He's beginning to take pride in good performance on whatever McJob he's doing.

Now, with Bernie and his son Kevin added to the household, Lynn's target shifts from me to Bernie. Adding a handsome eighteen-year-old boy into the mix intrigues her briefly, but Kevin has a girlfriend, and really, he quickly becomes just one more annoyance that Bernie's responsible for. I naively thought at first she'd be happy for me, but at sixteen, she just reacts against the encroachment on her house and her mother, shared only with Alan for most of her life. Her passive-aggressive treatment of Bernie nearly succeeds in driving him out, but not quite. Despite the bumps, I'm happy: I have my kids and my new love and plenty of career interest. I continue singing in the Unitarian Church choir, which for the past few years has been my one refuge from the responsibilities of career and childrearing.

2006

I'm retired from the university (2002), but there's nothing "finished" about my life, which is the best ever. The shock of my sister Sally's and my Dad's deaths far apart geographically but on the same day in December 1997 is well behind me, and it's strengthened the bonds with my other two sisters, Nancy and Mary. Lynn and Alan moved out into an apartment together the same year Bernie and I married, 2000. They moved not because of the marriage but because both decided not to continue in school that fall, so I figured it was time for that other school: the lessons of life that come with living on meager salaries. Both the move and the marriage improved the relationship between Lynn and Bernie substantially; now all is well among us. Alan has not returned to school after his two years in Mount Royal College's journalism program ("I just wanted to see if I could get good grades, and I did") and is now in a full time position with benefits at London Drugs. Lynn graduates this year with a degree in Justice Studies from Mount Royal. She married last year, and I have no fault to find with her choice. In fact, Ryan Thomson seems to me a blend of her two brothers, with Alan's tall, dark, handsome looks, Blake's focus on computing, and the intelligence of both. Her brothers "gave Lynn away" at her wedding, father Bill having died in 2003 where he was teaching in China. Blake married his beautiful, warm and vibrant Barbara Barton in 2002, celebrating a relationship that began the same year as Bernie's and mine. They've lived first in Santa Cruz, California and now in Bellevue, Washington, where Blake works at Microsoft. All seems well in my children's lives. There is also the distant delight of a grandchild, born to Bernie's daughter Jessica and her husband two years ago – but they live in Dubai, after four years in Kuwait, where Marina was born, so our access is limited. There's a change on the horizon though: they've bought a house in Calgary, which Lynn and Ryan will rent until Jess, Brent, and Marina move back to Calgary next year.

As to my life: the ten years since my sudden "fall" into love have justified that emotional leap. For the first time, I'm in a marriage that makes the institution seem like a good idea. Admittedly, we're not facing the challenges of rearing children together. And we learned a few things from the rocky roads through our earlier marriages. Third time lucky? More likely, a capacity to learn from experience; that must be what provides the "mellowing" of middle age, which seems a good time for true marital partnership.

I retired at sixty partly because the university no longer brought me the satisfaction it once did and partly because there were other things I wanted to do that take time. Over the years, university life gradually became more competitive, more driven, more about getting grants and less about education. There was no time for convivial collegial relationships. Student numbers and class sizes went up and up, contrasting with what I still feel was the ideal education of my own undergraduate years. The role of Associate Dean of Graduate Studies was great for exploring the cultural differences of different disciplines in the university and for rescuing students trapped by bureaucracy, but when my term was over, I really didn't see anything new I wanted to do on campus. My one regret about leaving was that I'd have liked to help develop an interdisciplinary degree in environmental studies that would draw on environmental courses in arts and social sciences as well as some in the environmental sciences program.

Some of my extra-academic activities felt more rewarding now than academe. The "activist" side of my teaching was paralleled by my participation in Calgary's Raging Grannies ever since the group was founded in 1998. I've enjoyed the fun and camaraderie of the group and the creativity of songwriting as well as the satisfaction of participating in peace rallies and actions combating poverty, supporting environmental responsibility, protesting government's underfunding of education and attempts to privatize healthcare, supporting women's priorities, challenging corporate greed. The Unitarian Church, also known for its social activism, offered constructive use of more of my time, including a term as Board President the minute I retired. I followed that by taking the chair of the Green Sanctuary Committee, created to increase congregational awareness of and participation in actions that could help slow and perhaps reverse our human path to self destruction.

Also compelling and very time consuming for several years has been Bernie's and my participation in Prairie Sky, a cohousing cooperative. In 2001, we and six other households bought land for an 18 home development in Calgary's inner city. For some years earlier, we'd been meeting, planning, hosting information sessions, developing a method for consensus decision making, and codifying group principles, priorities, and practices. Once the investment in land was made, the pace to completion quickened, with Bernie working intensively on site plans and I on recruiting the rest of the eighteen households we needed to buy in. Prairie Sky (originally called Wholelife Housing) was a project that appealed both to my idea of utopian living and to my wish to be a social change agent. In 2003, we all moved in and another time consuming work year ensued, as we'd decided to do our own landscaping to save, we estimated, $50 000, not counting the services Bernie donated as a landscape architect. Our Common House also needed a good deal of finishing work, not to mention our own homes. How could I have kept up my university work too?

Now, three years after move in, we know what "normal" life in our cohousing development is, and it easily lives up to our hopes. Our neighbors are all friends we can count on for help when we need it, and we're happy to reciprocate. Nobody needs to take a taxi to the airport or hire a pet sitter. It's like a large extended family, only better because we know we share values that support mutual respect, working for stronger community, and efforts to walk more lightly on the Earth. We learn from each other and get collectively "greener" as time goes on. We save money by sharing resources and creating home entertainment – our annual talent show is a favorite, as are occasional house concerts. Bernie and I have sold our second vehicle and instead have a share in a car owned by several families. We share hostel weekends, hiking and camping trips, canoeing expeditions, borrowing and lending equipment as needed. It's a good life.

Retirement made room for still other things I wanted. I'd done little or nothing in the way of fitness for most of my life; now there's yoga, NIA (yoga-dance-martial arts), deepwater workouts, cycling, walking. I still don't spend a lot of time on fitness, but certainly more than before. Outdoor recreation – hiking, skiing, canoeing – we don't get enough of, but at least some.

Equally important, my gradual movement towards activism, environmental activism in particular, took me immediately after retirement into Green Party politics. I had finally become a Canadian citizen in 1992, retaining my US citizenship, though I pretty much leave US politics to my sisters. There's more chance for impact in Canada, and I've become much more Canadian than American over the years. The Alberta Greens were small and much in need of time and energy from anyone who had them to offer. I became Deputy Leader in 2004 and ran in the provincial election that year – quite successfully for a Green, drawing 12% of the vote in Calgary North Hill. I was proud to have my daughter, Lynn, as one of my volunteers, along with lots of my Prairie Sky neighbors and fellow Unitarians. This year I'm President, working to strengthen the party further in anticipation of Alberta's next general election. I've been less involved with the federal Greens, but enough for some fun and interest. We've hosted Green Party Leader Jim Harris at Prairie Sky on more than one occasion, and he had a great press conference in our Common House to announce the energy plank of his 2004 platform. This year, he's stepped down as Leader, and I've worked as Alberta Organizer on Elizabeth May's successful campaign for Leader. Like Jim, Elizabeth stayed with us when she came to Calgary. My feminism reasserts itself in connection with politics both in the Green Party and in the form of membership on the executive of a fledgling southern Alberta chapter of Equal Voice, an organization dedicated to increasing the number of Canadian women in elected office.

So, what a good life, eh? Bernie and I are blessed with good health and wealth enough to sustain us and to share, thanks in part to my good university pension, in part to his continuing enjoyment of his career in environmental design focusing on wetlands, and in part to our choice to seek "enough" instead of "more." We are blessed in good relations with each other, his siblings and mine, and our children. We are blessed in the strength of our communities – Prairie Sky and the Unitarian Church. We are blessed to have time for volunteer work that feels useful and therefore rewarding. Now, if we and our fellow human beings can just get off the path we're on toward rapid exhaustion of the natural resources we all need for survival, we can count our lives well spent.

It's What's Below That Counts

Ilse Anysas-Salkauskas

55cm w x 41cm h Cotton fabrics, cotton and synthetic threads

My distress at what is happening to our Alberta environment led me to create this piece. The oil companies are only interested in getting our oil and are not concerned with how much pollution they create and leave with us in the process.

"It's What's Below That Counts" was featured in *Alberta Views* magazine (October 2006, p. 18).

Room for Me

Cathie Kernaghan

A woman needs money and a room of her own in order to write fiction. (Virginia Woolf)

The following is a fictional account of my life in the sense that all auto-biography is a re-imagining of one's life (Pinar & Grumet, 1978), a re-mem-bering (Estes, 1992; Kearney, 2002). I offer my story in the hopes that it will evoke memories in others; that they too might choose to share their own recollections of their lives, in the service of Others (Arendt, 1968). Stories, I have learned, are how we make sense of our lives, bringing meaning to what otherwise may seem like haphazard events (Arendt,1968 as cited in Kristeva, 2001; Kearney, 2002, Ricoeur, 1992). So it is that as I write this story for my readers, I am also making sense for myself, the series of events which have occurred in my life over the last number of years. I choose to risk sharing my experiences knowing that I have no particular claim to "truth" other than my own experience. I leave it to the readers of this text to decide if my experience has an element of truth for them as well (Woolf, 1928/2000; Merleau-Ponty, 1962). It is a decision which has required me to learn the humility of relying on my own lived experience as my voice of authority and it has meant unlearning previous cultural notions of what it means to be an author (Joy,1997; Ricoeur, 1981/2005). In light of reading the interpretive work of these aforementioned scholars, I prefer to name myself as the narrator of my life-stories, something of which I am learning is a continual process-in-the-becoming.

Virginia Woolf's fictional account of women writers in *A Room of One's Own,* shared with me by a colleague in our mutual studies through the Graduate Department of Educational Research (GDER) at the University of Calgary, has come to be very meaningful for me over the past six years of study. I am in the process of completing my dissertation, after daring to risk becoming a graduate student once again. I am a teacher by profession and I had initially thought that I would stay home with my first born for six months. However, having fallen in love with my daughters, six months grew into a year-and-a-half, then two-and-a-half and it was time for me to decide if I was going to go back to part time teaching or resign. I chose the latter. It was a choice which made all the difference in terms of depth in my life but it also led to many challenges. It is far too simple to name a single reason for one's life becoming "undone" as it were. But in my undoing, new possibilities of "becoming anew" also began to emerge. Every story is an interpretation, as I have said, and I qualify this interpretation as being skewed in the direction of the conflicts I experienced between wishing to provide the best for my children and being open to possibilities for myself and consequently my relationship with my husband.

In 2001, I applied to GDER to investigate the potential that oral storytelling and listening offered to human growth. I had fallen in love again with story through the phenomenon of oral storytelling when I was an active participant in a local storytelling guild, The Alberta League Encouraging Stories, (T.A.L.E.S.). I had come to realize what felt like magical experiences within me as I told and listened to stories, was an experience shared by others within the guild (Rosen, 1988). As a teacher I had an intuitive sense of appreciation for what this experience could potentially offer students and teachers in classrooms. It was not easy for my partner, Scott, to understand why I made the application to go back to university with very little conversation about my hopes and dreams with him. However, at the time, dialogue was not our strong point as a couple as we were both caught in a conflict which could perhaps be best articulated as our lived experience of trying our best to live within a society which valued reproduction of itself. (Grumet, 1988) In looking back I realize what I was raising as questions for both my Self and Scott were: "Just what is for the best for the family?" "Do we focus primarily upon accumulation of wealth in order to continue being a part of the societal pattern of reproducing itself?", or "Do we follow our path with heart, examining our lives and relationships in order to enrich our lived experiences and those of others?" I knew within my heart that I needed to follow my quest despite my trepidations of how things might evolve in my family relationships and my doubts on whether I was capable of meeting the scholarly demands of the doctoral program. I was accepted into the program and generously supported financially for the first year by the university.

My research in the first two years of my program opened up a world of research which echoed the transformational power of oral storytelling I had experienced: that our experiences as humans cannot be contained in objective analysis; that real learning and change occur at the deeper embodiment of lived experience and in conversation with others (Gadamer, 1989; Merleau-Ponty, 1962; Ricouer, 1992). Also as a result of my studies, new understandings of my life evolved and I came to feel (Gadamer, 1989; Merleau-Ponty, 1962; Ricouer, 1992) it was appropriate for me to find a dwelling that allowed me to: reflect upon my own lived experience in order to find better ways to communicate with Scott and my Self; and to continue to study while still actively fulfilling my responsibilities and desires as a mother and spouse.

At the time the university Married Student's quarters were not in the kind of demand which we currently find in this market of expansion in Calgary and Alberta. I was able to procure a two-bedroom apartment for myself and my children to stay should they wish while Scott and I worked through our communication issues. It was also an opportunity for me to study in a space which was truly "a room of my own," one which our home simply was not able to provide despite my best efforts to create such a space. The apartment became my studio-space, allowing me to grow in Self-awareness through my studies and the time/space to reflect through writing upon the interplay of my past, present and future relationships while maintaining my home with my family. The difficulty I found was that due to my felt need to work in the evenings as well as during the day on my studies, I spent more time away from my family than I and they would have liked. It became evident to me that I was experiencing too much alone time despite my best efforts to create a balance in my life through work, family and service in my community.

Over time Scott and I grew in our acknowledgement of each other's needs and I gradually came to question whether it was time to let go of the studio/apartment, but I had yet to find a resolution to the problem of creating a space in my home where I could actually productively write my thesis.

Because of the changing housing climate within Calgary's booming economy and my continued awareness that I was spending our family's funds on my studio space, I opened myself up to the question of how we could do things differently. That afternoon I bumped into a former officemate of mine, Lynn, now five months pregnant and in need of a home within ten days for herself, her spouse and her soon to be three-year-old son. By the end of the month Lynn had moved in to share the apartment/studio space and her husband and son were reunited with her within the month (adding to creative options they were implementing in the challenges of being an immigrant family with a mother-as-student). I offer sections from my journal as a summaried example of the process which unfolded from this point in my story.

May 31, 2007

Today I celebrated three-year-old Chen-Chen's birthday with his parents in the apartment we co-share. We ate noodle soup to symbolize longevity and sang *Happy Birthday* in Chinese; me, struggling a bit to get my tongue and teeth in the right places to produce the Chinese syllables to the oh-so-familiar melody. Today also would have been my Mother's ninety-fifth birthday if she had been alive. She has been gone for twelve years now, yet her breath for me today is as close as the crabapple blossoms which I picked off our tree . . . The blossoms don't last long, I am reminded; only moments, as are the moments of memory which come forth with their picking. My mother and I did not always have the ideal relationship but we tried the best we could with what we had been given by our cultural understandings. Yet we also had our moments of bliss just as these apple blossoms call up. Lynn and I shared stories of our childhood and hopes for our children as Chen-Chen played after lunch, Chen-Chen coming back on intermittent intervals to have another spoonful of noodle soup which his mother encouraged him to eat . . . anticipating the awaiting cherries.

I have tried in the last while to set myself up in a temporary office space in the Education Tower thinking that it would be wise to open up the apartment entirely for Lynn's family. At the same time, I have tried to set up spaces within my own home to write. I have only been minimally successful at both. It seems that I need a space separate from the calls of my responsibilities and my leisure in my home, and I need a space that welcomes my private voice. I thought if I brought the crabapple blossoms into the office along with some cherished memorabilia which symbolized my family heritage; . . . that the space would feel like an integration which honored both my inner and outer worlds. In actuality, I got very little done. I have surmised it was because I felt too content within my little cocoon I had created and the need to connect with the written word just wasn't there. So the flowers and the teacup and the stuffed heart with *Love* written on it came home. The office was an experiment and although I did get an article re-read I can't say it was a positive experience. In fact, having experienced the loneliness of working in the office in the evening, I packed up my laptop thinking I would write at home in the morning instead . . . but, I could not, I simply could not write there. So I packed everything up once again, and arrived, in gratitude, back at the apartment, with Chen-Chen's birthday celebration to look forward to.

Colleagues reassure me my discouragement is normal and that I will get back to the writing. So here I am, towards the end of the afternoon, back at my laptop in the upstairs bedroom of the apartment and yes, I am writing once again. What I note is that my writing is more connected to my lived experience as a result, I think, of my understanding that questions of how to live authentically live within me.

White (2000) speaks of a weak ontology that no longer tries to make grand statements about what it is to be human but instead focuses upon the lived experience of the learner. I still have a strong voice within me that questions whether my lived experience has anything to say to the topic of which I write. Yet, it is human connection that I crave and need: the singing of the simple happy birthday whose melody crosses cultures; the sharing of the birthday cake over a table which is also co-shared by Lynn and I as the public space in which to do our doctoral writing; a co-sharing of which we are still working out the details as we both recognize the need of its surface and location in our need for psychic space to think ; . . Writing in large quantities can be a difficult thing it seems on the human spirit; yet it is also very freeing when it comes forth in its own time and on its own terms.

I draw my writing to a close this afternoon, having come through a very anxiety-producing time and arriving at a deeply felt appreciation for those with whom I share this time on earth called life.

The current [ontological] turn might now be seen as an attempt to think ourselves, and being in general, in ways that depart from the dominant – but now more problematic – ontological investments of modernity. Ontological commitments in this sense are thus entangled with questions of identity and history, with how we articulate the meaning of our lives, both individually and collectively (White, 2000, p.4).

June 12, 2007

I'm back in my home to write after transforming my eldest daughter, Lindsay's, bedroom into a writing space; at least for the summer while she is away. I have arrived with a greater understanding of Virginia Woolf's (1928/2000) words: "every woman does need a room of [her] own" (p.6). Lynn's baby is due soon and the apartment we share as writers and her family is crying out to belong to her family at this time . . . I have had a pleasant surprise as I have been setting things up. The little portable stereo that I purchased so many years ago in order to be able to practice my singing, while preparing meals in the kitchen for my family, has become a lovely companion in this writing space. CBC FM radio is providing me with the sense of wildness, the out-of-doors otherwise provides, and allows my being to settle into the chair to begin contemplating "the next step along the way" with my writing. Megan, my youngest daughter, and friend Samantha are bustling about the house and I feel comforted by the sounds of their playful voices as I settle into this space which is reflecting a part of who I am back to me. I shall miss the company of Lynn and her family. However, I shall go back and visit; the work must be done and it must be done quickly now as my deadline looms ever larger. I would have liked to have been more effective at completing portions of the writing than I have, but ultimately it's been a tremendous opportunity of self-growth as I approach what feels more like what I have desired in terms of self-actualization. I have better integrated the masculine and feminine voice within myself consequently acting on my own behalf in a much more solid basis, which of course means I will also be more readily and solidly able to act on the behalf of others.

Paul Ricoeur (2005) suggests when we don't think we can do things it is only a defense mechanism telling us so. I would have to agree and also acknowledge that the resistance is found at the very level of language which also means I have realized a change in self-identity. What I have so long hoped for, I have also resisted all the way along; a deeper sense of self-actualization. I take this awareness into my future in all the many roles I will fill with a deep sense of gratitude and will always be grateful for the opportunity I created for myself in living in the between-place of my writing studio/apartment. I thank the University for their generosity and flexibility and I thank the professors I have had which have pointed me in directions which encouraged me to act on my own behalf that I might also act on the behalf of others. I wish every woman considering how she might achieve her goals while at the same time fulfilling the role of motherhood (if that has been her choice in life) the joy and energy to pursue that which she most desires. She may find that creating a room of her own makes all the difference, or at least find it is a fine beginning.

Epilogue

Life's pleasant surprises: Scott, who retired ten days ago has just baked his first chocolate chip cookie; not something either of us would have considered possible six years ago because of felt-constraints of roles. Isn't it lovely to see, when one takes those courageous first steps towards change that such interesting surprises can occur. Lindsay returns home in a week and the question of a writing space is once again opening up. However, I am confident our family can work something out for the short period of time I require to finish the dissertation, and who knows what will open up from there . . . Life lived, I have been reminded, is relationship in all its complexities (Grumet, 1988,

Merleau-Ponty, 1962; Ricoeur, 1992, 2005) and can be towards the good . . . life can be hopeful . . . Life can be change in process. Life, I have learned, gathers itself in stories; searching for a community of storytellers and listeners who are willing to risk revealing themselves in order to make a difference. Life lived, is a story in search of a narrative (Arendt, 1968 as cited in Kristeva, 200l).

References

Arendt, H. (1958). *The human condition.* Chicago: The University of Chicago Press.

Estes, C.P. (1992). *Women who run with the wolves: Myths and stories of the wild woman archetype.* New York: Ballantyne Books.

Gadamer, H.G. (2002) *Truth and method* (J. Weinsheimer & D.G. Marshall, Trans.). New York: The Continuum Publishing Company. (Original work published in 1960)

Grumet, M.R. (1988). *Bitter milk: Women and teaching.* Amherst, MA.: The University of Massachusetts Press.

Joy, M. Writing as Repossession: The Narratives of incest victims. In Morny Joy (Ed.), (1997) *Paul Ricoeur and Narrative: Context and contestation.* Calgary, AB: University of Calgary Press.

Kristeva, J. (2001). *Hanna Arendt: Life is a narrative* (Frank Collins, Trans.). Toronto: University of Toronto Press.

Merleau-Ponty, M. (1962). *Phenomenology of perception* (Colin Smith, Trans.). London: Routledge.

Pinar, W.F. & Grumet, M.R. (1976). *Toward a poor curriculum.* Kendall /Hunt Publishing Company.

Ricoeur, P. (1992). *Oneself as another* (Kathleen Blamey, Trans.). Chicago: University of Chicago Press.

Ricoeur, P. (2005). *Hermeneutics & the human sciences* (J.B. Thompson, Ed. & Trans.). Cambridge: Cambridge University Press.

Rosen, H. (1988). Epilogue. In B. Rosen, *And none of it was nonsense: The power of storytelling in school* (pp. 163-171). Richmond Hill, ON: Scholastic.

White, S.K. (2000). *Sustaining affirmation in political theory: The strengths of weak ontology in political theory.* Princeton, NJ: Princeton University Press.

Woolf, V. (1928/2000). *A room of one's own.* Toronto: Penguin Classics.

Gatherings in the Faculty Club in Earth Sciences
Program of Events 1985-1986

Executive

Honorary President	Mrs. Norman Wagner
President	Chelsyn Crites
Past President	Beth Davies
Vice President	Diane Zissos
Treasurer	Gail Copithorne
Recording Secretary	Rita Smeaton
Membership Convener	Pamela Harris
Social Convener	Loraine Seastone
Newsletter Editor	Gayle Trofimenkoff

Meetings

September 16	Welcoming Meeting Faculty Club, 7th floor
October 28	Fall and Winter Fashion Show by Melanie's Boutique Faculty Club, Bring your friends for fashions and refreshments.
November 18	Chinese cookery demonstration by Kay Yee Edna Lancaster's home, Conrad Drive N.W.
December 10	Christmas Buffet Lunch Red Dining Room
January 23	Lunch Box Theatre Bow Valley Square, Second Level
February 18	Annual Pot-Luck Dinner and Dance
March 15	Annual General Meeting and Election
April	Annual General Meeting Election of Officers – Bake Sale to follow

Prairie Sketchbook
Carole Thorpe

In 1976, I arrived in Calgary from my Birth City, Montreal. I discovered the glacial Bow River from the escarpment in Crescent Heights, and learned that I could walk downtown from inner city districts. In contrast, I left behind the wide, sea-bound St. Lawrence River and the St. Lawrence Seaway, which starts at St. Lambert.

I spent my early years in St. Lambert, then Dorval and back to St. Lambert, where Emily Dickinson became my creative muse. Today, I still read Dickinson almost every morning, when I practice meditation and yoga. In 2003, I wrote:

Emily Dickinson - writes
the psalm that tests
the prison-heart: cold
knowledge of the universe

dissolves. Everything instead
is white poetry, tiny
tentacles hope - reach into
Ambiguity and Waltzing.

Skyscrapers understand how
a woman writing – springs
to Each Generation mudboiled
rhythms. The business world

opens Attachments, folds
coffee grinds into cyberspace
just as emily announces that
Authority is Out to Lunch.

When I was a young student at the University of New Brunswick, in Fredericton, my mother wrote me notes on UNICEF cards. I became fascinated with UNICEF designs which inspired me to create collages. One day, I perched on my bed and a blank sheet of paper floated from the top of my dresser to land on its edge, perfectly balanced, on a partly opened bureau drawer. It was an epiphany. I decided I was also an artist as well as a writer. In 1974, Fred Cogswell at UNB published *The Story of Vixy Box*, a chapbook of poems and short stories with one of the collages on the cover.

Both sides of my family enlightened me about my heritage in Quebec, Ontario, England, and Scotland, as well as my Mennonite roots. At thirteen, I spent days wandering and exploring Expo 67 and this had a profound influence on my creative and intellectual development. As anglophones, we were exposed to complex issues that existed between English and French, and those tensions escalated when I witnessed the 1970 October Crisis. My mind opened up to current events, and history unfolding before my eyes.

Family heritage influenced my writing projects. I grew up listening to stories from my grandmother, Georgina Simpson Ross Roy, about our ancestor, Sir George Simpson, Governor of the Hudson's Bay Company. A major piece, *Letter from Red River Settlement*, published in *West Coast Line* ("Color, An Issue"), examines Simpson's racism towards Métis women.

By 1978 I was in Calgary and enrolled at the Alberta College of Art where I graduated with a diploma in printmaking. By 1986, I began to work with hot glass, and my ex-husband and I established a glass business, Double Struggle, in southeast Calgary. I discontinued printmaking, and instead, focused primarily on writing, painting, drawing, mixed media, and glass.

In 1989, I began creative writing courses in poetry and fiction with Fred Wah and Aritha van Herk at the University of Calgary. After completing a course in Women's Literary Tradition, I decided to do a BA in English. I was learning the difficult craft of hot glass and designed a range of marketable items that included jewelry, paperweights, vases, perfume bottles, votives, and bowls. As well, I assisted my partner with glass lamps, fish and bugs and Christmas ornaments. Creative projects and English courses were scheduled around a demanding glass agenda.

I began studying yoga at the Yoga Centre of Calgary in 1993. That same year, an experimental prose poem, "Calipers," was published in *Open Letter*. I adapted "Calipers" for Maenad Theatre, which promoted work by women. Different projects surfaced and resurfaced. Some faded away; others gathered in intensity. Around 1994, I began organizing writing material in response to the 1989 Montreal Massacre. Over several years, the December 6 writings developed a critical mass of complex inquiries and responses:

> where does violence begin. is it the cool
> ring around an empty hand hate? is it
> shameless? is it a teacher can't talk fear
> to a student can't talk here. does it wear
> white or purple only on memorial days
> then return to the crowd ribbonless.

In 1997, I did a December 6 reading in English and French with other women at a woman-focused gallery, the Centre Gallery, in Calgary. I participated in two more December 6 readings here in 1998 and 1999. The December 6, 1997 version weaves French and English into the text and expands the original, opening question:

> Where does violence begin? Où la violence commence-t-elle?
> Does violence begin on the small thumb of the child.
> Is it the cool ring around an empty hand hate? Is it shameless?
> Est-ce que la violence commence sur le petit pouce de l'enfant.

Est-ce que la haine n'est pas comme l'anneau froid sur une main vide? Est-ce sans honte?

While I attended University of Calgary classes, I dropped by the French Centre, or *le Centre français,* regularly, and practiced speaking French with monitors who helped me with the French translation of the December 6 reading. I participated in special events where I sold glass alongside other people, who were displaying their artistic wares. I began writing a playful piece called "my mother brings: ma mère rassemble un groupe de petites filles," which was published in *Tessera,* in 1997, for an issue on "Work / Le Travail." As a child, around the age of eight, I loved watching and drawing birds. This was fertile ground for creativity. My piece "my mother brings" explores this fascination with birds and connects it to early French lessons, my mother line, education and cooking. On one level, the piece looks at the problems I encountered trying to learn French in Quebec. My bilingual mother is acknowledged as a primary source of inspiration for learning French.

This piece was also another exploration of family stories and looks at my relationship to my great-grandmother, Mary Simpson Ross, who was the head of a *seigneurie* at Saint Patrice de Beaurivage, south of Quebec City. The Beaurivage *seigneurie* was purchased originally by my ancestor, Captain Alexander Fraser, who fought with General Wolfe on the Plains of Abraham. The Quebec government purchased the *seigneurie* in 1936. Significantly, my great-grandmother could not vote until 1940 in Quebec, in spite of her position of power. Once again, I became fascinated with these stories and continued to collect numerous things from my family that sometimes led me to red herrings. Unexpected discoveries are often the rewards of creative work.

The Centre Gallery, which closed in 2001, became a testing ground for experimental creative projects and public readings. During a four-year period, I participated in several exhibitions which included mixed media, paintings, drawings, and installations. I engaged with other women in thematic exhibitions that challenged cultural norms and stressed feminist practices. We struggled to keep the gallery going with numerous fundraisers. I sold a considerable amount of hot glass items and the gallery took a percentage of sales.

In 2001, I divorced after a seventeen-year relationship with my partner. I began to realize how our glassblowing business had taken over my life and caused problems for my creative and academic interests. When I separated in 1999, I discovered the Women's Centre of Calgary, which had moved to Bridgeland-Riverside in the northeast, a few blocks away from my house. In 2000, the Women's Centre published "Centred: The Women of the Women's Centre," an anthology, that includes a piece that I wrote about the difficulties of separation and transitions.

September 11, 2001 stands out as a significant event that affected me and others profoundly. I was still working at the glass studio, as part of my divorce settlement with my partner. I learned to work more independently and made conscious steps to work on skills that reflected my singleness. I was driving to the glass studio and first heard the news on the radio in my car. By the time I got to the studio, it became evident that something major had happened. Over the next few days the skies were silent, and I walked on Tom Campbell's Hill, in Bridgeland-Riverside, searching for creative direction and solace. Slowly, three poems emerged. The first one focused on the cell phone, with its ubiquitous presence:

an empty cell phone
calls to no return –
a place so dead

handprints can't
   touch final claims

what's down so deep
overflows in spring

this speechless autumn equinox
   disarmed night equal to
      unquiet day

in this western place
   receiving photographs
satellite maps of
   ground zero

we look further away
towards forest fires
   rooted in glacial dust

   our voices call over
      black autumn trees
asking green earth to restore

   natural birth rights
of each fragile voice

As the 2001 Christmas season approached, I was searching for a spiritual community with global connections. On Christmas Eve, I attended a carol service at the Unitarian Church of Calgary. As I left the carol service, the Unitarians left me with something magic that would take a while to understand. I was christened as an Anglican, and confirmed in a United Church; however, I quietly rebelled most of my life against Christianity, and had not been to many church services throughout my adulthood. During my thirties and forties, my ideas and attitudes changed. This was partly because my yoga teachers instilled values in me which I felt were within my reach. And my courses at the University of Calgary taught me the value of understanding Judeo-Christian heritage and other cultures. These were conditions that preceded my discovery of the Unitarian Church of Calgary. I didn't attend another service, until Easter 2002, although by September of that year, I started attending services regularly at the Unitarian Church. This was a surprise. After all, I had spent years working at a glass business on Sundays.

During this post divorce period, I was struggling with another difficult situation. In 2001, I had an episode of uveitis, an inflammatory eye disease, in my left eye. The trauma of altered vision and the fear of blindness affected my perceptions of daily living. By 2004, I was worried about how this would affect my ability to work and perform numerous daily tasks. I went to the Canadian National Institute for the Blind in Bridgeland-Riverside and became a client. Curiously, I had spent many years walking around their building with its special fragrant gardens: eye-catching to outsiders, and an aromatic haven for visually impaired or blind clients. It happened that the CNIB was setting up a pilot program for employment retraining, called "Bridges" and I was accepted into the program. Staff members encouraged us to develop positive attitudes towards our disabilities.

Uveitis was teaching me strange lessons about One-Eyed Vision with its loss of depth perception and balance. I also learned how the right eye compensated for the left eye with its relatively better vision. In spite of the challenges of uveitis, I became fascinated with the science, art and psychology of human vision. By researching uveitis on the internet and at hospital libraries, I empowered myself. This helped me beat the Uveitis Blues.

These repeated attacks resulted in two surgeries performed simultaneously; the trabeculectomy would drastically improve the drainage from my eye and significantly lower the intraocular pressure. Throughout this period I practiced meditation at home to calm myself while taking so many eye drops. On February 15, 2006, a few hours before surgery, I stood on my morning yoga mat facing north. Each morning, I study different aspects of the eight limbs of yoga philosophy. On this morning, I wrote a special pre-surgery meditation on a green index card and read it quietly to myself by winter candlelight:

(1)

Goodbye to my left eye lens
Thanks for showing me first light
when I was a wee baby in
    Montreal, in St. Lambert
Hello to my new bionic lens
Thanks for restoring me to light
    as a wee adult babe
        in Calgary

(2)

Goodbye to the wee snippet of
    tissue gently being removed
        in my left eye
Thanks for prismatic light

Hello to the primal fluids
   seeking balance

Water
The Universe and her
Magic Light-in-Darkness

Fortunately both surgeries continued to bring excellent results. The acuity in my eye gradually improved and the intraocular pressure stabilized within an acceptable range. I could now read more quickly and drive again at night; thus, with renewed perceptions came an appreciation of enabled vision.

My father died August 16, 2006 and my mother, older brother and I gathered in Montreal in a small grieving circle. There are some special things that my father gave me just before he died, including a final note to me on the back of a postcard from Newfoundland and Labrador with a photograph of partridgeberries or redberries: "Dear Carole – Not quite cranberries – but interesting. . . ." a reference to my writing and visual arts business.

My academic interests have often been put aside because of events and conflicts that made it difficult to pursue further studies. On the other hand, there are many people around the world who are living in poverty with no access to education. I have had excellent teachers and educational privileges at all levels of education, in spite of rebellions. I now live within walking distance of the University of Calgary and the Alberta College of Art and Design. I considered going into Environmental Design at the University of Calgary.

In the autumn of 2003, when I experienced the most serious incident of uveitis, I felt my perceptual world changing dramatically. Slowly, I had to work through issues of fear and isolation. That autumn, I retired from my glass-blowing career. In December, I wrote out twelve ideas in my sketchbook, based on the Twelve Days of Christmas. I then chose three of those twelve ideas to develop, as guidelines for my creative work. These three core ideas are statements of my passionate interests.

The First Idea is to actively engage in environmental and peace work. The Second Idea is to continue exploring gender issues and feminism. The Third Idea is to follow my interests in conventional and experimental publications.

Before eye surgery, I began an eclectic vision project. I began photographing subjects that represented my experience of vision impairment. I met the writer, Robert Creeley, in 1995 and purchased several of his books. Creeley was blind in his left eye, and died in 2005. I photographed *The Collected Poems of Robert Creeley* with a blue papier mâché bird that I made several years ago. A photograph of Creeley shows him with his left eye closed on the front cover of the book. The blue bird's left eye is cock-eyed. In my photographs, Creeley and the bird are communicating with their left eyes.

Glassworks – *Carole Thorpe*

Quietly, my eyes are opening doors to places, people, and communities. It is possible to read Prairies and Mountains with Braille. These words can be constructed with magic tactile dots. In printmaking, embossing creates an ink-less white field with subtle shadows. Inside my Prairie Sketchbook, doors are embossed, and snow drifts over pages.

In Search of Composure, Community, and Clarity amid Impermanence, Liminality, and Transformation

Bev Mathison and Melissa Mathison

Preamble

This chapter primarily consists of excerpts from a tape recorded conversation that led this mother-daughter team down the "path less travelled," to the landscape where uncertainty and tentativeness reside, the place that petitions honesty, vulnerability, and entry into the personal containment chamber which holds hopes and fears, doubts and dreams – also known as liminal space. Within this "liminal space" – that which is explained in psychology as a state characterized by ambiguity, openness, and indeterminacy – one's sense of identity dissolves to some extent, subsequently bringing about disorientation. Liminality is also described as a period of transition. The term comes from the Latin "limen," meaning threshold. The "liminal" is present in our many similarities in our quests for degrees, yet at the same time, due to our arrival to postsecondary institutions at different time periods, there are also some significant temporal and cultural differences.

As we pondered and meandered through personal journeys into and through education, we drew from the safety net that close friendships, family, and collegiality engender. The existence and creation of a strong and supportive community facilitated groundedness in a space where there was no ground to stand on.

How Did We Get Here?

We came to "liminal space" via conversations from our experiences in which we have felt thrust into a state of anomie: neither here nor there, disconnected, caught in a seemingly endless process of coming to be. It is this space that we decided to enter into and explore, if for no other reason than it was highly familiar territory, though difficult to map, for both of us.

One leisurely Sunday afternoon, we shared stories, laughter, gratitude, and a glass of our favorite red wine. Bev was in a PhD program and teaching as a Sessional instructor in the Faculty of Education and Melissa had just finished her undergraduate degree and was transitioning into the "real world." Though our situations were very different, we had one very important thing in common – we had no idea where we were going. Having each found ourselves at a transitional point in our lives, the discussion of being neither here nor there and at the point where – as Bev "optimistically" described – "that point where you're entering into something, and you don't know what it is and the ground falls away, and you find yourself spiralling into hell," existing in liminal space was something that was very close to home.

What follows is an abbreviated and revised account of our conversation, which we have broken down into several categories based on a few preliminary questions we devised to focus our conversation. Although the liminal may be experienced in numerous ways, we have kept the focus on our journeys through education. Our identification of ourselves as being mired in liminality is something that we have both experienced at several points in our lives. It is a space that we have moved in and out of, through our various meanderings through degrees and something that speaks to our experiences of postsecondary education.

Loss of Self in the Liminal – The Transpiring Transition

Melissa – For me the first couple of years of university were an extended period of liminal space. I didn't choose a major, didn't know what I was doing, I just needed time to figure out what I needed to pursue.

Bev – I was really apprehensive about beginning a Master's degree but it was, at the same time, more so a continuation, a progression. In the doctoral program, however, where you were able to float [in your undergraduate degree], I wasn't. As was the case with each time I started another degree, I had a lot of outside encouragement. Not knowing what was going to come at the end or [initially] even what I was even going to do while I was there, the excitement had a somewhat diminished effect. During that initial entry into the program, for me the liminal was a place of angst. Making matters even more difficult, within the uncertainty, after a two year leave of absence from my job, I had to make a decision: either return to work and put the PhD to rest on the back burner, or resign outright and continue full time on my doctoral study. I eventually resigned, but it was an extremely difficult decision. My job was my security, my touchstone, everything I had to that point understood my life to be. It was my identity. I knew that quitting would remove the solid ground beneath my feet and even though I was surrounded with a very supportive family and friends, I felt truly on my own, isolated, alienated, and really, really tense. Anxiety had become my close friend. My entire sense of self had been wrestled loose and became wrapped up – no, trapped inside a space. As I'm transitioning out of that I'll be standing on another threshold as I move back into the workforce but I think that's going to be a lot easier than my first few years in the PhD program.

Melissa – What stood out to me the most about the liminal space when I began my undergrad degree was the confusion and the discomfort. It wasn't ever a place of terror; I'm sure I had my moments of freaking out, but that was more so confusion. However, the liminal space I moved into when I finished my undergraduate degree felt like the bottom dropped out. I didn't know what I was doing for about six months. That space was a very dark and terrifying space, and it was much worse than the liminal space that I existed in when I was beginning my undergraduate degree. I experienced a lot of anxiety about leaving university and entering the so called "real world." It's kind of strange because it would seem that finishing a degree would be a time to celebrate, and while it was, at the same time I sort of experienced a mini identity crisis. I had identified myself as a student for the majority of my life, so it was a really difficult transition for me. It was as though I had fallen off my "path," so to speak – as though I was taking a wrong turn or setting myself up for some sort of struggle or difficulty. It was difficult for me to accept that it was a temporary place and that I would be able to move beyond that.

Bev – Was there a point where you moved out of that liminal space, a point of clarity? [Melissa, having felt interrogated to this point because she had been hammered with questions from Bev – many of which have been removed – responded with: "I think it's your turn to go first." Hearty laughter followed.]

Bev – I don't think I can pinpoint because for me it was much more of a progression. And I stayed in that no-place for quite a long time. Even after

I arrived at a topic for the doctoral study, there was still a lot of uncertainty. My candidacy exam was extremely traumatic and it was the antithesis to what I believe "good" teaching and mentoring should be about. I was shocked at how some people – former teachers! – could be so utterly callous, aggressive, and mean spirited. So even with support – and believe me, that support is absolutely vital, even if it's just people saying, "You can do it," as simplistic as that sounds, it really is meaningful when you are standing on shaky ground – it's easy to slip, because, ironically, it's pretty familiar in the insecure. And the thing about slipping in this space is, there's a slipping into a nothingness. So as for a specific point of clarity or through-it-ness, I think it was much more a gradual progression. When I took on a Sessional teaching position, my experience in the unknown took on a new dimension. It was only a couple of courses, but that was a bit daunting at first, again it was a sort of altered sense of self . . . it seems like this past six years has been a series of sense of selves coming into being and passing away, letting go (reluctantly) of old beliefs. That's hard to do, to let go of "I'm not sure I can do this."

Melissa – It is hard to do, especially if you really do solidly believe you can't do it, that is a seriously limiting belief and one that is difficult to get over.

Bev – Because it is your identity, even though it is dysfunctional. You get happy in there though.

Melissa – No, it's not happy, it's more like you accept that as your reality and it starts to feel like you can't change it. We create an entire belief system around the assumption that we can't do it, we're not good enough, and we can't change it.

Bev – The achieving, the changing beliefs is an individual thing, something you have to experience?

Melissa – Ultimately, it is an individual thing but I think it's necessary to be surrounded by some sort of support system while you're going through that. Otherwise you can quite easily slip through the cracks, get mired in your own ugly [unreal] reality, not being able to overcome those things.

Bev – What has been your greatest learning from this?

Melissa – My greatest learning is to trust myself. I knew I had a goal and that was to pursue higher education. I had the support system, I had the assumption that I would just somehow get in so it was just a matter of trusting that I could overcome all the obstacles that were in my way. How about you? What did you learn in the liminal?

Bev – What did I learn? That we can do it. If we can ride it out, we can do it. It's hard, though, to be in that space because it really binds you emotionally, it's hard to pull out and recognize it for what it is. It is very difficult to rationalize and see that it will come to an end at some point. I've had enough life experiences where I can backtrack and know that if I got through this or that, I can get through this.

Through the Liminal: Self Re-Discovered, Re-Articulated, Re-Located

Bev – How will your experience impact the next phase of your academic career?

Melissa – If I could overcome my fears and anxieties with the right motivation, I can overcome anything. That was a huge hurdle for me and it's also allowed me to develop my own sense of self to a point where I feel like I can help others overcome similar challenges.

Bev – So this is like a stepping outwards from having the support system to being the support system?

Melissa – You can't share something that you don't have yourself, so now that I do have self esteem and self confidence and solid ground to stand on, I know what to say to people who don't. My entire plan for my Master's comes from my ability to overcome my lack of self esteem and self confidence and identity. What I plan to study and write about I hope will inspire others to find whatever it is that will help them to work through their own challenges. How will this influence the next phase for you?

Bev – Well, similar to you, I think it's broadened my perspective enough that if I encounter someone who's resting in that same uncertain space, I might be able to act as some sort of support. It's true that the journey is an individual one as you're making your way through it, but from my own experience of just knowing that people were "there" for me really helped. Have you moved through the liminal, through the threshold?

Melissa – I definitely think I've moved beyond the threshold, that very dark period between when I first finished my degree. I don't necessarily know that I'm through the liminal, I feel like I still have a lot of stuff to sort through but it's more personal than professional or academic. At least I know where I'm going. I don't know how I'm going to get there but I know where I'm going. Although, what is very strange and interesting about liminality is that once we become entangled in it, it becomes very difficult to recognize that it is a liminal space. It's sort of like a sub-liminal space if you will – we are so embedded and it is so packed with uncertainty and confusion that it becomes difficult to try to move beyond that or even recognize where we are.

Bev – Having a support system is very important, whether it's someone who knows you or at least understands the situation. About moving beyond the liminal, yes, most of the time I can see the light, but the slippage is always easy, it's easy to default to the "comfortable" place.

Widening the Lens: Words on Community

Bev – Community, as it relates to my experience with the University of Calgary, has evolved in two ways. One involves the small but tight graduate realm – the friendships that developed, the conversations we had as we were all united in a common dilemma, through the uncertainty, and a solid understanding that there are people there who can offer support, who will just be there. The second is about the support system that arises in taking on something new professionally. When I stepped into my position as an instructor, along with feeling some sort of expertise from having dwelt in a particular career for a number of years, there was also an accompanying loss or perhaps reworking of identity. The shift from classroom teacher to university teacher was not smooth and transparent. It was fraught with all the challenges that arrive with undertaking something new. Again, the support system is really important.

Melissa – I feel like I had two separate communities that helped me along my path. One was within the university, particularly within the Faculty of Women's Studies where I was supported by my peers and my instructors. Within this community I felt it was okay to explore, recreate, and develop personally and academically. The second community would be through extracurricular activities, particularly dance. My involvement with Middle Eastern dance over the past three years has exposed me to a support network in a place where I didn't expect to find one and it is through this experience, in combination with my academic study of gender in a cultural context that has inspired me to pursue a Master's degree. What is interesting is, both of these community support systems that have been so significant to me are coming together in my pursuit of a Master's degree. My topic is such that it will draw from both those support systems in terms of explaining my own experience and defining who I am. This has been an unexpected intersection but one that speaks to my own experience and one that I hope will be inspiring to others. I believe that to move beyond the liminal you need two things. One is a solid support system. When you are feeling confused and lacking a clear focus, sometimes all you really need is to talk it out with someone who is willing to listen. The other piece of that however, is that you have to be strong enough to face whatever fears or uncertainties that facilitated the creation of your own existence within the liminal space to begin with. In order to do this, it is necessary to have enough strength of character to work through those the difficult times. Then it becomes your responsibility to share that with your support system – your community – in an expression of gratitude to those people who have helped you along your way.

Expressions of the Post Liminal

While it is difficult to describe the ambiguous, the confusing, the not knowing, not coming to understanding, we feel it is appropriate to draw some sort of conclusion from our considerations of the liminal and the (sub)liminal and how this relates to our experience in a community of academia. As we have touched on in the previous section, it is clear that it takes a lot of courage in order to work through some of those feelings of not knowing, not understanding, and not being in control. The strength that we have both had to develop as a part of this process will aid us in all that we pursue in the future, personally, professionally, and academically. In addition, it is clear that we couldn't have overcome many of the challenges that we faced without our support systems. This was instrumental in our own process of coming to grips with our multiple selves – in the constant coming to be and passing away – and it is clear that it would have been near impossible to see the light in the darkest realities that we created without each other, and without knowing that we had strong support systems on which we could rely. Therefore, it is important to express gratitude to those people who helped us through the fog and mist of the uncharted territory, that place we came to understand as the "liminal." We cannot possibly name each one individually, but we are fairly certain they know who they are. The one name we would both like to include is Ann Yaremko, mother of Bev, grandmother of Melissa. Through the example she set, one of quiet strength, unfailing courage, inimitable humor, and indomitable hope, we find our hallmark.

From a card from a dear friend, Carol, we would like to end with:

Beware ~

A strong woman lives here. To you she may seem aggressive. Prepare to be challenged, to ponder, to wonder, to have your beliefs reflected back to you, to speak of deep feelings to pass through confrontation and find understanding, to find common ground, to laugh, to teach and learn, to search for the truth and be accepted, to howl at the moon. (Lynne Hunter-Johnston, 1992)

Unpacking My Baggage After a Long Journey Home
E. Lisbeth (Betty) Donaldson

I arrived at the University of Calgary during the summer of 1990 with a lot of baggage. Like all baggage contents, some were new items, some were cherished, and some things I never should have brought with me. This is the story of how I unpacked much of that baggage during the years I moved from instructor to tenure track to full professor, and finally in 2005 to professor emerita. It also is a case study of the larger narrative about women in academia: their trials, tribulations, and triumphs. It took me some time to realize that what I thought was individual is really collective; you also may recognize similar experiences stored in the mental suitcases of your mind. If so, I hope you will do some immediate recycling.

When I arrived, I was a professional neophyte. My new doctorate from the Department of Educational Administration, Ontario Institute for Studies in Education, University of Toronto was a passport to academia but I knew I had to prove myself as a scholar. And, I had to present evidence of this proof very quickly because, while I was a young scholar, I was nearly fifty years of age. I'd had earlier opportunities to do graduate work but life intervened, partially because in spite of mentors' recommendations, I wasn't at all certain I could be successful in such an intellectual hothouse. Finally I realized that I might as well attempt the challenges presented by the university environment because I'd come to the conclusion that the commitment would be no more difficult than anywhere outside academia and now knew that hard work was only part of the equation. I still didn't understand the exclusionary history of women in postsecondary education.

I was so much more fortunate than many women! The University of Calgary is a young university in a pulsating city. I like to say that U of C respects the academic tradition but is not necessarily a traditionally academic institution; it is situated within an eager city that strives for excellence, one that is edgy and entrepreneurial. These values suited my ambitions and goals. It took another fifteen years for me to accept that neither I, nor the University, nor the City itself, could succeed in our aspirations, unless first we absorb and acknowledge the contributions of women. So, gradually I evolved into a feminist and an activist.

When still a graduate student, I'd ignored warning signs. For example, it was easy to obtain statistics about how many women were administrators in the K-12 educational system; with a little more difficulty I collected similar stats about the college system. But, no one anywhere was publishing research about women in universities; it was "too close to home." My dissertation research database, that tracked the transitions of students from school to work, clearly indicated very different trajectories for females than males. But I had been head hunted after graduation, only to discover that most women in governmental administrative positions were token appointments. As a junior faculty member, I noted that the University had one female Vice President, no female Deans, and very few female Department Heads; the women who had the most power seemed to be Administrative Assistants. Not long afterward, the Women in the Nineties Report appeared, facilitated by appointed Advisors on the Status of Women to the President (2001).

The women's movement will eventually be recognized as the greatest social change of the 20th century. At the beginning, few survived the child-bearing years; too many pregnancies, chronic diseases and infections, plus harsh living conditions made the ratio of women to men about 124:1000 between the ages of 15-45 years (Donaldson, 1996). By midcentury, antibiotics, contraceptive pills, and new labor saving appliances such as electric irons, plus the vote had generated sufficient affluence and leisure for women to obtain more education and to develop careers as well as families. Divorce rates escalated; single mothers struggled with too many responsibilities, and adult women demanded the right to sign for mortgages and loans as well as to invest. Throughout the world by the end of the 20th century, more women had more health, more education, more money, and more opportunities than ever before in history. But few of us understood this historical wave of change and the subsequent power it offered. Our educational systems and our leaders were but imperfectly prepared. While "Ms" was accepted, "feminism" was a flashpoint word.

By the mid 1990s, I was in mid career and, to use the slogan of the period, "I'd come a long way, baby." Within the University, I was a tenured Associate Professor, Coordinator of the pre-service communications program, and later of the graduate leadership specialization. Nationally, I had been elected president of the Canadian Association for the Studies of Women in Education and served on several other Boards as a Director. Internationally, I was offered a sabbatical fellowship in Aberdeen, Scotland and was completing award winning research projects. Obviously, I'd unpacked some of the irrelevant clutter in my mind and sharpened my profile. What caused this change? One motivator was the 1989 Montreal massacre of on campus female students and staff. I simply could not believe that I lived in a country in which women who wanted an education could be shot. I'd lived in Montreal during the 1960s and appreciated, perhaps envied, the vibrant bilingual culture. When in Toronto, I'd been a member of the Voice of Women and we had made beeswax Canadian peace candles to gift and sell. As a repatriated Westerner, I wanted to ensure that our new region would become a place that tolerated and appreciated diversity, including girls and women, so I got involved. Every December 6, when a memorial service is held at the University of Calgary, handmade beeswax candles are sold to raise scholarship funds that assist women who want to study at this campus: it has become a well established tradition in a university that just celebrated its 40th year.

Another motivator was the consistent results of my own research that clearly indicated differentiated participation in education with consequent discriminatory outcomes and identified institutional biases that perpetuated these inequities. Data from a longitudinal study of first year chemistry students revealed that female students worked longer for less money at part time jobs; that they used the secondhand bookstore more and recreational facilities less than men; that they considered marks as an indicator of intelligence so if they received a lower grade in a hard science course than in a social science one, they would withdraw rather than persist (Donaldson & Dixon, 1995). They knew of few role models in atraditional careers, and they had few advisors who would discuss potential difficulties in juggling career and family responsibilities. For many, opportunities for financially remunerative careers were limited because more females graduated in baccalaureate programs, such as psychology, sociology, or humanities, than in economics, physics, or computer science; at graduate levels, the greatest numbers of women students were in education and many of them were seeking leadership opportunities in their schools. Although increased female participation had sustained enrolment at both undergraduate and graduate levels, most female students took classes at night or during Spring or Summer terms when institutional services are more scarce (Donaldson, 1998).

A third motivator for me was the Women in Education course that I inherited from Dr. K. Skau who had initiated explorations into how women might make decisions differently than men because their moral values and personal perspectives were not identical nor always complementary. I had become convinced that until women were self consciously living from a woman centred perspective, they never would maximize their innate talents and potential, thus their contributions to society would be limited and narrowed. There is not much point in trying to be "one of the boys" because we are "one of the girls;" therefore, let us be active, generative women who teach girls about social silences, anonymity, and isolation. We must engage in the curriculum to learn to be analytical, then disengage to reflect about the biases, and finally actively re-engage to shape a more equitable and sustainable planetary culture. However, I needed to teach this course for about ten years before I had the insight that patriarchy is a system that also warps and distorts men unfairly, and many pay a very high price for their unquestioning acceptance of power and status (Johnson, 1997). After twenty consecutive years, the feminist course was not offered in 2006, but a shorter course in "Gender and Leadership" attracts both female and male educators who are astounded at how much they don't know about this topic. Two books in particular had influenced my development: one was a novel, *Mists of Avalon* (Bradley, 1982), and the other was an historical overview, *The Creation of Feminist Consciousness* (Lerner, 1993). I now understood that spirited women might also image themselves as females with a "spark of the divine" within them, a spark that could be cultivated and that infused innate talent, not a perspective that most religions nurture. Furthermore, contributions from the few acknowledged women geniuses were limited to their time period because their intellectual work was outside of the mainstream or subsumed by men.

My final motivator was the success of an unusual project, *Images of the Goddess* (1995). Adapting R. Murray Shaefer's concept of "theatre of confluence," together with some very talented artists, I produced a sold out event in the University Club that included thirteen dance, sculptures, dramatic vignettes, media clips, and an aboriginal talking circle. It began with a $4000 budget and resulted in a donation of $14 000 to the new Gender Studies Institute. Both the project script and the follow up video won international awards: the 1995 Unitarian Universalist Feminist Theology Award and the 1997 Communicator Crystal Award. This venture was a huge professional risk but my timing was perfect: President Murray Fraser enthusiastically influenced the Deans, the "town" arts and cultural community supported the "gown" innovation, and audiences of curious women were willing ticket purchasers. Shortly afterward, I was promoted to full professor upon the recommendation of internal and external reviewers of my portfolio.

In many respects, I surfed the crest of the second wave of feminism that has now ebbed and crashed. I doubt such a project could be staged in the climate of this first decade of the new millennium. Canadian feminism, which means to recognize the position of women in society, is in a trough (Donaldson, 2004).

During the 1990s, Canada was ranked by the United Nations as the best country in the world in which to live but the status of women never was higher than 9th because there were too few women in leadership positions and too many in "pockets of poverty." Since then we've slipped to 40th position and in fall 2006 the federal government slashed funding for the National Status of Women's office. During the final years of the 20th century, the Alberta legislature passed a policy motion that established the male "he" as the only official pronoun to be used in provincial government documents, while The City of Calgary approved gender inclusive language for all employees but retained "aldermen" for elected Council members, a discrimination that persists. Although much is made of how well girls are performing in schools and postsecondary institutions, in 2005 most women earned seventy-one cents to every dollar that men take home according to a recently distributed Statistics Canada Report. Middle income families make difficult decisions about how to balance income, career time, and quality of life activities, but lower income parents are the working poor who have latchkey kids. Canada is becoming a one child state because our society is confused about how to raise children properly, how to support mommy's ambitions, and how to apportion daddy's schedule. Nevertheless, when it comes to developing countries, everyone knows that the most effective strategy is to provide support to women because immediately it improves the well being of the entire community. Do you see blind spots in front of your eyes, dear reader? We are very short sighted, it seems to me!

At the beginning of the new millennium, I was in the final phase of my academic career. As a consequence of continuous work, averaging 70-90 hours per week and many truncated holiday breaks, I had achieved most of my teaching, research, and service goals. My briefcase was heavy with articles, reports, books, reviews, and student dissertations: it was time to reclaim a personal life. The luggage I wanted to pack included toys for the godchild living in England, swimsuits for the beach in Mexico, and periodic time outs from aging parents. The University's phase out plan seemed a good way to avoid long winters. I kept quoting Allan Fotheringham's comment that Calgary was a great place to live, but it was too long between seasons.

Six weeks after I signaled my intentions, I was offered a two year secondment to central administration as Director of the Teaching and Learning Program. The University of Calgary had rallied after severe budget cutbacks had not only cut institutional fat but threatened amputation of vulnerable initiatives. I'd been an early member of the Strategic Direction team and believed that we had articulated the best plan in Canada to involve faculty members, students, and staff in a bottom up redefinition of our academic culture. Exercising leadership amongst a group of motivated colleagues who represented all the academic disciplines on campus was a challenge I couldn't resist. It remains one of the most stimulating activities in which I've ever engaged. Before coming to the University, I'd been president of the Canadian Recreational Canoeing Association and that previous experience gave me confidence that I could endure whitewater crosscurrents as well as facilitate diverse subcultures. Consequently, I had confidence in my ability to accomplish these institutional goals; more importantly, by now I knew that the profiles of most women leaders often had similar types of experiences in sports and recreation.

I had observed many women demonstrate competence as Associate Deans or Department Heads before they'd earned full professorships; unfortunately often they could not be promoted further because they were not competitive against men who had better scholarly track records. I'd watched six women deans present at an Academic Women's Association lunch and in the process realize they were not institutional competitors, but women who had survived discriminatory situations, chilly climates, and learned successful strategies. I'd fought for women who were being denied tenure because broken marriages, young children, and other personal responsibilities consumed energy that detracted from publishing; some perished while others got extensions. I'd read about retired women academics that had sued to obtain equitable pensions. From my service on the Women's Action Committee of the Humanities and Social Sciences Council of Canada, I knew that the percentages of women scholars appointed to research chairs were much lower than those of men and that the numbers of senior women academics and administrators were minimal. And, I'd had long conversations with many intelligent women who were slowly carving out a career path but who genuinely had doubts about how well they were doing because of low self esteem.

In a coauthored paper, I discussed the need for "critical mass," a concept that is not well understood by women in the academy (Donaldson & Emes, 2000). According to the United Nations, social change is attainable only when the percentage of awareness reaches 35-40 percent. That is to say, not only must the numbers of involved people be sustained at a certain level, these participants must be aware of the issue and willing to act accordingly. It is a falsehood to argue that women are succeeding because the numbers of female undergraduates is more than 50 percent of the total enrolment. If they are not aware of their own interests and talents; if they do not know how to persist when faced with difficult challenge; if they are not knowledgeable about the historical exclusion of women from professional, public, and political life; if they do not see other women as companions and colleagues but regard them as competitors, then the women's movement for societal change and greater equity is stalled. Worse, a negative ripple effect will detour and warp many lives; individual talents will remain underdeveloped and utilized. It is not enough to be accepted; the individual must have an informed consciousness. When a woman enjoys achievement, it is hard to acknowledge that she is an isolated success story. But until women collectively change the mainstream current of intellectual life in Canada and elsewhere, their individual efforts will flow and ebb like the daily tide, continuously shaping the edges of shorelines but usually invisible in the process unless an angry storm generates forceful high waves.

Doctoral level studies result in an individuated career path. An academic is hired because of the potential to make a unique contribution to knowledge, not because one has become certified in a profession. In the effort to attain a scholarly profile and privilege within a timeline that is based upon a male achievement pattern, few women comprehend that they are unwilling members of a marginalized group. However, although women are being appointed to assistant professorial positions in greater numbers than ever before in history, the withdrawal rate of women from tenure track positions is 50 percent higher than that of male appointees (Donaldson, 2004). Furthermore, the numbers of very senior administrators remain tiny because few women gain apprenticeship experiences as Department Heads until they are older than colleagues while others are place bound because of family responsibilities. As one bright new Dean remarked to me, "I'm too busy to learn about how I am discriminated against," but noted her challenges seemed to diminish when she shares difficulties with peers. Women have been members of the academy for approximately 100 years. It's such a short period of human history but our efforts are reshaping human contributions to life on Earth.

As a retired professor, now I occasionally am reminded of my possible legacy. Recently I received an email from a woman student I probably never will meet. She is interested in student transitions and, having located some of my publications, wanted more references. Many of my Master's graduate students have become administrators who know how to facilitate greater gender equity within schools; their leadership seeds future changes. Others I've supervised have completed theses or dissertations about various aspects of women's lives and their work is being disseminated. Sometimes junior colleagues ask to have coffee so they can check how their perceptions of academic life align with mine. In 2005, I was awarded an Alberta Centennial Medal for my contributions to society. I'm now on the Executive of the Emeritus Association and listed as an "emerita." This female Latin form was denied to a friend who retired several years earlier and was not requested by older women in the Association.

As a woman who likes to write, I've just published my first novel. It's based upon solid research about real people who lived during the fur trade era but I wrote the letters which form the book. Had I continued as a historian, the topic would have been part of my scholarly trajectory. Instead, as a seasoned researcher and academic, I'm using my experiences to interpret and narrate the lives of an accomplished brother and sister, *The McLoughlin Correspondents* (2006). It is a very exciting project and I'm having lots of fun marketing the book to readers, developing a latent entrepreneurial streak, and learning to promote my work in a very different way. If everyone has a book inside of them waiting to be birthed, then I am a fortunate "mother." My "baby" seems to be having a very good first year.

As a senior citizen, I lobby for more inclusive language. Why should the English version of the national anthem ask that "true patriot love in all our sons command"? The original version was "all of us command" but this wording was changed during the carnage of the "Great War." During our lifetime, women serve as professional soldiers, as reservists, and a few die to sustain our common values. But most of us are quietly loyal, having made personal decisions to work for the quality of life in Canada. However, I am appalled at how many women seniors live in impoverished silence. Some elderly women in Alberta must decide between food supplies and financial statements. They worked part time or as homemakers and therefore have little or no pension. Their husband's pension was reduced or terminated when he died so their cash flow is reduced but at the same time, taxes and inflation corrode small fixed incomes. Also, I've developed the family female diseases, an inevitability I should have prepared for decades ago but didn't. It is scary to learn that the first longitudinal studies for osteoporosis have just been designed and that women's heart diseases are frequently misdiagnosed because symptoms are different than men's.

As I get older, I want to have less heavy luggage to cart about but it seems each stage of life demands new types of courage. How many little old ladies have been caught with bombs in their carry-ons, but standing in long lineups does make me a fatigued rebel! It is getting more difficult to climb in and out of small boats, but I can stop traffic anywhere with my touring stick. One thing I am learning is that I need to carry less and less as I travel through this life. I just wish I'd learned some lessons about how to pack what truly is valuable much earlier, to be a more healthily self-centred woman. At the height of my physical powers when I was still an immortal twenty-year-old, perhaps I might have done better if I'd looked about or ahead at other women travellers and shared more stories about the trip in which we all are engaged. Nevertheless, the University of Calgary has been a highlighted transit station, and I hope many more women have an opportunity to make this stop along their journey.

References

Bradley, M.Z. (1982). *The mists of Avalon.* New York: Alfred A. Knopf.

Donaldson, E.L. (2006). *The McLoughlin Correspondents, with great affection: Letters between a brother and sister during the fur trade era.* London: Athena Press.

Donaldson, E.L. (Ed.) (2004). *Coming of age: 100 years of educating Alberta girls and women.* Calgary: Detselig Enterprises.

Donaldson, E.L. (2004). *The transition of women educational leaders to doctoral study.* Paper presented at the Canadian Student Experience: Patterns, Prospects, and Policies Conference, York University, Toronto, November 12. Available on web page: http://www.educl.ucalgary.ca/research/academic/donaldson/html/

Donaldson, E.L. & Emes, C.G. (2000). The challenge for women academics: Reaching a critical mass in research, teaching and service. *The Canadian Journal of Higher Education, 30*(3), 33-56.

Donaldson, E.L. (1998). Three markers on the waves of the women's movement. *Interchange, 29*(2), 237-240.

Donaldson, E.L. (1996). Imaging women's spirituality. *Comparative Education Review, 40*(2), 194-204.

Donaldson, E.L. (1995/97). *Images of the Goddess.* Production and vignette script available from the author. Video available from UC ComMedia Department. See also: Spiritual aspects of the women's life cycle. *Canadian Women Studies Journal, 17*(1), 36-39.

Donaldson, E.L. & Dixon, E.A. (1995). Retaining women students in science involves more than course selection. *The Canadian Journal of Higher Education, 25*(2), 29-52. (Winner of the "most excellent article" of the year award.)

Johnson, A.G. (1997). *The gender knot: Unraveling our patriarchal legacy.* Philadelphia: Temple University Press.

Lerner, G. (1993). *The creation of feminist consciousness.* Oxford: Oxford University Press.

Women in the Nineties Report (2001). Updated Recommendations are available from the ucalgary.ca webpage search engine.

Travelling

Jennifer Eiserman

I hang in the air, a blanket of white below and a canopy of blue above. This nowhere place between leaving and arriving, between having been and becoming. I have been in this place often before, each time is the same and each time is different. One is. One waits. One anticipates and sometimes one dreads that which awaits when the aircraft finally touches down. This is a story about the waiting, the anticipating, the dreading, and finally, the arriving.

Twelve years ago I sat in such a seat, on such an aircraft, hanging in space. I was full of anticipation as I waited. I was rejoining my husband from whom I had been separated for two years as he and I pursued our Master's degrees. With our daughter we would be a whole family again. I was beginning a doctoral program at the University of Calgary. Although bemused by the idea that *I* was going to be a scholar, the journey ahead thrilled me like nothing I had ever known. I was so excited I couldn't read, I couldn't sleep, I could only look down at the clouds and mark the minutes that passed with the beating of my heart.

Many trips away from the University of Calgary and back again fill the time between that first flight and the one I now take. Golden in memory is my first conference trip to Brock University to present a paper at the Congress of Learning meetings. Just as the five-year-old feels "all grown up" as she leaves her anxious parents at the classroom door and walks into a world of her own, so too did I feel, kissing my family goodbye at the airport. I was going to share *my* ideas with scholars from all over the country – people who taught me were going to listen to *me.* It never occurred to me that I was "just a grad student," any more than the five-year-old thinks she is "just a kid." As I hung in the air that day, waiting, I was proud and excited to be taking up my place in the academic world.

I listen to the unhappy cries of an infant in a row somewhere in front of me. How miserable the small person seems! I think of my own son, now ten years old. The child born during my gestation as an academic. In his way, he spent a great deal of time waiting, as I do on this plane. He slept in a crib in my office as I wrote my proposal for my doctoral study; he nursed while I discussed Kant and Heidegger with my aesthetics study group. He drew and played Nintendo in my office as I prepared lectures and graded papers. With his older sister, he has learned to live his life within the world of academe: secondhand clothes, hand-me-down furniture, the desk and the computer the centre of our domestic universe. Camping trips and days at the lake preciously hoarded from the days needed to write that grant, prepare that paper, travel to share my work with colleagues on the other side of the world. My children will always have to share my passion with my work. Sometimes they have to wait, hanging in the space between the times I delve into my studies and the times I arrive back into their world.

Six years ago, I boarded a plane to present my first paper as a professor. On the program I was listed as "Dr. Jennifer Eiserman." I had not yet become accustomed to the title. I felt shy and uncomfortable with the moniker. Unlike the flight five years before, I was anxious about facing my peers. Would my paper be good enough? Were my ideas really that interesting? Would I be able to defend my position? As I waited in the air that day, I wondered if this whole enterprise really had been such a good idea! I was content to wait, to put off the arrival for as long as possible.

That paper went well, as did many that came after. I became part of a group of scholars from across North America that work together and meet once year at our annual conference to share our ideas, our work, and our lives. I attend other academic gatherings and fly to far off centres to conduct my research. With the University of Calgary as my home base, my academic home extends from coast to coast and from the Gulf of Mexico to the 60th parallel. Soon it will include South Africa. The time I hang in the air has become time to think, time to dream, time to rest. These aircraft are my study, a place where I live. I think of medieval scholars who travelled the countryside to teach and to learn. A highway of clouds has replaced the dusty path, and great cosmopolitan cities have replaced the villages, but a scholar is still a traveller.

Today I sit in my window seat and wait to return to Calgary. So much has changed since that first flight. I am now a tenured professor with national al funding. I am returning from a research trip that has left me full of won-

Microcosmology – *Jennifer Eiserman*
Microcosmology is about the ways that worlds exist within worlds and that our sense of individuality is really just a matter of scale and perspective. It is about how our worlds interact and nourish each other. It is about how jewels of understanding, wisdom, and compassion, are exchanged.

derful questions to ponder. But from time to time, my breath catches in my throat and tears fill my eyes. The life of a scholar can be hard on the people we love. As I wait in the air today, I know that the father of my children will not be coming to pick me up and take me to our home. I will take a taxi to the house I share with my daughter and son. The husband I waited so eagerly to join twelve years ago now lives a life separate from mine, immersed in his own studies. The academy can be a difficult place for families to thrive. Too little time, too little money, work that demands one's full attention wore away at the delicate fabric of our marriage. Eventually, the threads pulled completely apart.

This is my story of being a woman, a student, a scholar at the University of Calgary. It is a story of travelling, of waiting, and of being. It is a story of deeply satisfying success and equally deep sorrow. It is the story of a life being lived within the academy.

The Early 1990s
A Special Time for Feminists On Campus
Mary Valentich

I was very happy a few years ago when FIRE – Feminist Initiative to Recognize Equality – emerged on the main campus at the University of Calgary. This student run venture has continued to offer support to women students, programs of interest to women, and advocacy in relation to traditional women's issues such as sexist advertising. More recently, after efforts of numerous individuals and groups over several years, the Women's Centre has been reborn in a fabulous setting with resources for all women on campus. One can only hope that these are signs that feminism has not been abandoned in the dust bin of ideologies.

Why am I guarded in my outlook? Because I know what it's like when women of every constituency at the University join together to call for social change. The early 1990s was one such period. After describing this special time for feminists on campus, I will ask whether women once again will become drivers for needed changes.

In 1989, President Murray Fraser, following his earlier step of appointing a Women's Advisor at the University of Victoria, appointed Dr. Susan Stone-Blackburn (now Stratton) as his first Advisor on Women at the University of Calgary. She and her Status of Women Committee produced Women in the Nineties, an update of the 1977 Blair Report on the Status of Women at the University of Calgary. This report presented a factual picture of women's status at the University of Calgary with respect to rank, position, salary, representation in administration, and numerous other aspects. Overall it was not a particularly inspiring portrait. Further, little progress had been made in increasing the number of child care spaces. There were, however, three university committees dealing with women's issues – the Status of Women, Employment Equity, and Sexual Harassment Committees.

In order to bring about change, President Fraser requested recommendations. In 1991, Women in the Nineties: Recommendations, was presented to the University. There were 123 recommendations for change in the relationship between professional and familial well being; the intellectual and psychological environment for women, recruitment of more academic women, women's career progress, pay equity, and administration. Twenty-five were assigned high priority, fourteen higher and nine highest.

I became the second Advisor to the President in 1991 and my task was to shepherd these recommendations throughout the entire University community and to issue regular reports on progress. This I did three times, each time reporting on the moderate improvement in various Faculties and units throughout the University. The Recommendations document had been accepted in principle by General Faculties Council; it was up to each unit to find the appropriate way of implementing or working toward implementation. I found my days filled with meetings with individuals and groups, some of whom clearly understood the recommendations whereas others were puzzled, if not defensive. In particular, some male faculty feared that they might be obliged to take sexual harassment seminars. Clearly an infringement of their academic freedom! Some departments were not very keen on making changes, but to their credit, they engaged in lengthy meetings with me and Carol Clarke, Employment Equity Advisor, in attempts to understand why women on campus were so unsettled.

While I might not have used the word "heady" at the time, I now realize that the ferment was exciting and there was a promise of change. In 1991 the Women's Academic Association (AWA) was formed followed by the Academic Women's Council of the Faculty of Social Sciences. Susan Stone-Blackburn (Stratton) was involved in the emergence of the former as well as the first informal gathering related to the December 6 massacre of fourteen women students at École Polytechnique in Montreal. Julie Kearns and I continued with grassroots organizing efforts and oversaw the emergence of the Network of Women Staff (NEWS) and the Women's Graduate Student Association. Women in Science and Engineering (WISE) continued to be active during this period. Finally, with pride, I was able to call together all committees and organizations on campus, at one point, consisting of twenty-seven units, into the Women's Council and Network (WCAN) which replaced the former Women's Network. This umbrella organization was designed to give women a powerful voice on campus. While we met only for approximately one and a half years, the effort was a noble one.

Additionally, there was visibility for women leaders: Dr. John Kendall, Dean of Science had appointed an Advisor on Women's Issues. Prof. Donna Ferrara-Kerr was the first Sexual Harassment Advisor, followed by Ms. Shirley Voyna-Wilson. Media reports were issued about sexual harassment and I was called on regularly to comment on a diverse range of women's issues. Generally, media response was quite women friendly, with a few exceptions that one soon learned to avoid, for example, *Alberta Report.*

The overall response of Faculties and units was quite supportive in promoting institutional change to achieve gender equity. All identified the importance of developing creative, productive environments where individual differences were respected and women and men were treated as equals. A prominent viewpoint was that women's issues should be considered in the context of equity for all persons. There was widespread support for recommendations related to child care and all feasible initiatives to create an environment conducive to combining career and family life. Improvement in leave policies was seen as desirable as well as clarifying expectations when women went on leave for childbearing purposes. Many recommendations related to improving the climate for women faculty and students and to this end, there were many showings and discussion of the video, *The Chilly Climate.* Undoubtedly there was greater recognition of the importance of ensuring equitable recruitment and hiring practices, albeit the desired increases of women in faculty and senior administration positions proceeded slowly.

Looking back, I can state that organizational change did occur. I did feel as if we were prodding a slow and sleepy elephant that had learned its routines a long time ago and was very reluctant to change. But there was goodwill and administrative support, including resources, from the President. Somehow, the tempo or the times changed by the mid 1990s. We lost a President very committed to equity and women's issues. Some later Advisors on Women's Issues did not engage in grassroots organizing, perhaps leaving relatively new organizations in an unstable state. The Status of Women Committee, a university wide body, disappeared. The liaison role between the Women's Centre and the President's Office was not maintained, leaving the Women's Centre without guidance and support, thereby likely contributing to its ultimate demise. Other women's organizations started to fail, including the AWA, despite valiant efforts of Dr. Janice Kinch in more recent times to give it new life. One cannot ignore that the wider society also began to question whether feminist organizing was really necessary: after all, hadn't women achieved important goals? Women on campus also found themselves very stretched with respect to their assigned and volunteer duties; there were, after all, only so many women who could sit on various committees and ensure that, at least, a female voice could be heard. Further, attention was increasingly being given to diversity issues, with discrimination toward women becoming more of a background issue.

While the first half of the 1990s was a boom period in terms of feminist organizing with a pervasive sense that "times are a-changing," the period from 1995 to 2000 has, in my view, seen a diminishment of such social action. This is not to suggest that there have been no worthy initiatives. Research on women's situations has been undertaken by various Advisors and committed feminists on campus. President Weingarten has remained very supportive toward gender equity initiatives and there are signs of resurgence, such as this book that may show us that social change involves ebb and flow. I'm glad I was involved in a time of heightened social awareness and action. I look forward to the next feminist storm!

A Soft Spot for Underdogs

Corinne Borbridge Austin

Nearly twenty years have passed. Yet, I can still feel myself standing at that small gathering of people huddled together at Memorial Park that bitter December night. My mittened hand held a burning candle with a red cup around it, vaguely reminiscent of the mini-torches we held at the Olympic closing ceremonies the year before. I was twenty years old, a third year Psychology major trying to make sense of my horror and sadness that fourteen young women had just been killed at Montreal's L'École Polytechnique.

The speakers at the memorial talked about what happened in Montreal. And how they felt about what happened. And why they thought it happened. They cried and shouted as they talked about the continuum of violence against women that this gunman's act represented. To them, he was acting out a cultural hatred towards women. To me, he was acting out a defective mind and spirit. It was a shocking bout of brutality, yes. But I didn't see the connection to any kind of everyday experience or view toward women; I didn't want to see the connection to my life as a woman. What was this misogyny they were talking about? These people were crazy. I blew out my candle and went home, feeling alone with my ideas and emotions about the murders.

That feeling was familiar. I was surrounded by people; I'd always made friends easily and had a large extended family. But I often felt different, just outside of any "group" even if I had connections with random individuals within it. I thought too much. I was hypersensitive. I had a too big soft spot for stray cats and underdogs. It seemed like some of the things I wanted to talk about, wanted to understand, made people around me uncomfortable. I wanted to dig deep and yet I also wanted to be in relationship in my hockey-draft-picks-and-Uncle-Pete's-knee-surgery-discussing family. Balancing my sensitivity and my silence wasn't new, so walking away from the intensity of that memorial with a sense of aloneness didn't beg much thought from me at the time.

Two years later, I was in my final year of my undergraduate degree at U of C. I'd completed nearly all my credits, despite a tendency toward mind-freeze during exams and a couple of encounters with $29 bank balances when rent was due. I'd been elected as a representative for the Students' Union. I didn't know at all what I was getting into when I handed in my nomination forms and began seeking votes. But now I was a few months into this part time position in student politics and I found myself excited by the work and by the possibilities for change. After four years of university, I was having a whole new experience of being a student.

One of my roles was as a member of what became known as the December 6th Memorial Committee. Our job was to plan the second memorial of the Montreal Massacre, to commemorate the killings and to bring awareness of violence against women. We were masterfully guided consensus-style by Mary Valentich, then the President's Advisor on the Status of Women. We discussed the impact of the killings and our desire to have the women, not their killer, remembered. We debated where the service should be held, what voices should be heard at the service, and who should stand in representation of each woman's lost life. I listened to the views of the women on the committee, each touched by the event in different ways. I agreed with some and not with others but I felt honored by and connected to their passionate expressions. I read the killer's suicide note and let myself learn about what had happened that day that fourteen women were separated from their male peers and murdered for being women, for being women who dared to educate themselves in a male-dominated field. I educated myself on the lives of these women – women so much like me – and opened a door to learning I had not anticipated.

I allowed myself to see how women were still struggling. I allowed myself to feel sadness and anger about the ways that being a woman had brought me hot-faced shame and worse. I let myself experience a deep connection to these other women, to feel the power of our circle. I opened myself to knowing about suffering and the ways in which privilege and power – certainly not only related to gender – are part of that human picture. Thinking too much became truth-seeking. Hypersensitivity became intuition. A soft spot for underdogs became passion for empowerment and emancipation. And this is how I became a feminist.

I spent many more years at the University after that. My grassroots feminist beginnings on that committee expanded as I took on other opportunities to grow and connect and effect change. As I worked through masters and doctoral studies, I found others – among them Lorna Cammaert, Kathy Cairns, Judy Chew, and enduring mentor, Mary Valentich – who nurtured my academic feminism. I became a Psychologist and found counselling and teaching would-be counsellors offered a new home for growth, compassion, knowing and expressing. Now, as mum to three little boys, the integration of my feminist self continues. After all, what better mission might I find than the raising of wonderful men?!

My years at university did as it should; it guided me to "lift up mine eyes." This happened in classrooms and boardrooms and offices and laboratories. But it always happened in connection, in circles where I was lovingly seen and passionately encouraged to see, where truth-seeking, intuition, and a desire to bring light are just plain beautiful things.

Full of Spirit and Laughter
Remembering Dorothy Groves

Dorothy was born in Dartmouth NS in 1924. She trained as a nurse, then did post-graduate work at McGill where she met Trevor when they were both acting in a production of Ibsen's *Ghosts*. They moved to Calgary in 1966 when Trevor joined the Mechanical Engineering Department of the U of C. Dorothy had incredible enthusiasm and energy. While raising her six children she plunged into every aspect of public life, especially women's and health issues. Adroit at managing meetings (she was an expert on Robertson's rules) she was on numerous committees: Status of Women, the Local Council of Women, Unemployment Commission of Canada, Calgary Board of Health and the Calgary Birth Control Association, of which she was a founding member. In later years she volunteered with the Planned Parenthood Association of Canada, Parkinson's Society, and Elizabeth Fry Society. Throughout her life she worked for the Liberal Party, and three times was a candidate for the Alberta Legislature. In 2002 she was awarded the Queen's Jubilee Medal. She was an active member of the Faculty Women's Club from 1966-2004, serving as President in 1971-72. At her 80th birthday party, hosted by her children, she was full of spirit and laughter as her son read a humorous poem about life with such a busy mom who still found time to support them all. It was a great loss when she died after a relatively brief illness in November 2004.

Faculty Women's Club Archives, January 2005 Newsletter

Jo-Ann's Christmas Balls
Dorothy Groves

1½ cups   candied cherries
1 cup   almonds
1 cup   shredded coconut
Few drops almond flavoring

2   egg whites, beaten stiff (whites at room temperature)
10 Tbsp   icing sugar

Put cherries, almonds and coconut through meat grinder. Add a few drops almond flavoring. Form into balls, gradually beat 7 Tbsp icing sugar into beaten egg whites; fold in 3 more Tbsp icing sugar. Dip the fruit balls into egg mixture. Place on greased pans. Bake in 250ºF oven for 45 minutes – but prop door of oven open.

Faculty Women's Club Favourite Recipes (1969). (2)1, p. 47

Academic Women's Association
Musings over Recent Years
Janice Kinch

In 2001, Dr. Annie Katzenberg prepared a report on the status of women at the University of Calgary, an update on the recommendations from the Women in the Nineties Report. Of 123 recommendations made by the authors of that report to the University Administration and General Faculties Council (where the report was accepted in principle), Dr. Katzenberg found that there had been progress in some areas. Individual university units had been expected to work on the recommendations, but women's issues remained much as they were before the lengthy report was presented to the university administration and GFC.

Recommendation #84 of the Women in the Nineties Report stated "That an Academic Women's Association be developed to promote career progress of academic women: continuing staff, sessional staff, and graduate students and that the Association organize workshops for academic women." Dr. Katzenberg reported in her 2001 update, "There is an Academic Women's Association on campus. It meets regularly, sponsors a mentoring program for new members and holds occasional workshops." The AWA was first established in 1991 through the work of Dr. Susan Stone-Blackburn (now Stratton), in one of her last acts as Advisor to the President on Women's Issues.

In the larger scheme of things, the Academic Women's Association was established to provide a forum for academic women to meet, network, and begin the movement toward improving the status of women on campus in areas such as salary equity, campus childcare, progression through the ranks, and achieving gender balance. Through the foresight and commitment of academic women of that time, Dr. Susan Bennett, Professor Helen Holmes, Dr. Aradhana Parmar, Dr. Jeanne Perreault, Dr. Elly Silverman, Dr. Susan Stratton, and Dr. Mary Valentich, among many others, the AWA became a force on campus that welcomed new faculty members, initiated a mentorship program, and provided a place to meet colleagues and find much needed support.

It was in 2001 that I was introduced to the AWA in one of the orientation sessions. I attended an AWA social meeting shortly afterwards, pulled to the collegiality of the women who attended the session. Several months into the year, I had heard nothing further, and made inquiries about how I might become involved with AWA. I was informed that if I wished, I could try to muster the membership and resume the activities of the Association, which had more or less "gone to sleep for a while."

Connecting with academic women whose names I acquired from the very wonderful Gail Daniels, I put out a call for women who might be interested in resurrecting the Association. Ms. Daniels played an integral role in the Association, when as administrative assistant to the Advisor to the President on Women's Issues (and leading figure in AWA), Dr. Mary Valentich, she took on the responsibilities of managing the membership coordination and communication activities. Response from Drs. Mary Valentich, Lorraine Radtke, Susan Stratton, Jeanne Perreault, Minnie Joldersma, Fiona Nelson, Heather Kanuka, Betty Donaldson, Kristen Pullen, Kamela Patel, Jennifer Eiserman, and Julia Murphy resulted in a renewed steering committee and our first membership gathering. We gained momentum as we added to membership by welcoming new faculty. Ms. Joan Hedstrom, who became the administrative support for the Advisor to the University for Women's Issues, took over responsibilities from Gail Daniels. Without strong supportive backup, we would have been lost!

Over the following two or three years, we met fairly regularly. Some of our activities included a panel presentation about promotion and tenure, with participation by Dean Gayla Rogers, Dr. Susan Rudy, and Dr. Ida Wierzba, and another panel with three political candidates who discussed women in politics. We continued to strategize new ways to make our voices heard more clearly as we pushed for salary equity, campus childcare, and progression through the ranks, to name a few issues. Dr. Jeanne Perreault continues to pursue resolution to the issue of salary equity. Through our AWA email list, we forwarded interesting and sometimes important items to members about women's issues, academic concerns, and campus activities. We supported AWA member Dr. Fiona Nelson and her cadre of students, as they lobbied for a women's space on campus. Due to their persistence and strength, we now enjoy the new University of Calgary Women's Resource Centre.

Our steering committee grew for a while, but it soon became increasingly difficult to entice members to attend planned meetings and participate in membership gatherings. Research, teaching, and service responsibilities were heavier than before for us all. Family responsibilities kept many of our colleagues away, even though they responded that they were interested in the organization. We encouraged women to bring their children to meetings, and some did, but even that idea fizzled after a while. While I continue to forward selected items of interest to the membership, nothing has replaced the "old times" passion and desire to advance women's status at the AWA level at the University of Calgary.

So, we are now back in sleeping mode. AWA is resting, waiting for some new spirits with high energy to come along to tackle the persistent issues within our University community. Women continue to lag behind in salaries, progression upward through the ranks, and presence as heads of faculties and departments. One recommendation that I make here is that graduate students be included in AWA. As they enter or continue in the academy, it is they who will carry the torch – if it is not to be extinguished.

Thanks go to the many women who have contributed their time and energy to bolstering the status of women on our campus. They know who they are. Until we once again awaken from our slumber, I wish all of our academic colleagues success, satisfaction, and above all, the recognition that they so richly deserve. There is so much work to do. Our most important work is to look after ourselves, and be cognizant of the fact that we must also look out for each other. As long as there are the same and continuing barriers for women in academia, we will need to be vigilant, to guard against being completely silenced. We must continue to speak out, to use our voices (loudly) to affirm our presence as equals in academia and our right to be here!

Promoting Equality and Building Community through Sharing, Learning, and Teaching: The Women's Resource Centre

Stephanie Garrett

Within the walls of the Women's Resource Centre delicate layers of women's stories and experiences weave together much like the quilts that decorate its walls. Quilts are integral to women's history and transcend cultural boundaries; they tell stories, they preserve history, and they protect and comfort. The Women's Resource Centre is the culmination of women's interwoven histories at the University of Calgary in addition to representing the site for the future challenges and successes of women students, faculty, and staff on this campus.

Women's Centres have existed in varying capacities at the University of Calgary since the 1990s. Always housed in closet-sized, secondhand spaces, always volunteer run, always representing women's continuous struggle to be recognized as equals at the U of C. While pockets of stories exist, the history of struggle to establish a women's centre is not well documented and therefore, the weaving of this quilt begins only a few years ago with a group of young female students in Dr. Fiona Nelson's Women's Studies class. Given the task of translating their knowledge of feminist theory into practice, they chose to campaign to the Advisor to the President on Women's Issues and the University President of the time. Although their voices grew in number, the political foundations had not yet been laid for the establishment of a women's centre. Undergraduate and graduate students from across faculties campaigned in the years to come and eventually one determined woman within University administration was found to champion the cause.

In 2006, Sheila O'Brien, then Advisor to the President on Student Life, took the need for a Women's Resource Centre to heart. Along with the Coordinator of Women's Studies, Dr. Fiona Nelson, the Advisor to the University on Women's Issues, Dr. Claudia Emes, and Catherine Fisher of the International Student Centre. As a group, they worked hard to create the political environment necessary to found a women's centre that would become sustainable. O'Brien not only convinced the President and fellow Advisors of the need for a women's centre, she and her husband, Kevin Peterson, made the financial contribution necessary to have the newest incarnation of the centre built. She was determined to create a new and beautiful space reflective of the beauty of the women that would become a part of the centre. O'Brien believed that women had spent too long organizing in secondhand, rundown spaces and needed a place that reflected their beauty.

Thus, on October 18, 2006 – Persons' Day in Canada, and the 40th Anniversary of the University of Calgary – the founding women opened the doors to the Women's Resource Centre (WRC). Every aspect of the WRC has been touched by women's hands and hearts. From the Centre's stainless steel sign created by Calgary welder, Gina Bewski, to the Centre's beautiful architecture, designed by two female Environmental Design students, Georgia Houston and Livia Antakilova. From the WRC Fair Trade merchandise sewn by a single mother's cooperative in El Salvador, to the art pieces by female artists that decorate the Centre's walls.

As the founding Executive Director of the Women's Resource Centre, I have had the privilege of not only shaping the WRC's identity, but also seeing firsthand the way this Centre has grown and flourished in just two short years as a result of the dedication and hard work of hundreds of women. Walking into the WRC is like walking into a second home for most of the women who visit. There is a creative energy that flows from every corner, and the entire space is shrouded in an air of safety and calm. It has become a breeding ground for community, friendship, and social change. I see my personal goals for the Centre achieved on a daily basis when women come into a space where their voices are heard and their experiences are valued in a way that reflects back to them their beauty, strength, and potential.

The Women's Resource Centre has a vision to achieve equality at the U of C and to create a more inclusive campus environment where each individual's agency and voice are nurtured to contribute to the collective spirit of a community where citizenship and leadership is made possible for all, regardless of gender. We provide a safe and supportive place to advance women's equality and build community through sharing, learning, and teaching where all experiences are valued, and everyone is offered the resources necessary to make informed choices. The Women's Resource Centre is first and foremost a place of kindness. We celebrate diversity based on – but not limited to – gender, ethnicity, race, class, ability, age, and sexual orientation, and we believe that the key to achieving empowerment is through the cycle of reflection and action, creating positive social change.

The Centre has evolved enormously over the past two years and five pillars support the core of our work; Peer Support, Mentorship and Leadership, Diversity, Health and Wellbeing, and Internationalization. We begin with the most profound of women's experience around self esteem and self confidence. Without this strong sense of self, women find it challenging to realize their potential. Issues of self esteem seem to be at the core of all other major issues women face. Through one-to-one peer support, workshops and various events, we focus on valuing women as they are and helping them to see their inner beauty. From this foundation, we build on women's leadership capacity through a unique mentorship program and through the availability of leadership positions within the WRC. We recognize that women's experiences are diverse based on a number of factors and we are sensitive to the needs of as many diverse women as possible.

It is an interesting time for women at the University of Calgary. At no other point in our history have women challenged traditional gender norms as much with an increase in tenured female faculty, female deans, and young female students entering nontraditional fields. And yet, never have the challenges towards achieving equality been as great. Our campus continues to lack adequate childcare services or accommodation for women's unique roles as mothers. No formal university charter exists to protect women's rights, and women continue to face discrimination at all levels as faculty, students, and staff with few mechanisms for recourse. The Women's Resource Centre exists to remind the University of Calgary of the work that still needs to be done. The WRC Advisory Committee, a group of individuals representing all of the major WRC stakeholders, is chaired by the Advisor to the University on Women's Issues – currently, Dr. Claudia Emes of the Faculty of Kinesiology. Dr. Emes has been instrumental in creating a strong link between the Advisor on Women's Issues and the Women's Resource Centre in order to facilitate advocacy work at a university level. It is our hope that with time and the growing support for the Women's Resource Centre, the University of Calgary administration will become more receptive to championing women's issues.

The Women's Resource Centre is not only a resource and service provider, but has built a bridge with the program of Women's Studies, offering community service learning courses to undergraduate students. Developing academic legitimacy is vital to the Centre's sustainability and it is hoped that one day the WRC will grow into an institute of world class gender and feminist research alongside the provision of key resources and services.

The Women's Resource Centre is dedicated to honoring women and profiling those women that are shining examples of wisdom, resilience, and compassion. Each year we honor one female alumna, and one student who demonstrate professional and academic excellence, who have trail-blazed for women, overcome great challenges, and who give back to their communities, in particular to marginalized women. When I was an undergraduate in Women's Studies at the U of C, I remember walking into our library and looking around the walls at the paintings and photographs of mostly male leaders on our campus. I envisioned a day on our campus when an entire space would be dedicated to pictures of phenomenal women who have graced this campus. With the WRC Awards celebrating women's wisdom, resilience, and compassion we are doing just this — we are creating a physical and social space to recognize the achievements of women.

Although great uncertainty exists with regards to the future of women's struggles at the University of Calgary, the Women's Resource Centre will continue to grow and evolve with the needs of the women of this campus. We will continue to honor the stories and lives of those women who have brought us to this point while nurturing the great potential of the young women who become a part of our community each academic year. And so our quilts continue to grow.

The Principle of Universal Franchise
Developing a Constitution

Of course you would like to know how we decided on our name? Whether to call ourselves "Faculty Women", "Women's Faculty Club", or "Faculty Wives" provoked a lot of discussion. We wanted to include women on our staff but we didn't wish to imply that the Club was for women of our male staff. You understand the delicacy of the problem.

Next, we had almost as much trouble as Canada is having today settling our constitution. Our special problems were our objectives, membership eligibility and categories, and what we should hazard as dues. We agreed that the Faculty Women's Club should have two purposes: to give the wives and women members of the faculty an opportunity to become acquainted with each other, and to assist the University in any appropriate way. In the matter of membership, we must have had legal aid. To quote:

All women members of the faculty, all faculty wives and all other adult female members of faculty families who indicate their interest shall be invited to join. Also, wives of deceased or retired members, or retired members of the faculty, will be eligible for membership. . . .

and,

Honorary membership may be extended on occasion to women whose interests lie with the University and who are approved by a majority vote of the active membership. Honorary members shall be exempt from payment of dues and special assessments, and shall have all the privileges of active members except those of voting and holding office.

The appropriate financial commitment (dues) was $1.25 per year.

In our first revision, three years later, interested members of faculty families were no longer eligible. However, we now included the senior administrative appointments who were women and the wives of senior appointees. Our executive expanded from table officers to include social committee chairman and phoning committee chairman. Dues jumped to $2.00 per year. In 1964 we specified an official crest; added fund-raising as a new purpose; designated the wife of the President as our Honorary President; and invited Chaplains' wives to become associate members (a new category). Because our club was becoming a very active one we clarified some of the executive roles. The Past President was to be coordinator of the projects committees. Social committee chairman was to be in charge of meeting reservations and refreshments. The new position, special events chairman, specified responsibility for all social functions.

Our last two revisions in 1967 and 1971 broadened the eligibility for both active and honorary membership. As of 1971, our Honorary President became eligible for active membership. Annual dues are now $7.00.

One of the awful ramifications of having a constitution is that you just might have to uphold it! This happened to me some years ago during election of officers when I had to dissuade our Honorary President from exercising her strong belief in her right to vote because she had also paid dues. My strong belief, as Parliamentarian, was to the contrary. In retrospect, it would have been better to let subordinate clauses lie and yield to the principle of universal franchise.

Norris, p. 1-3

A Society Becomes a Society

Polly Knowlton Cockett

Language for the Times

Only recently have I begun to realize a certain (in)disposition: editing seems to be a way of being for me. Clarify this, revise that, enhance, expand, expound. Although it's not always a desirable trait (certainly not from my children's perspectives), whether as a columnist, classroom teacher, community activist, or doctoral candidate, I do seem driven to edit the human constructs around me, to question the details, to search for integrity of purpose until I find some modicum of peace with nuanced notions. When these fleeting moments of peaceful mindedness fall my way, I revel in discovering the extraordinary in the ordinary, and am then compelled to voice the profound I've found in the humble.

So, when I received the several and hallowed dusty boxes of presidential files and folders and fonds, including a wooden calling-to-order hammer, a small volume of *Robert's Rules of Order,* and a golden pin for the Faculty Women's Club, handed along from outgoing President Sue-Ann Facchini in 1999, I began to rummage through them searching for insight into the role where I now found myself humbled. I began wondering just what this organization was really all about, what its place was as we approached a new century and new millennium, whether its papers fully reflected its spirit and intent, and whether its words were ones that I could live by if I was duly going to represent it.

Not exactly surprisingly, I don't think anyone had looked closely at the Constitution and By-Laws in quite a while. The most recent visitation appeared to be in 1984, with revisions newly ensuring that any dues paying member could vote and hold office, that any member may continue membership irrespective of separation, divorce, or termination from the university, and that there shall be annual financial audits. There were other revisions, specifying who should do what, and when and how it should be done. It was comforting to realize, not only that there may be others with editing afflictions, but that the women who had crafted these documents were voicing their ongoing commitment to clarity, accountability, and inclusion. I could live with that.

But the assumptive language of gendered roles: NO! The time should be well past for any document that said, "The wife of the Chancellor and the wife of the Chairman of the Board of Governors" are eligible for Honorary membership, or assumed that, "The wife of the President of The University of Calgary is the Honorary President." These words had to change!!

At the very first meeting I chaired (though I didn't use the wooden hammer), I put out a call for volunteers to revise the bylaws with me! ... Sigh. After a year or so of measured silence later, my faithful and beloved friends who'd stayed on or returned to the executive to serve with me, despite glazed over eyes, stoically suffered through my idealist enthusiasm as we not only merged the old Constitution and By-Laws into one set of simplified bylaws, we became an Incorporated Society with Alberta Registries on April 2, 2001.

Primarily, our revisionist efforts were to update language by substituting "spouses or partners" for "wives," and allow for positions such as president or chancellor or chair to be filled by women (just imagine!). We also simplified duties and clarified flexibility for the Executive, including allowing the validity of communications via email: another iteration of streamlining for today's version of multitasking women. It did take a bit of convincing for some of the older members, who already knew well that FWC operated with integrity, ethics, and accountability, to understand that, in the current times of public liability and litigation, and in the words of Alberta Registries, formally incorporating a group afforded it "a more definite and permanent status than an unincorporated group." For these painstaking efforts, I particularly thank Kate Bentley, Eileen Lohka, Lorri Post, Ann Rohleder, Jane Steele, Tannis Teskey, and Sue White for their forbearance and perseverance. Together, in becoming a Society, we became what we were, and had always been.

Inclusive Practice

Some questions linger, and old discussions emerge yet again. Still tripping up on the possibly antiquated connotations of our own name, and perhaps a certain lament for the historically prominent role of the club, one wonders what lies ahead, how might we continue to expand our inclusiveness, what is our current relevance, how might we manifest ourselves in an uncertain future?

In early September 2006, not dwelling on such questions while we were preparing for our Golden Anniversary year of special celebratory gatherings, an email from Dr. Fiona Nelson filtered through the ether and landed in my inbox via the FWC email, with the subject line, "Urgent question."

> Dear Faculty Women's Club,
>
> The Women's Studies Program here has received a couple of 50th Anniversary Membership forms from your members (because we tend to receive anything with the word "women" in it). One has included a cheque. I opened them both to see if there was a mailing address for your group but didn't see one. Do you have a campus address, or even an off-campus mailing address that I can forward these to?

The misdirected mail was duly redirected, along with making new direct connections. Fiona invited me to attend the grand opening of the Women's Resource Centre, which led to my meeting its new Director, Stephanie Garrett. This led to a joint meeting with Stephanie, me, and Janice Kinch of the Academic Women's Association. We swapped stories of past and future visions for our various women's organizations, and we planned a shared gathering.

On March 29, 2007, a Golden Anniversary Campus Tea was held with members and friends of the Faculty Women's Club, the Academic Women's Association, and the brand new Women's Resource Centre. Our woman Chancellor, several women deans, women faculty and women spouses or partners of faculty, and women staff and women students joined together in multigenerational circles of friendship spanning over fifty years. Many of their stories can be found in this book. Together we inaugurated the potential of a new era of collaboration and connection amongst all University of Calgary women's groups, both on and off campus.

The Women's Resource Centre has since offered us a home for our meetings and a place for our mail – even though some missives have mysteriously ended up in the Gauntlet office across the hall. Yet still, the questions resurface. Does our name define us or confine us? The University of Alberta, Calgary Branch has changed its name along with the dropping of the "The" and periodic logo changes to express autonomy and an evolving identity. The Faculty Babysitting Swap, when numbers were low, incorporated a neighborhood swap without changing its name, but later dropped "Baby," not because they'd thrown out the babies and bathwater, but because watering plants, pets, and gardens were newly included as swapped sitting opportunities. Campus Child Care Co-Operative spent a year on campus and then moved around to various nearby churches and schools for several years before settling in Capitol Hill. At one point they tried, without success, to change their name to Northwest Preschool Co-Op, and thus later formally incorporated as Campus Preschool Association of Calgary, eventually having found value in name recognition over time and in honoring the heritage of their literal place of origin. (Although, when I was a Registrar for the preschool, we did still get calls wondering where on campus we were located!) BP has moved beyond petroleum, and the Young Men's Christian Association is now fully inclusive of all comers and is still the YMCA.

In 1956, the Faculty Women's Club was careful to ensure both female academics and female spouses of academics were included equally, and together they became a welcoming and community building tour de force for the university and the city. In 2009, although this extended family of the university is now largely an unrealized resource, that early spirit of equality and inclusiveness continues.

After more than fifty years, the Faculty Women's Club will no doubt now remain titled as such for its duration. However, once our Golden celebrations were concluded in spring 2007, FWC again began to scrutinize the inclusiveness of its terminology and eligibility clauses for membership. With Eileen Lohka at the helm, along with Brinsley Fox, Marie Gailer, Elizabeth Marko, Lynn Williams, and me, after a year long process developed to ensure all voices were carefully heard and honored, possibly final (here's hoping!) revisions to the bylaws were made.

Unanimously blessed by those at the annual general meeting in April 2008, the changes were made to facilitate inclusiveness, simplicity, and flexibility within our organization. "I have to admire their willingness," says President Eileen Lohka regarding the longtime members "going along with our streamlining suggestions to reflect the new realities of women in the workforce." Our membership process is now open and straightforward, and we welcome any interested woman whose interests may also lie with the University of Calgary to join us in increasingly greater circles of friendship and service.

FWC: For Women in Community

Exploring

Doing Everything Ourselves
Convocations, Catering, and Catalepsis

In those early years we really functioned like a ladies' auxiliary, or considering our youth, 'handmaiden' to the University: hostessing the convocation receptions; assisting with the sale of crafts to raise funds for WUS (World University Service); arranging Christmas parties and pot luck suppers.

Convocation receptions were just spring affairs then. We prepared all the food ourselves, getting together in a member's home (usually Vi Doucette's) to have a sandwich-making bee. Vi had the best filling recipe – Three Decker Chicken Special – which required thirty slices of brown bread, sixty of white, and could be cut into either ninety or one hundred twenty sandwiches, depending on the crowd. I remember the cost of preparing sandwiches in one of our first sessions was $14. For quality control, certain staff wives were known for their reliability in making special squares – Penny Storey: walnut slice; Bernice Gibb: Nanaimo bars; and so, we always asked them.

Not only did we make the food but we also served it in high style in the lower foyer of the Jubilee auditorium. Ladies selected from the higher ranks "poured" from loaned silver tea services set on lace tablecloths graced with our own china brought from home. As we were trying to do everything ourselves, time was always critical. I remember once, the feeling of catalepsis, when ONE convocation address was brief, and the gowned and renowned descended the broad staircase for a reception while we were still in an adjoining room cutting the squares. Our local support of convocation was soon recognized, for we were allocated and escorted to a special section near the back of the Auditorium so that we could slip out discreetly to assemble the food on time.

A few years later, when our University moved to the present campus, the food services department gradually took over food preparation and we were relegated to a low profile modification. As the size of the receptions

Various coffee entries in FWC ledger, but who is counting beans . . . or coffee urns . . .

Income from urn rentals:

1971-1972 - Treasurer's report and budget
Urn rental: $4.00 income

1972-1973 - Treasurer's report and budget
Urn rental: $11.00 actual income; $3.00 budget projection

1973-1974 - Treasurer's report and budget
Urn rentals: $5.00 est. income: $1.00 actual income: $10.00 budget projection

1974-1975 - Treasurer's report and budget
Urn rentals: $3.00 est. income: $7.00 actual income: $5.00 budget projection

1976-1977 - Treasurer's report and budget
Urn rentals: $10.00 est. income: $3.00 actual income: $5.00 budget projection

1977-1978 - Treasurer's report and budget
Urn rentals: $5.00 est. income: $2.00 actual income

1979-1980 - Treasurer's report
Urn rentals: $6.00 actual income

1980-1985 - Treasurer's report
Urn rentals: $0.00 actual income

Expenditures from urn rentals:

July 1, 1977 - FWC year ending Club Budget
Urn repairs: $15.00 estimated: $7.60 actual repairs

grew, the hatted pourers, who formerly sat before silver services, now stood over ungainly coffee urns with heads bowed, releasing liquid into crockery cups as required. Job satisfaction waned. Furthermore, those of our members who had "graciously agreed to pass food around" couldn't because they were immobilized by the crowds. In the words of Milton, "They also serve who only stand and wait."

Norris, p. 4-5

Chief Usher Has Best Volunteer Role in Calgary
Featuring Judy McCaffrey

The 12 convocation ceremonies held on campus each year – nine of which take place June 11 to 15 – simply wouldn't happen were it not for the efforts of nearly 100 volunteers who ensure each event runs smoothly.

As chief usher on behalf of the Alumni Association, Judy McCaffrey, BA'82, is responsible for ensuring the volunteer team is in place to greet guests, answer questions, address any safety concerns or emergencies and make it an enjoyable experience for the fresh graduates and their families.

"I have the most positive volunteer job in Calgary," McCaffrey says. "It's particularly rewarding for those volunteers who work on campus as faculty or support staff because it gives them a different perspective and they realize that this is what it's all for."

The ceremonies can also take on a special meaning for an usher when they know a graduating student. Last month's convocation for the faculties of law and medicine, for example, included a graduate who, as a six-month-old, was a guest at McCaffrey's wedding.

McCaffrey's convocation experience has broadened her involvement elsewhere in the community. She is an honorary member of the Faculty Women's Club and is involved with the Canadian Federation of University Women – Calgary, an organization that promotes education and advancing the status of women and human rights.

McCaffrey has recruited members from both organizations to the convocation team. U of C alumni also comprise a significant portion of the volunteer group.

It's obvious the volunteer family enjoys the camaraderie and laughter. There's usually a story making the rounds about reuniting an elderly grandmother with her family, or someone recognizing that the pipe band's appropriately subdued music welcoming the students into the Jack Simpson Gymnasium is actually a Scottish drinking song.

Reprinted with generous permission from the University of Calgary: Fox, M. (June 8, 2007). Chief Usher has Best Volunteer Role in Calgary. On Campus (4).

Louise Guy Has Done it Again!
Carole-Lynne Le Navenec

At age 80++, with knee braces, a survivor of an aortic valve replacement which works just fine, and broad smiles intact, our very own inspirational Louise Guy climbed the 802 steps of the Calgary Tower FOUR times on Saturday April 21, 2007 in support of the Alberta Wilderness Association (AWA). We are so very, very proud of Louise and her ninety year old spouse, Richard, who despite having a pacemaker, climbed the tower six times!!!! Le Navenec (a professor in the Faculty of Nursing, in a 2007 article) believes that knowledge of their activities contributes enormously to understanding approaches used by older persons for health promotion and personhood well-being across the lifespan, and the centrality of the concept of creativity in that process.

Here's how Louise composes the meaning of creating health and well-being, and enhancing quality of life through what I call "rhythmic movements" and "connecting with nature." I believe they celebrate Earth Day every day of their lives, not just near April 22.

> The climb is good fun if anyone out there would like to do it too! Schools and groups paint delightful murals on the landings, good places to rest and contemplate! I am only too pleased to encourage people to take exercise.

> Both Richard and I had parents who were active . . . And when we met, we were delighted to share our love of mountains and enjoyment of walking and scrambling, at first in the English Lake District and then wherever we went around the world. When we had the chance to come to Calgary we soon joined the Alpine Club of Canada, and have had nearly forty years of climbing our beautiful mountains. I have had breast cancer, lung and heart surgery, and I am sure my eagerness to resume outdoor activities has always contributed to my recovery.

> I am interested that you consider the importance of rhythmic and dance movement in health. Ballroom dancing has always been another activity we have enjoyed together.

Editors' Notes: Carole-Lynne's article above appeared in *The Canadian Gerontological Nurse* in 2007, vol. 24(1), p. 3, and she has shared it with FWC. She also organized a Faculty of Nursing public presentation in June 2007 by Dr. Russ Hepple, Faculty of Kinesiology, entitled, "Effect of Exercise on Aging: Enhancing One's Healthspan," and featuring Louise, FWC Member, about how she uses exercise over her lifespan. Of note, Louise and Richard Guy, both in their nineties, climbed the Calgary Tower as recently as April 2009, 4 and 7 times respectively, easily winning the Awards for most climbs by senior male and female. The FWC has supported the Alberta Wilderness Association by sponsoring Louise in her annual climb.

Towering Meditations
Interwoven Threads of Friendship
Polly Knowlton Cockett

> To regain our full humanity, we have to regain our experience of connectedness with the entire web of life. This reconnecting, *religio* in Latin, is the very essence of the spiritual grounding of deep ecology. – Fritjof Capra, *The Web of Life.* (p. 296)

Perhaps the subtitle of this piece should be called "Treads" of Friendship, rather than "Threads," for it is a journal of musings on interconnectivity arising from iterated ascents of the 802 steps of the Calgary Tower, something I've done annually with my family since 1999. Each April, the Alberta Wilderness Association (AWA) hosts a fundraiser in Calgary in the form of a Tower Climb and Run. Participants collect sponsorship monies in order to climb, with all funds going to the AWA for its education and advocacy on behalf of our province's special spaces and species. Those with substantial pledge money may climb the Tower as many times as they wish, or can, during the five hour period the stairwell is open on a Saturday close to Earth Day. The event is a high spirited occasion, with music, entertainment, and children's activities, both at the top and bottom of the Tower, and a Wild Alberta Expo featuring all sorts of environmental organizations from around our city and province.

One year, friends from the Faculty Women's Club who've generously sponsored my children to climb, asked *why* we would spend a beautiful spring day in the confines of a windowless stairwell instead of with them on our annual Easter Saturday multifamily hike in the unconfined beauty of the front ranges of the nearby Rocky Mountains. I didn't have an immediate reply, although we did of course join our friends later for an evening meal and swapped stories of our day's ascensions. But I have since thought that it's not about experiencing the sightless stairwell; it's about supporting a vision to help create a sense of environmental awareness in others and an ongoing *re*-cognition of a sense of place for my own and my family's life/lives in Calgary and Alberta – outside the stairwell. It's about finding ways to promote an understanding of the ecology of networked systems and interdependency, and thus, for me, the grounding spirituality referred to in the quote above. And, ultimately, it's about friendship, even if occasionally forgoing a shared hike: affirming and reaffirming relationships where we can come to terms with our interconnected place in the web, and our responsibility toward it, ourselves, and each other.

Understanding ecological interdependence means understanding relationships. It requires the shifts of perception that are characteristic of systems thinking – from the parts to the whole, from objects to relationships, from contents to patterns. A sustainable human community is aware of the multiple relationships among its members. Nourishing the community means nourishing those relationships Capra (p. 298).

One, Two, Buckle My Shoe

8:30 a.m. Shoes tied, not buckled. No Velcro. Ready to go.

This heading's counting rhyme for children may need updating.

She's off, my daughter, speeding ahead of me as I amble along for my initial ascent and first repetition. She is once again tackling these stairs as many times as she can in the allotted time. Only five hours to go. She started with 2 climbs in 1999 at age seven, and has climbed as many as 20 times in subsequent years. Will she match her own record? She's rapidly grown taller in recent years, with a consequent greater mass to hoist, to will, up those stairs. Why does she do this?

She was asked this question by the AWA several years ago, to which she replied, "So I can practice my 15 times table." The flights of stairs within the main column have 15 steps each, and the landing numbers and cumulative steps are indicated on each level: 1:15, 2:30, 3:45, 4:60, etc. Optimism surfaces around 50:750.

The first AWA volunteer I knew was Joanne Wyvill. I'd met her, Barbara Birtwistle, and Sue Stodart immediately upon arriving in Calgary in 1991 – all spouses of Computer Science faculty, the department which my spouse, Robin, had just joined. We'd emigrated from an Australian winter warmer than the late June day we landed at 51°N, our heads ringing with stories we'd been told of eleven month winters and cars that needed engine block heaters to be plugged in before driving (resulting in half cords dangling off the fronts of cars with the other halves found in spring's sublimating snowbanks). I awoke the first morning horrified to see large white fluffy balls drifting past the window of the Village Park Inn where the University put us up for our first three days. But my pulse soon eased when I realized it wasn't snow, but seeds from the female poplar trees seemingly ubiquitous in Calgary as it prepares for Stampede.

All three of these women's families were in the Faculty Babysitting Swap and encouraged us to join, which we of course readily did – always ready to swap support time rather than scarce money – with my first meeting at Sue's home. Robin and I had helped to found the Preschool Cooperative of Knoxville in Tennessee where our two sons were born, and we had enrolled Grayson in parent cooperative kindergartens in Australia. So I now wanted a parent cooperative preschool for Rowan here, and Barbara recommended Campus Preschool Association, where her kids had gone. Having bucked the then current trend for women by choosing to parent my children full time rather than find outside remunerative employment, I wanted a school for Grayson which had a reputation for parent involvement and that he could walk to, and Joanne recommended Dr. E.W. Coffin where her kids went. It was Barbara who took me and the boys in after the Inn – Robin, having now officially taken up the job, promptly went off to European conferences – until I could find a place of our own near both the University and Dr. Coffin School, which I soon did, thanks to her driving us hither and yon.

Shortly thereafter, having determined our new life was stable enough to create an in situ Canadian, I became immobilized with all day morning sickness which went on for months. Robin, thus attending solo all the various autumn Welcoming Parties for new faculty and their partners at the University, met Kate Bentley due to their English accents. He must have woven quite the tale of woe, as Kate proceeded to phone me regularly in my bedridden state. Finally we met, when I shakily ventured forth for *American* Thanksgiving at her home. She introduced me to another new arrival, Lorri Post, and they made sure I joined the Faculty Women's Club along with them. The rest is history, and I have kept a saying from a fortune cookie that came my way around that time: "Rely on long time friends to give you advice with your present question." And so, thanks to these several brand new long time friends, we were set for our Calgary journey to unfold, including shared hikes and holidays with these and many other very special Sitting Swap, Preschool, and Faculty Women's Club families.

9:00 a.m. Emerging at the top of the Tower, I see gulls flying over the Bow River to the north. Having grown up on the New England coast, I naturally assumed that all gulls were seagulls, including Jonathan Livingston Seagull. Well, imagine my surprise when I moved to landlocked Alberta and found gulls. In fact, early on in my time in Alberta, I awoke one gusty chinooking morning, to the ringing slap, slapping of the halyard on the nearby school's metal flagpole, and heard the distinctive cry of seagulls.

In that strange semi-conscious world of awakening, I entered into some other personal construct of my whereabouts, somewhere on the coast, a harbor, with the slap, slapping halyards ringing the metal masts of moored yachts in a morning breeze filled with crying seagulls excited by an outgoing tide and their innate assumptions that this ebbing would offer up a fine breakfast. But, no, as I awoke more fully, my startled thought was, "What the heck were seagulls doing in Alberta?" And so, I whipped out my bird books, and tried to make sense of this new reality. I duly discovered that myriad gull and other bird species migrate up and down the vast interior waterways of North America, and that many a California gull may never have been to California, nor ever have seen the sea.

I loved this discovery! It shook me out of my own thinking about seagulls, which I am now very careful to describe simply as gulls. For me, my use of this shorter word represents a personal transformation, a paradigm-shift if you will. And it, or even the sight or sound of a gull in Alberta has become a personal metaphor, a personal reminder actually, to try to remain open-minded, to remember that there is more to be discovered about almost everything.

Circling westward along the observation level, I encounter the now familiar view of the Bow valley unfolding across the prairie, rising to the foothills and mountains beyond: the classic Alberta view. The same view from Nose Hill Park near where we now live and call home; the same view I laboriously embraced between my knees for innumerable hours in the Foothills Hospital giving birth to my daughter in April 1992, the first Canadian in the family.

Iteration

9:30 a.m. My daughter passes me by. Says she's not feeling well; may not get to her usual total. Take it easy, I encourage; there's no need to go so intensely. Sip water. Breathe evenly. Well, I used to give her advice when she was little; now she knows it herself and/or doesn't want to hear anything from me.

With 15 steps per flight, that's 53 flights plus 7 additional steps; there are a few extra steps near the top as one passes by the Panorama Restaurant with its high ceiling, though the risers on these public stairs may be slightly shorter as well. We had lunch in this restaurant on the day the rest of the family became Canadian citizens in 1995, an orbiting view of our new country. My daughter celebrated her 16th birthday by *taking the elevator* to the observation level with friends, and for her 17th she took friends to the restaurant here. I've always wondered what cues the servers use to find their assigned tables on the revolving floor after they come out of the fixed-point kitchen. What is their frame of reference?

In preparing for the publication of this book, I referred to many archival materials: with Marjorie Norris at MacKimmie Library for the first twenty-five years of FWC, with Claudia Gomez at the Glenbow Museum for the Preschool in the 70s and 80s, with Debbie Hall in her role as the final President for the Babysitting Swap, and with Kate Bentley through general records still held by current members and the Club (to be archived one day!). Kate and I discovered a perplexing (to me) entry in the March 1998 FWC Executive minutes under Current Business: "Tannis Teskey, as past president, contacted Polly-Lee Knowlton-Cockett who accepted the job of Vice President for next year." *Not true!*

What is true is that we were on sabbatical in Cambridge, England for most of that year, and Tannis had sent me a note via my husband's email at work, asking if I would consider joining the Executive. I do remember Robin coming home and telling me about the message, but as we were about to complete our eight months there and go to Australia for the next three months, I didn't reply. I thought, "Phew, I will be too busy when I return, and I wouldn't ever want to do that job anyway!" – as at that time, being VP meant being President the following year, and then staying on for a third year. Round about May, when we finally had email set up through the telephone at our next home in Sydney (easier to do in Australia than in England at that time), I used my husband's email to write back to Tannis, secure in my knowledge that the offer had successfully expired, to let her know that, with apologies for my tardiness, I couldn't take it up just now, thanks anyway. She emailed back to say, "Too late. Robin accepted for you. You're in!"

10:00 a.m. I reckon this type of interaction arises as a women's identity issue when email first went beyond the business setting: wives often sharing family email addresses under their husband's name! Perhaps this was part of the impetus when I did become President in 1999 (it was my husband's fault) for ensuring that FWC become e-literate. I obtained a U of C email and website domain for the club – though that required intervention by Sue White to convince IT that her husband, the U of C President, said it was okay, we really were a valid U of C entity. I also started Egroup, a free listserve for members, friends, and alumni of FWC. At first, any listees' postings went to the whole group rather than to Sender Only as is now the case. When we were planning our 45th Anniversary in 2001, Lynn Williams, using her husband Hugh's email, sent an Egroup message to the entire membership confirming the luncheon details for noon at the University Club. There then came a message back from Ann Elliott's husband, Robert, saying he'd be delighted to meet Hugh for lunch, but could they please meet at 1:00 p.m. in the Oak Room at Scurfield Hall, as it better fit his schedule.

In perusing the archives, it struck me how right into the 1970s, many women were still being referred to by their husband's names, e.g., Mrs. Stanley Norris was in charge of the University Ball, Mrs. C.E. Challice set up a Music Program at Campus Preschool. It wasn't until the 80s that these women's first names began to regularly appear, e.g., Mrs. Margaret Oliver, and even later still until appearing without the "Title," e.g., Marg Oliver, or even simply Marg, in various records. Even in the 2000s many of us are having trouble deciding what to do with our own names if we marry or start families or make changes thereafter. Should I keep my own, take my partner's, combine the two? And if I combine, should I hyphenate or not, and if not, under which should it be alphabetized? And then our answers to these questions evolve with the changing dynamics of our lives. If one didn't know some of the people behind the names found in our archives, one would be confused by the Loov, Tulloch, Crites, Zissos, Dunwoody, Lancaster, Lancaster, Stone, Stone-Blackburn, Stratton, Anderson, Marko, Solecki, Roma Flint Eiserman Reynoldson, Borbridge Austin, and Barron Norris combinations which refer to far fewer women and even fewer spouses (in the end) than one might suspect.

Five, Six, Pick Up Sticks

10:30 a.m. I've been lapped by my daughter again, and by my spouse, whose surname I added to mine, without a hyphen, alphabetized under "my" K, as we joined to build a family together.

In 2005, at age fifty, I really pushed myself, doing 15 ascents in the five hours. And my knees have been hurting me ever since! I have not climbed again with the intent of doing anything like that. I'd be happy with 5. But I'll probably do my standard 10, an average of 2 per hour, and I'll still have time to chat and think along the way. I'm moving toward sustainability in my approach to this annual event, and to life in general. Or at least I'm trying to. Although I do have soccer afterwards, and I'd better go, as those women have all generously sponsored me to climb, too.

While resting at the top once more, rehydrating, listening to the live musicians, I gaze southward through to the perimeters of Calgary's Cartesian quadrants of streets and avenues, noting the railroad tracks laddering between Canada's east and west coasts at the local $y = (-9.5)$. The Tower sits at about $y = (-9.25)$, with $x = (0)$, right on Centre Street, the y axis. I've been yo-yoing up and down the z axis in my contemplations for this writing: grids as frames of reference for enhancing communication. Still, people get lost in Calgary.

11:00 a.m. Now at the halfway point in time. She's passed me again, maybe a couple of times. I'll have to say she is more cheerful this year. Perhaps she is also moving toward sustainability, toward balance in her life.

The Raging Grannies are singing a few tunes now. Well, they don't actually claim to be musicians; their emphasis is on the words, and they consider themselves social activists, not entertainers. Here they sing on environmental themes of course. Several are from the U of C and the Unitarian Church of Calgary (UCC) and even used to be in the Preschool or Swap or FWC, and several have stories in this book. It is pertinent to mention the UCC connection here, as that is where I first heard about the Tower Climb, and it's the extended group with which our family climbs. Ward Neale was an energetic octogenarian before he died in 2008, forever raising awareness and motivating others to participate in social and environmental justice activism. He was associated with the Chancellor's office at the U of C, a judge at the Youth Science Fair, and a rather famous Canadian geologist. But I first met him as a professed atheist and humanist and activist at the Unitarian Church, getting everyone there to also climb the Tower, or to sponsor someone else, especially the UCC youth.

Ward used to lead informal church group hikes up to the Burgess Shale, to ponder the mysteries of Cambrian life left behind in the magnificent setting of Yoho National Park in British Columbia. When there, he liked to search for evidence of Pikaia, the earliest known chordate, and bring the group to ponder this distant human cousin and the foundations of consciousness.

The UCC is also where, in 1996, I became acquainted with Ann Kyle and Jennifer Eiserman, both then also associated with the U of C. We first met while co-teaching a Sunday School class which explored human traditions which respect and celebrate our Earth home and each other. Jennifer and I went on to co-facilitate a discussion group on the U of C campus for three years, entitled University Unitarians, and it was also an Interest Group of the Faculty Women's Club and open to all comers. We had an interesting mix of attendees and together we explored contemporary issues in a context of liberal humanist ideas, bringing into consciousness a greater awareness and respect for nuance and complexity. I have learned much from those conversations, including about science and aesthetics, and daughters.

Seven, Eight, Don't Be Late

11:30 a.m. And she's lapped me again, right hand pulling on the rail, left hand on her hip. Determination.

Speaking of aesthetics, there are dozens of Alberta wilderness murals in the Tower stairwell, painted by various youth, school groups, and adults, to brighten up the experience of the fundraising climbers. In 2009, the UCC Church School won an award for theirs. In 2007, they became the first Sunday school in Canada to become a Green School through the SEEDS Foundation which generally provides environmental programming for schools. I had spent some time consulting for SEEDS, after Margo Helper "discovered" me in 2004 when Dr. Coffin School became an Earth School after having completed 1000 environmental projects over a 10 year period. Karen Gummo, Barbara Sherrington, and I had been involved on the Environment Committee at the school throughout that decade, and I had presented a poster session about all those projects at the International Geoscience Education conference at the U of C in 2003 – connecting community and place-based curricula. As I was also involved in the Green Sanctuary program at UCC, I suggested to both Margo and UCC that they could/should cross over into each others' realms, as perhaps it would be another effective avenue for environmental education to go through churches as well as schools. Margo, always ready to build community connections, of course agreed, just as she also readily agreed to have SEEDS act as the registered charity to host FWC's grant through The Calgary Foundation for this book. With trust, one thing leads to another.

Noon. The bells are going off in the Tower.

One step leads to the next. Haven't actually seen my daughter in a while, but the mural called Fractal Blooming on Level 14 was painted by women, including Rachel Collins, the daughter of a U of C prof and a UCC family. She was also a "sittee" in the Faculty Babysitting Swap, as noted by her mother, Marie, in this book. The petals of the mural's blossom feature handprints and footprints of various fauna, including humans. Footprints of chaos?

Well, my life has become increasingly chaotic over the last few years – with community anti-graffiti murals, and schoolground naturalization and interpretive signage projects, not to mention home renovations. Oh, and then I turned fifty, and got so inspired by the amazing people involved in these community environmental projects, that (while my husband was safely away on sabbatical without me this time) I just had to apply to do a doctorate in Environmental Education at the U of C with Dr. Bonnie Shapiro! Yes, with trust, one thing does lead to another. I remember sitting bolt upright very early on New Year's Day 2007 (in one of those menopausal sweats no doubt hastened on by becoming a "mature" grad student), wondering how to get through the next 365 days. Just about everything I had been involved in over the last few years suddenly had the same end of year deadline: we had to use the provincial grant to complete the interpretive signage through the Friends of Dr. Coffin, we had use the community grant to finish this FWC book, and I had to complete my candidacy exams. Not comprehending how it was all going to happen, I decided to start the year by cleaning the washrooms instead.

Indeed, none of those things were completed that year. Thank goodness for extensions. But the signage was completed in spring 2008, with the Grand Opening of course being right in the middle of my candidacy exam period. . . . And if you're reading this, The Book is finally finished too!

Nine, Ten, Let's Do it Again

12:30 p.m. There she goes again.

The signage is a unique set of interpretive panels in a suburban grassland and aspen parkland setting in Brentwood Heights. Students, teachers, parents, and community members, including current and alumni FWC, Preschool, UCC, and Sitting Swap members (several are also in this book!), worked together with The City of Calgary Natural Area Parks department and Dr. Coffin School to produce the original art, poetry, and text for thirty-four amazingly beautiful and provocative signs for both school-based and public education. Prairie conservation, invasive alien species, environmental stewardship, deep time, geomorphology, and conservation landscaping are but a few of the natural and cultural history concepts and issues touched upon by this grassroots public environmental education initiative. As a set, the resulting signs speak closely to the complexities of our ecological context and our place in the web of existence, especially at the precious and precarious intersections of our natural and built environments. What a great destination for a walk!

As I emerge from the stairwell at the top of the Tower for my penultimate 360° view that day, I look east, across the prairie. With Alberta declaring rough fescue the provincial grass emblem in 2003, and with our native fescue grasslands becoming increasingly fragmented and/or invaded by alien grasses, with resultant area and biodiversity losses, I have become quite interested in this indigenous ecosystem for which this province is visually renowned.

A few days after becoming a Canadian in 1995, I checked the citizenship box on a form for the very first time when I signed on to be the community liaison for an Adopt-a-Park involvement that Dr. Coffin School and the Brentwood Community have with the City of Calgary Natural Areas department. We have adopted a small natural area adjacent to the schoolground, called Whispering Woods, as named by students at that time, although half of it is grassland, a small outlier of Nose Hill. We've been working with the city since then in basic stewardship roles, as well as issues to do with pathways, invasive species, and restoration work. Together we have created a sandstone amphitheatre which is used as an outdoor classroom for local schools – and even Bonnie Shapiro's U of C environmental education class! – as well as providing a quiet seating area for the public. We have also engaged in native plant rescues and a grassland reclamation project in the schoolground, and of course the interpretive signage. My children have done science fair projects in the park, and in summers we host community weeding bees, with our greatest attendance always at the final evening bee followed by a potluck wine and cheese.

1:00 p.m. I've lost track of my daughter with all my window gazing. I shall succumb to base 10 temptations by climbing once more. It'll all be over, for me, when I get to the base of the tower after climb number 10.

Friendship and refreshment goes a long way toward (re)discovering and restoring the world and ourselves, no matter what else we're (over)busy doing. When my daughter was young, we participated in a Mothers and Youngsters (MY) Group with the FWC and the Swap, weekly enjoying each other's company and discovering our children as they grew anew before our eyes. We also developed a Walking Group which arose out of a prenatal exercise class at the U of C. Most of us also helped found the Brentwood Cooperative Playgroup and joined Campus Preschool, and from all these developed a Mother/Daughter Book Club. Many years of drifting into different schools and activities later, several of the same mothers recently regrouped with urgent restoration needs as MY Group gone MAD – Mothers with Adolescent Daughters. I'm very glad to have shared these perplexing last years of our daughters' childhoods with others as baffled as I have been, and I would never have had an opportunity to know any of these women and their precious daughters, nor many of the other multiple generations of women represented in this book, if it hadn't been for the example set by the Faculty Women's Club's tradition of welcoming and developing an interconnecting community.

Recovery

1:30 p.m. The five hours have elapsed, and so, I am thankfully done with the Tower Climb for another year. My daughter, Audrey Lane, again climbed enough times to secure the most climbs by a female youth. All the "most climbs by a youth" categories started with Grayson and Rowan. When they climbed some ridiculous number of times when quite young, there wasn't even a youth category. So AWA started a youth category, and then male and female youth categories. Then, when my kids kept winning those, they developed older and younger youth categories. My daughter has but one more year to climb as a youth, though she might find herself challenged by some amazing newcomer, like Rowan was in his last year as a youth. Grayson likes to say that the only events we win are those that no one else competes in. Instead, I view it as another example of pushing the boundaries of perception for what children can do and how they might be included as individuals, together with their families and communities around them in support.

And now I'm back to communities and support. Alison Prentice (2006) looked at the work of faculty wives and their clubs in the twentieth century, and the decline of these clubs over recent decades. She "wonders if the sense of community they tried to foster was really a viable goal," given the increasing size of universities and the changing nature of women in the workforce (p. 292). It seems our FWC has survived longer than those at some of our sister universities, and it remains unclear how much longer it will survive as such in its ever streamlined form. But as I carry the pledges of friendship and faith along with sponsorship monies up these stairs again and again on behalf of our shared wilderness, I know there is tremendous potential in the permeable boundaries of an interconnecting community.

I also know with great certainty that together we do absolutely make a difference. And I know that *friendship* is never out of date.

Make new friends and keep the old,
One is silver and the other gold.

References

Capra, F. (1996). *The web of life: A new scientific understanding of living systems.* New York: Anchor Books.

Prentice, A. (2006). Boosting husbands and building community: The work of twentieth-century faculty wives. In P. Stortz & E.L. Panayotidis. (Eds.). *Historical Identities.* University of Toronto Press.

Polly Knowlton Cockett was awarded the Alberta Centennial Medal in 2005 and an Alberta Graduate Citizenship Award in 2009 for her Community & Environmental Education Leadership.

A Centennial Hike Along the Bow

FWC Hikers Support New Trail for Calgary

From Marg Oliver's Scrapbook

FWC's Tuesday Hikers strode 15 miles from Bearspaw Dam to St. George's Island on April 29, 1975, in support of the new 30 mile trail system proposed by the Devonian Group and the City's Parks and Recreation department in honor of Calgary's Centennial Year.

Tuesday Hikers: A Fall Resume
Marg Oliver

We're all gathered here, the reason –
The end of the fall hiking season.
  It's Christmas too, the time for holly,
  And we, on wine, are feeling jolly.

Fifteen times I've called the roll;
Many and varied have been our goals.
  The weather grand, went on so late,
  The longest season we've had to date.

Barrier Lake at 15 miles –
The longest walk yet on our files.
  At Sundance Creek, oh weren't we sodden
  As through the rain we kept on ploddin'?

Tho' Norquay peak eluded us,
The goat trail gave adventure plus!
  Larch Valley in its golden hue –
  A repeat visit, yet always new.

Pigeon Lookout and beyond,
With sweeping views of which we're fond.
  Another lookout, Eisenhower –
  The mountains held us in their power.

Just had to try the pass called Cory;
Lots of sweat, but sure not sorry!
  Up Carrot Creek we crissed and crossed;
  Many wet feet, but no one lost!

Hella's ridge, tho' not ambitious –
Distinctly pleasant and delicious.
  Mount Allan posed a challenge mighty;
  After the maps we all took flighty!

Bowness Park to Bearspaw Lake;
A picture woods and snow did make.
  Hoar frost clung to bush and grass,
  Then suddenly was gone, alas!

'Long McLean Creek we walked through snow;
Five hunters there as well, you know!
  Trap Creek was not without a hitch –
  Slipped off the road into the ditch!

On Livingston Ridge the limbers grow.
And over it the wind does blow.
    Only Ann had above all shone,
    Only 14 hikes in a row she's gone.

All the others she has outdone –
In miles she's totalled 91.
    Determination – that shows in measure
    How she likes to spend her leisure.

So here's the prize she's won with ease;
We hope she enjoys her rosehip teas!
    The fall season o'er, we look with glee
    To when we start to cross country ski.

Ode to the Thursday Hikers

Betty Schofield

It was September '76
We met at Maya's house.
We thought we'd like to hike a bit,
Tho' we hadn't got much nous.

Marg Oliver instructed us
Because we were so green,
And Peg Magee came out with us
To help us set the scene.

Our hikes were pretty modest –
Skogan Pass and Ribbon Creek.
The Larches of Larch Valley
Caused stiffness for a week!

And then we took up skiing-
We found it rather hard,
Although we only skied the verge
Of John Laurie Boulevard.

But fifteen summers later
Our hikes are not so tame.
And some have left, and some have joined,
And some have stayed the same.

We've climbed up steepish mountains
And come down slippery rocks,
Crossed icy streams on tree trunks
Or doffed our boots and socks.

Our leader, who shall be nameless,
Fulfills some curious need
By leading us up cutlines
Where none have walked or skied!

We've had some overnights as well-
O'Hara and Skoki,
But best of all is Windermere
With Ollie and Marjory.

We've seen some glorious wildflowers
And learnt a name or two.
Of goats and marmots, sheep and elk
We've seen more than a few.

We've all of us had sorrows,
And some were hard to bear.
But as a Thursday Hiker
We knew the group was there.

We've shared so many joys too,
And every week rejoice
That we live in this wonderful country
That gives us so much choice.

So when the last trump soundeth
And St. Peter at the Gate
Asks, "And what did you do?"
And you tremble at your fate . .
You say, "I tried to do my best,
And though not free from sin,
I was a Thursday Hiker."
And he'll smile and let you in!!

*Composed on the occasion of the 15th Anniversary of Thursday Hikers,
November 14, 1991*

Memories of the FWC Thursday Hikers

Louise Guy

Many of the Faculty Women's Club members have always been enthusiastic outdoors people. In fact the proximity to the Rockies was quite a factor in bringing many staff to Calgary!

Marg Oliver started a Tuesday Hiking group in 1971. This soon grew too large to handle new members, so in 1976 Verna Sorensen started the Thursday Hikers, who in 2006 celebrated their 30th year. I joined the group two years later at Betty Schofield's suggestion. I had gained a certain amount of experience in the backcountry with the Alpine Club of Canada, and since Verna was very busy with her three little daughters and the Girl Guides, she asked me to take over the leading of the group. This soon became one of my major preoccupations, and the source of great friendships.

Over the years, we climbed most of the hikable peaks and passes within a day's drive, in sun and rain, in winter on skis. Perhaps because we were a very chatty lot, we had very few encounters with wildlife. A couple of times we detoured or ran from menacing looking moose in the rutting season, or retreated carefully from a grazing bear. In the spring, we greeted the emerging flowers as old friends, reminding each other of the names we had forgotten. In the winter, we marveled at the glistening peaks, the glittering flowers of the hoar frost, the ice formations in the almost frozen streams. In summer, we occasionally had a cooling skinny dip in remote lakes . . . but as Verna reminds me, still with hats on!

When Gillean Daffern began publishing her hiking guides, Betty would pore over them suggesting new places to go. We started making a wish list at the beginning of each summer season, old favorites and new hikes, to which everyone contributed. I would be teased about taking them on short-cuts up steep cutlines (I'm sure it only happened a couple of times), and it wasn't a really exciting day unless there was some bushwhacking. I sometimes carried a rope if there was some exposure on the route, but really only used it seriously once when we did a circuit over Ribbon Falls. This involves a short climb up an exposed cliff, where there is (or was) a chain, but no holds. So to be quite safe, Jean Pawson tied each person in turn to the rope and I belayed them up.

We would occasionally plan a two or three day trip, to an Alpine Club hut or a Lodge, which were great fun. We started celebrating important birthdays (decades) on the trail. Someone would carry up a cake, rush ahead and surprise the birthday girl with a, "Happy Birthday!" Probably the most memorable one was when Marjorie Taylor became the first of the group to reach eighty, on Burgess Pass, above Emerald Lake. (Sadly, Marjorie died recently at the age of ninety-two) Word of that birthday reached the late Peter Gzowski and we were invited to take part in his morning talk show. This was great fun; four of us sat in a studio here and chatted with him in Toronto. He reproved us for all talking at once! We were astounded at the number of people from across the country who happened to hear our brief moment of fame.

Over the years we have welcomed visitors to the University, sometimes for as long as a year, and still keep in touch with them. Members move away, we grow old, and new younger members join in. In 1998, I was very happy when Mary Vermeulen volunteered to take over the lead, which she has done so very competently. They've even done trips to Nepal and Peru! Now I enjoy an occasional little ski or walk with them, and all the social occasions and slideshows of their adventures. Long may they keep up the good work!

Swan Lake Vistas

Ilse Anysas-Salkauskas

Swan Lake Vista III
51 cm w x 66.5 cm h Cotton and synthetic fabrics and threads

Swan Lake Vista II
56.5 cm w x 55 cm h Cotton and synthetic fabrics and threads

Swan Lake, Alberta, is a place that I love. We have fished there for many years as a family and I have enjoyed observing the colors of the scenery around the lake change from one season to the next. Over the years I have photographed these changes and have created my art works to keep those memories alive.

Golden Larches

Mary Vermeulen

Prairie Creek – Powderface Creek Loop
Journal Entry: September 14, 2006

This was supposed to be our "Golden Larch Hike," to help the FWC celebrate their big 50th anniversary. The weather simply did not cooperate, so we changed our plans. We started at 9:00 a.m. (wow!), with vague plans to go to the Kananaskis instead of Burstall Pass. However, even that seemed too far to drive in the miserable weather. So we opted for the Bragg Creek area – parking at the Powderface parking lot, hiking UP Prairie Creek, across Prairie Link, and back down Powderface Creek (11.5 km). This was quite enough for all of us since the going was rather difficult. The snow started right at Bragg Creek. We started out in about 2 inches of heavy wet stuff, with more coming down all the time. Starting at 10:00 a.m., the trail up Prairie Creek was tough, because it was rocky and over umpteen tree roots, most covered by snow. By the time we reached the pass on Prairie Link we were in about 10 inches of it, but that at least made the traction a bit better. Lunch at noon was a quick affair at the bridge over Prairie Creek – even under the trees it was dripping! Both Prairie and Powderface Valleys are quite lovely with lots of aspens already turned color – but these poor trees were almost completely bent over with the weight of the snow, making beautiful arches. But no one bothered to dig out the camera in the snow. We were all quite wet by the time we reached the cars (about 2:15 p.m.), and all willing to stop in Bragg Creek for coffee and goodies. Spent half an hour there, warming up and sort of drying out, before continuing on to Calgary. Home by 3:30 p.m. Quite a satisfying day, although wet.

Mary Vermeulen & Mila Vesely – drivers; Linda Jackson, Verna Sorensen, Wendy Ehlers, Kathy Paulsen, Naegi Nigg

Volunteers Make Calgary Great

Linda Heidemann

The University of Calgary Faculty Women's Club has had many great volunteers. Dorothy Groves led the charge with Calgary Birth Control Association. Marg Oliver helped the Calgary Field Naturalists' Society with its activities. Others were involved with Inn from the Cold, the Calgary Drop-In Centre, the Calgary Zoo, the Glenbow Museum, the Calgary Philharmonic Orchestra. Some volunteers like Dorothy and Marg were or are long time members of the University of Calgary Faculty Women's Club. Others came and went. Their contributions to the greater good of Calgary often went unnoticed, but their deeds lived on to make Calgary one of the best cities in the world.

Anne Aiken, for example, was part of the Tuesday Hiking group in the 1970s, and every time I looked at her recipe for the Wenkchemna Pass cookies, which she brought on one hike, I remembered her comments about ARBI.

Anne used to volunteer at ARBI, the Association for the Rehabilitation of the Brain Injured. ARBI works with individuals who have received or sustained such a severe brain injury that they are not expected to have much of a recovery. Anne worked with only one individual at a time when she volunteered at ARBI. She carried out the physiotherapy and occupational therapy program under the direction of a qualified therapist. She was never interested in the inner workings of the organization but she wanted to help the fledgling group. "Just the basics," she said when I asked her about ARBI recently. "I was not an upfront person. I worked with a girl who had been with the RCMP and had received a severe brain injury on the job. Later I worked with Bill." Anne enjoyed the hands on experience and was thrilled to see the improvement in muscle tone. She was into Yoga, and she used some of those techniques to help.

I hadn't seen Anne for years when my own son Doug sustained a brain injury in 1996. We were told that he would never walk, talk, or know us again. Somewhere in the back of my mind I remembered Anne talking about ARBI. I wondered if it still existed and if it could help my son. I had no idea where Anne was but I checked the phone directory for ARBI.

It did indeed exist. A year or so after my son began attending the day program at ARBI, I ran into Anne at the Westside Club. When I told her that her stories about ARBI had affected our lives she seemed embarrassed. "You first heard about ARBI from me," she said in disbelief. "I thought everyone knew about ARBI. I only wanted to help."

And she did. By volunteering her personal time to help one individual she was one of the contingents of volunteers who helped a small community-based rehabilitation facility grow from the basement of Woodcliff United Church to one of the nation's top organizations to assist persons with brain injuries. By 1990, it had expanded and moved into its own facilities in Spruce Cliff. Later its founder, Audrey Morrice, was awarded an honorary degree and the Governor General's Medal for her pioneering work.

My son attended rehabilitation classes at ARBI for seven years. Many volunteers – some from the University – worked with him. Today he's able to talk on the phone and be understood. In summer 2006 he audited his first university course since his injury. In January 2007, more than 10 years since his injury, he took his first wobbly totally independent steps. The University of Calgary Faculty Women's Club volunteers have supported, enriched, and sustained many lives – often quietly – sometimes one at a time. Each, in her own way, has contributed to help make Calgary a great place to live.

Anne Aiken's Wenkchemna Pass Cookies

```
4 cups      brown sugar
1 ½ cups  oil or 2 cups melted shortening
4              eggs
3 cups      whole wheat flour
2 tsp        baking soda
1 tsp        salt
2 tsp        vanilla
6              large flake oatmeal
(1 cup      raisins)
(1 cup      dates)
```

Linda Heidemann was awarded the Alberta Centennial Medal for her work on behalf of individuals with brain injuries.

Intimate Circles

Special Interest Groups

One of the most successful innovations has been the introduction of the Special Interest Groups in the mid 60's. Although the atmosphere at our regular meetings was lively and friendly, these smaller groups provided an intimate circle for members with common interests. In fact, they provided such an attraction that our Executive recommended membership in the Club as a prerequisite. Here are the histories of a few in the words of their own members:

THE AFTERNOON BOOK CLUB
By Ruth Miller

The Afternoon Book Club has challenged and informed its members since 1964. It was one of the four original interest groups formed that year, with Beth Carson as its first chairman. An evening book club has operated occasionally, but this report deals only with the afternoon group.

Each year books and plays are chosen representative of different periods, nations, and schools of literature, including for example, the work of Sylvia Plath, Tennessee Williams, Shakespeare, Chekov, Dickens, Attwood, Ibsen, Mead, Shaw, Oates, Lessing, Davies, Hesse, Solzhenietszn and Eliot.

Meeting in members' homes the first Wednesday of each month, we enjoy coffee and cakes and a report which includes comment on the author's life, an outline of the work and its place in the literature of the period, and the initial reception of the book. As the group includes members from many national backgrounds, reading of such works as Boll's *The Clown,* Dûrrenmatt's *The Visit,* Faulkner's *The Rievers,* Nedezha

Mandelstam's *Hope Against Hope,* and Grass's *The Tin Drum* is enlivened by first-hand comments on the physical and political background, the effects of translation, and personal anecdotes of locales used in the books. Occasionally, there is a cry for help, as when a professor of modern literature spent an afternoon exploring Kafka with us.

As December is a bad month for reading, January's meeting can be the reading of a play, examining everyone's favorite children's books, or Marlene Peattie's wonderful collection of cook books. We have also sampled Lunchbox Theatre, and the June meeting concludes each year with a delicious pot-luck luncheon..

Sometimes the year's reading follows a theme, such as the literature of the women's movement, but members usually prefer a variety of books each year, from classic novels to biographies, to current novels, to plays and major essays. We like controversy, and how the arguments have soared over Simone de Beauvoir's *Memoirs of a Dutiful Daughter*, or the worth of historic fiction, or Shakespeare's viability in his own time.

The warm friendships that develop from participation in the group would be reward enough in themselves, but we have, in addition, the stimulation of reading a wide range of books and the opportunity of discussing them with a group of interesting and aware people.

THE BRIDGE GROUPS
By Marilyn Goodman

The bridge players have been an active entity within the Faculty Women's Club since the mid sixties when Groups were first introduced. Our bridge groups during the academic year, have traditionally met every second week and, you might say – morning, afternoon, and evening! During the years 1971-76, . . . our husbands joined in sharing many enjoyable evenings as members of a mixed couples group consisting of three tables which met once a month. At times dinner was served first and at other times bridge came first, with tea after. Although only a morning group has been meeting during the past year, we have experimented, since term-end in May with a summer bridge. For us who love the game, it can be considered a year-round pastime. Eight of us met weekly for an afternoon of relaxed playing.

An observation appropriate to our Club's 25th anniversary history is that some of the charter members of our first group are still with us. Because bridge is an international pastime, many newcomers with a variety of ethnic backgrounds have found pleasure as members of the Bridge Interest Groups.

We keep organized by heading each group with a chairman, a volunteer or appointee, whose responsibility it is to arrange a schedule for the homes in which we play and to help arrange for substitutes.

As a long-time participant, I can assure you that our groups have been very sociable and cohesive. They continue to be a viable and enjoyable way of integrating new faculty wives into our University community. Many of our members have served with distinction on the Executive of the

Faculty Women's Club. It can be truly said that this Group has engendered among its members a feeling of belonging and loyalty in relation to the activities of the Faculty Women's Club as a whole.

TRANSACTIONAL ANALYSIS
By Berta Fisher

Over a three-year period in the mid 70's, a number of our members participated in six and eight week sessions of transactional analysis, usually gathering at my home. Essentially, transactional analysis is the concept that within each of us are three states of the ego: Parent - Adult - Child (PAC) which must be brought into balance. In a very relaxed and informal way, our group members analyzed transactions within themselves and between people by reading Eric Berne (*Games People Play*), Muriel James (*Born to Win*), Jess Lair (*I Ain't Much, Baby - But I'm All I've Got*) and the relevant studies of Wilder Penfield, our eminent Canadian. Thomas Harris, the well known author of *I'm OK – You're OK*, became the focus of our explorations. My recollection of these sessions is a gratifying one because we were stimulated and intrigued by the anecdotes of those group members who came to us from very different national and cultural backgrounds. Today, transactional analysis is used in such fields of human endeavor as education, religion, psychology, and daily living skills.

Norris, p. 24-30

Editors' Note: Over the years there have been many other interest groups covering a wide range of topics. A sampling would be Physical Activity, Food, Art, Self Improvement, Service Groups, Newcomers, Investment, Gardening, along with Quilting and Out-to-Lunch Bunch.

Book Club Moments

Carol Marica

I now live in Victoria, BC, and remember a few particular moments with our FWC Book Club. It must have been in the 1970s, and W.P. Kinsella was teaching one year. He writes delightful stories about First Nations people. He came to our Book Club one day and read from his latest book, and then answered our questions. One of us "knowledgeably" asked Kinsella, when you wrote such and such, didn't you really mean this and that?

"No," he said, "I write only for the enjoyment of the story."

Another book club moment: Marlene Peattie gave us the history of cookbooks. It was fascinating and when she was finished, we spontaneously broke into applause. That never happened before or since, during my time there.

A Potpourri of Programs at General Meetings

Since 1997, Speakers and Programs have been Sponsored by Interest Groups.			
Sep 1997	Karen Serrett	Literacy	Adopt-a-Family
Feb 1998	Louise Guy	Climb Every Mountain	Hiking
Apr 1998	Liz Westbrook	Creative Science Fiction	Book Club
Sep 1998	Pat Morgan	Lighten Up Your Life	Mothers & Youngsters
Feb 1999	Sharon Tate	Healing Scents	Newcomers Plus
Apr 1999	Kathy Hansen	Environmental Illness	Out to Lunch Bunch
Sep 1999	Art Laurenson	A Visit to Antarctica	Yoga
Feb 2000	Millennium Tea	Memory Book	Executive
Apr 2000	Fundraiser	Silent Auction	All Members
Sep 2000	Marg Oliver	Wandering the World: Nepal to the Yucatan	Bible Study
Apr 2001	Margaret Brown	Spring in My Garden	Book Club Too
May 2001	Sue White	Farewell Tea	Executive
Sep 2001	Val Warner	Secrets to Saving Your Sanity	Revolving Potluck
Apr 2002	Tim Goddard	The Kosovo Educator Project	Bridge
Sep 2002	Sharon Sullivan	Bees and Your Garden	Coffee and Chat
Apr 2003	Fundraiser	Silent Auction	All Members
Sep 2003	Gail Niinimaa	Cochrane Tapestry	Quilting
Apr 2004	Sally Goddard	Subbing in the City	Arts Sampler
Sep 2004	Isobel Dixon & Verna Sorensen	Hiking the Himalayas in Nepal	Hiking
Apr 2005	Sheldon Smithens	Antiques and Memories	Executive
Sep 2005	Gisèle Villeneuve	*Visiting Elizabeth*, a reading by the author	Book Club
Apr 2006	Susie Rod & Ilse Salkauskas	Celebrating the Fine Arts	Executive
Sep 2006	Eileen Lohka	Inscribing Memory…in Bits & Pieces	Executive
Apr 2007	FUNraiser	Dress through the Decades	All Members
Sep 2007	Debbie Marshall	Finding Roberta MacAdams: A Writer's Journey Into the Great War	Book Committee
Apr 2008	Polly Knowlton Cockett	Whispering Signs: Art, Science, & Local Landscapes	Executive
Sep 2008	Adriana Guarinos	UNICEF: Who we are? What we do?	Executive
Apr 2009	Readings by Authors	Golden Threads: Women Creating Community	All Members

Restaurant in Review
Vera Simony

Silver Inn Restaurant – 2702 Centre Street N

On November 1st, 1983, eight members of the Out-to-Lunch Bunch enjoyed a variety of Peking cuisine dishes. The meal began with green tea, followed by "3 kinds of meat soup" ($6.50 for 4). Entrée choices tried were: deep fried fish in sweet & sour sauce ($6.95), quick fried prawns with baby corn and mushrooms ($7.95), quick fried chicken slices with broccoli ($5.95), deep fried shredded beef with chili ($7.50), four vegetables – gr. pepper, celery, mushrooms and bamboo shoots ($5.95), plain fried rice ($3.75) and steamed rice ($2.00). There are, of course, many more choices in all categories. Those tasted were very good. For dessert we had mixed toffee apple and banana ($7.50). No coffee is served. There are a few parking stalls behind the restaurant. By the time you read this, we will have enjoyed the annual Christmas buffet lunch at the U of C Dining Centre in December.

Faculty Women's Club Newsletter, January 1984

Cratering Cakes and Willing Takers
Dorothy Krueger

They presented it to me on the last day of classes in 1959; the Grade 10 girls came to my classroom with a well-chosen gift – a black and gold glass cake tray and eight matching glasses "for entertaining the professors," they said! I was leaving this beloved high school to marry and go "out west" to Calgary where a new university was in its initial stages.

We did entertain professors to evening coffee and desserts (Lady Baltimore cake!!) and soon realized they were much less formidable people than I had imagined! Although I was unfamiliar with the altitude of Calgary I baked three cakes from my mother's prize sponge cake recipe, all rising beautifully, and then cratering as they cooled. Not until I read directions on a cake mix box did I realize one had to "adjust" the recipe for the altitude or accept the fact that some "eastern" (Canada!) recipes would not work at all!

In the 70s as the University grew, FWC spread out to initiate various Interest Groups. When I proposed starting a Bible Study Group, the questioning voice of program director Betty Schofield resounded, "Will there be any takers?" In spite of my very real doubts and with much trepidation, I announced the group at the fall general meeting. Cathie Nicoll, a seasoned teacher of university students, agreed to lead the inductive style studies in a non-threatening, non-judgemental manner allowing freedom to question and inquire. It has been a most positive, rewarding endeavour which, after thirty years, continues to this day. As well, Book Club and Yoga classes have been wonderfully informative and constructive.

A Calgary Psalm 2005

Kitty Gillott, Anne Paul, Evelyn Braun, Dorothy Krueger, Betty Giles, Ruth Armstrong, Martha Singh, and Beth Young

Let everything praise the Lord and give thanks,
The university, the professors and students, the secretaries and technicians,
Let them praise Him with music, with guitar, organ and singing.
Let the great city praise Him for corn, cattle and oil
And all the people who live therein.
Let the mountain passes praise Him,
The bear, moose, elk, wolves and swans,
Let all the wildlife praise Him.

Let us all give thanks to the Lord
For the riches we possess in scholarship,
In food and in resources.
And let us all give thanks for the Faculty Women's Club fellowship
Which we have so enjoyed.
Praise the Lord!

For the magnificence of your creation
We praise and thank you.
For the unity in diversity we see around us
We praise and thank you.
For Art and Literature, Music and Science
We praise you, O Lord.

Lord you have blessed us all these thirty years,
We have rejoiced in your mercies
But sometimes we have doubted and
You seemed far away from us.
We have grieved over the deaths of Valerie, Arlene, Edna, Rita, and Ainslie
But are confident they are with you.
You remind us so often that you are always present,
Always loving and always sovereign.

Lord as we come to Thee asking for help
Our problems are many and distressing
And cause us needless worry,
Unless you give us a light and direction.
Help us to resolve them with your help.

God is good!, we cry, when the fruits of Summer fall into our laps.
God is good!, we find out, when we dig for the sweet roots
Almost frozen in the ground in Fall.
God is good!, the same yesterday, today and in His tomorrow.
Where there will be no more death or sadness, pain nor tears.

Written on the occasion of the 50th anniversary of FWC and the 30th anniversary of the Bible Study Group.

Commemorating Our Fortieth
Program of Events: 1996-1997

Executive

Honorary President	Sue White
Past President	Linda Crouch
President	Tannis Teskey
Vice President	Karen Serrett
Secretary	Eileen Lohka
Treasurer/Membership	Kate Bentley
Social Convenor	Lorri Post
Newsletter	Martha Laflamme
Member at Large	Jennifer Bushman

General Meetings — Olympic Volunteer Centre

September 26 — "Parade of Past Presidents"

April 24 — "Bid for the Boxes" Silent Auction
Revives and old Alberta Tradition

Special Events

October 23 — 40th Anniversary Commemorative Dinner
Faculty Club, Husbands are Invited

December 4 — Christmas Luncheon
Crowchild Inn

February 20 — Blues Beater
Judy Hunt, co-owner of J.B. Bags
"How to Choose and Pack your Luggage"

Rising from the Ashes
Ilse Anysas-Salkauskas

I live near Cochrane, Alberta, on a hill with a view of the Alberta Foothills and Rocky Mountains and am strongly influenced by my visually rich ever-changing surroundings. In 2002 there were several fires burning in the area for a month and I was surrounded by a grey haze, smelled smoke and watched little pieces of burnt embers fall from the sky. Two years later I saw those same burnt areas rejuvenated by the spring and summer rains creating new visually rich colors, textures and moods. This rejuvenation inspired my 3D leather tapestry.

I create my representational leather tapestries using colorful overlapping layers of hand cut split cow hide strips that are knotted together and attached to a wooden header. These tactile, free -flowing layers create sculptural depth and when moved, undulate and change just as my environment changes from day to day.

In 2006 the Alberta Craft Council invited me to exhibit this tapestry in their "All About Alberta" exhibition. The exhibition travelled from 2006 to 2009 to the following venues: Smithsonian Folklife Festival, Canadian Embassy and Organization of American States, Washington, DC; Alberta Craft Council, Edmonton, AB; Nickle Arts Museum and Gallery, University of Calgary, Calgary, AB; Salon des métiers d`art, Montreal, QC; Cheongju, International Craft Biennale, Cheongju, Korea; Saskatchewan Craft Council Gallery, Saskatoon, SK; Devon House Gallery, St. John's, NL.

122 cm w 204 cm h Leather

Hiking and Travelling
Marg Oliver

Hiking – what is it? It's getting out on a trail in the mountains, hills, or even the prairies, breathing wonderful fresh air, trading the hustle and noise of the city for the peace, joy, and quiet of the mountains, woodlands, or meadows, enjoying the profusion of wildflowers and birdsong, eating lunch while perched on a rock, with a grand panorama spread out before you. For me, it has also been discovering new trails and new destinations and, from a ridge or mountain top, surveying areas already visited, and many more possibilities for future exploration. What two activities could be more enjoyable than hiking and travelling? Most of my friends associate me with either or both.

Hiking has been a very large and important part of my life since I discovered mountains in the summer of 1952, on days off from working at the Banff Springs Hotel, slinging hash in the Beanery (working on the line in the staff eatery). The Canadian Rockies were my first ever mountains, and they claimed me, as I hiked and explored on my days off.

The "travel itch" actually struck after university graduation in 1949, and two years working in the University Science Library and a medical research lab. My friend Hilda and I said "enough" and, via "thumb" in the summer, ended up in Whitehorse, Yukon. We soon took the train to Skagway and got steeped in the history of the Klondike Gold Rush. Hilda returned home to England, but I loved the north and stayed until February, experiencing a long, dark, cold winter. I worked in an office for the Canadian Army, and enjoyed new friends and activities. Little did I know that this introduction to the north would induce me to travel four more times to Canada's northern extremities in future years!

The "itch" was getting active again and so, from Juneau, Alaska, I sailed the Inside Passage to Seattle, and by bus moved on to California, Oklahoma, and Kansas (to visit old neighbors and new friends met in the north). Then it was home to Winnipeg. I was enjoying this wandering life and sailed in April for England to meet some home friends in London. The Queen's coronation in 1953 was a grand occasion – I even had a seat on the Mall to witness the pageantry. Having arranged waitressing jobs for the summer on the Isle of Wight, a friend and I spent our time off exploring the island – I was discovering history. Four of us cycled through southwest England, Wales, the Lake District, and Scotland in the autumn, before I returned to London for more visiting. Home beckoned and I returned in time for Christmas with family, and to resume a friendship with Tom, whom I'd known since high school, and with whom I'd maintained a correspondence since university. The rest is history.

We were married in 1954 and lived in Edmonton for two years before settling in Calgary. Tom left the oil patch in 1959 for the University, establishing the Department of Geology. Family life somewhat curtailed hiking and travelling activities, although there were many excursions to the mountains usually accompanied by "Carry me, Daddy," "How much further?" or, when the children were older, "Which way did they go?" as we reached a trail junction, and found no one in sight. Our 1967-68 sabbatical in England gave great opportunities for exploratory trips in all directions.

Back home, life continued as before, until the Faculty Women's Club embarked on the formation of Interest Groups in September 1971, and I started the first Hiking group. After a meeting of interested persons, the group got underway immediately, with five participants: Margaret Johnston, Linda Harrington, Patricia Krasinski, Sheena Davidson, and I as organizer. Tuesday was the chosen day – the only one I had free! Four hikes were held until the group recessed for the winter.

In the spring of 1972, the "word" had spread, and every week saw new ladies joining the ranks until there were twenty-eight on the roster (although not all were FWC members). There were three months of spring hiking, exploring the prairies, hills, badlands and mountains, and mountain hikes in the summer and autumn. The group continued enthusiastically and November found us cross country skiing, although the winter was much like this recent one (2006-07) when we walked more than we skied. Over the next few years, numbers fluctuated as lungs and legs were tested, until we settled at twenty-five. Since then, the group has been on the trail fifty weeks of the year, with two weeks off at Christmas.

And so the Hiking group continued its outings, hiking or skiing as seasons and conditions dictated. Seasonal windups were held (four seasons – four windups), usually at a mountain restaurant after a special hike with attendance prizes awarded. The Fall Windup/Christmas parties were potlucks in a member's home. Annual summer backpacking trips began in 1974, and winter and summer lodge trips in 1976 and 1979 respectively, all progressing from one night to four, which have taken us to destinations near and far, always seeking new experiences.

In the early years, the Hiking group had many "outsiders" in its ranks, but the University women who participated, once or many times, included: Estelle Boak, Dorothy Groves, Marjorie Freiberg, Peggy Magee, Barbara Laychuk*, Dorothy Sharman, Jan Gregory, Jana Stevens, Penny (Bayer) Morris*, Joan Wing, Sharon Fairborn, Judy Truax, Joyce Sugars, Jean Gaucher*, Dorothy Linder, Dot (Conklin) Hughes*, Ilse Salkauskas, Pam Morrow, Regina Shedd, Linda Heidemann, Angela Rokne, Ruth Love, Penny Storey, Linda MacCannell, Barb Stevenson, Hella Friedmann, Sharon Gladman, Louise Guy, Vreni Gretener*, Judy (Heintz) Hurd, Mary Vermeulen, Grace McGregor, Meta Mamo, Edith Zwirner*, Betty Dahlie, Helen Tavares*, Verna

Sorensen, Charlotte Bachelor*. (*indicates those still active in the group). Several visitors to the University also hiked with us: Betty Abetti, Uta Bohl, Anne Graham, Rosemary Penner. The Tuesday Hikers, now numbering twenty-six, have continued with many of the earlier members, plus Ruth Becker, the only new University associate. Some of our ladies have reached the "non-active" or "not-too-active" stage, but maintain their membership and attend parties and meetings.

Leading the Tuesday Hikers for 35+ years has been a labor of love – planning weekly hikes, major trips, meetings, keeping records, etc. The Tuesday Hikers have hiked or skied fifty weeks of each year (taking two weeks off at Christmas; in 35+ years we have made over 2000 hikes, totaled over 23 000 kilometres on the trails, and climbed almost 600 000 metres of altitude. Over the years we have celebrated birthdays with: "your birthday – you bring the cake," and with special songs for 65th, 70th, 75th and 80th, memberships of 20, 25, 30, and 35 years (with a certificate and various awards); and, of course, the club's anniversaries, starting with the tenth and each successive five years until the 35th in September, 2006 – all in the form of a special lodge trip and/or a city dinner gala event. Did I ever dream, in September 1971, that we'd still be out there 35 years later?

In 1976, with a keen, active, and congenial group of twenty-five, we decided to close membership and secede from the Faculty Women's Club to become a private club, henceforth known as the Tuesday Hikers. We have continued, as the Tuesday Hikers, ever since. I suggested other names – The Tuesday Skikers (to include the skiing activity) and Oliver's Twits, but neither took hold. A new FWC Hiking group was formed at the time and continues every Thursday to this day.

Once the children had fledged, Tom and I enjoyed many years of escapes in our trusty Volkswagen campervan to western and eastern Canada and US. For three months in 1986, with a rented campervan, we explored and hiked in both islands of New Zealand; Hawaii and Fiji were visited enroute and on return.

Tom never cared for off-the-continent travel (NZ excepted), but always encouraged me to scratch my travel itch with an annual foreign trip. The first such was to Nepal in 1986 where I hiked the three-week circuit of Annapurna, climbing to an altitude of 17 771 feet at the Thorang La (Pass). To traverse so much country on this route and to be exposed to the changing topography, habitations, customs, and religions of the various ethnic groups was quite eye opening, and set the stage for future perambulations and discoveries.

The Austrian Alps, Tuscany in Italy, the Cotwolds and Hadrian's Wall in England, Patagonia in South America, and the Chilkoot Trail in Yukon, were primarily hiking trips – and what a variety of terrain, history, and cultures! Cruising down the Mackenzie River and rafting the Nahanni River were more novel ways of exploring the north.

My interest in ancient and other cultures, and nature in general, has taken me to Mexico, Africa, Belize, Costa Rica, Turkey and Greece, China, Ecuador, Bolivia, Peru and the Galapagos, Madagascar and Indian Ocean Islands, Australia, Greenland, Baffin Island, Egypt, Thailand and Cambodia, and Honduras. I revel in ruins of all kind – what stories they tell!

Mostly I've travelled with a friend, but often "alone" in a group where I have made new friends, with many of whom I still correspond, and some I have visited over the years.

Since Tom's passing in 1997, I see no reason to stay home when my love of travelling and discovery can be satisfied with one to three trips a year. 2007 will see me rafting and hiking in the Grand Canyon, hiking in Switzerland, and cruising the St. Lawrence River. There are still many places in this world which beckon, and I hope to make many more journeys before my final "escape" from this world.

Into a Land of Fire and Ice, Mosquitoes and Grizzlies: Russia's Kamchatka Peninsula

Pamela Harris

In July 2001, I was privileged to visit a part of Russia that few people in the west have ever seen – the Kamchatka Peninsula. I travelled there with my husband, a University of Calgary geography professor.

Three tectonic plates meet at Kamchatka to produce a spectacular chain of about 200 active volcanoes, a thousand kilometres long, which are part of an island arc stretching from Japan to the Aleutians. Some of the volcanoes have been extinct for millennia, often filled with aquamarine crater lakes, but about 20 are erupting at any one time. Mt. Klyuchevskaya is the highest volcano at 4750 metres. It lies in the northern part of the peninsula and last erupted in 1994, when the ash disrupted flights from North America to SE Asia.

Some of the volcanoes have smoking fumaroles, and the discharge of heat and energy in this way relieves the pressure within the ground. Many are snowcapped, even in summer, as Kamchatka has extremely cold winters and short summers. Kamchatka is separated from the Russian mainland on the west by the Sea of Okhotsk. To the south lies the Pacific, with the Bering Sea to the northeast. We visited all three coastlines, studying coastal plant communities.

You have to have special permission, written on your visa, to visit this part of Russia. On entry, the authorities at the airport were sure we must have been with other seniors who were on an icebreaker tour. We finally managed to convince them that we were participants in a seminar and that the organizers were to meet us.

We were taken to one of the two best hotels in the city. It was fairly old and bare, but reasonably clean. The view from our window was of high concrete apartment buildings, often in need of repair, with a football field between. Many of the buildings were covered with graffiti, giving an impression of despair. The thin mattresses were covered with uncomfortable wire mesh, but since I have arthritis, I always carry an air mattress and that proved invaluable.

Young people on the street looked fairly happy and attractively dressed, the girls with big bows in their hair and wearing miniskirts. Older people looked as if they have had a very rough time, with alcoholism rife. Remnants of the communist system remain, with people having to get permission to leave town even for a weekend, since the Peninsula is the main military training area for Russia.

The 10 000 or so brown bears on the Peninsula are obviously well fed and don't bother people on the whole, though there was one instance of a Japanese scientist who was pulled from his tent by a bear, and eaten. There has been at least one TV documentary on Kamchatka. Charlie Russell and Maureen Enns have spent several summers studying the bears, and have written an interesting book, *Grizzly Heart: Living Without Fear Among the Brown Bears of Kamchatka.*

One of the day trips we took was the journey of a lifetime. We boarded an army helicopter and flew 150 kilometres north to the Valley of the Geysers, one of the three largest areas of boiling mud pools and geysers in the world. We flew through the valley with snowcapped volcanoes on either side, some topped with craters. It was awe inspiring and we took many photos. At one point the pilot chased a bear, which seemed rather mean.

We landed at the head of the valley and had a salmon lunch. Then we were taken on a conducted tour up and down rickety wooden steps to view the many mud pools and geysers. On the way back, the helicopter landed in the Uzon caldera, containing a ten kilometre crater with steaming lakes, ringed by berry bushes. I'm sure there were bears hiding in the bushes as they had left plenty of tracks in the mud.

A small group of us accompanied the leaders on a two week plant hunting trip. The organizers had to change the itinerary due to low snow and erupting volcanoes and our three nights of wilderness camping turned into ten. Our two leaders did their best in the way of comfort and cooking. Our usual fare was buckwheat porridge, rice pudding, tinned meats, and lots of potatoes, tomatoes and cucumbers.

The first campsite was on black volcanic ash, close to a volcano which had erupted in the 1950s, with the subsequent ash killing the surrounding larch forest. This site was bare of vegetation which means there were no mosquitoes. Water for cooking had to be trucked in from many kilometres away. A small container was hung off a large stump so that we could get a drip or two to clean ourselves. Our toilet was behind a collection of dead larch trunks with mother and baby bear tracks all around. There were tiny poppies and other colorful flowers struggling for life in the ash. As the Bible says, "The desert shall blossom as a rose."

Between the first campsite and the second, we stayed in a town called Esso in a hotel, where underground water heated the whole area. The inhabitants grow vegetables in greenhouses, even out of season. The people of Esso greeted us warmly and one lady prepared a delicious salmon meal. We were also treated to a wonderful song and dance show put on by the local Evian people, a group of Indian-Eskimo extraction. They wore beautifully handcrafted leather and fur costumes. Their dances were vigorous and noisy, but others, like the swan dance, were like a poignant ballet. We counted ourselves lucky to be able to include this wonderful performance in our trip.

Our next campground was at the site of a stream, which meant vegetation and many more mosquitoes. Our last campsite was in the high vegetation near the Sea of Okhotsk. In order to pitch our tents we had to crush down the enormous iris, rose, and lily plants, which seemed a crime. We also found the attitude toward bears rather cavalier. The young son of one leader slept in an open tent among mosquitoes and food, and one couple found they had pitched their tent close to a bear "nest." An injury to my husband's foot prevented us going on the final hike of the trip. The rest of the group crossed a boulder strewn stream with water up to their waists. The richness of the flora on these hikes was simply amazing – some of the species have crossed the Bering Strait into Alaska.

Although we spent ten days sleeping in a tent and coping with mosquitoes, it was a wonderful trip.

Pam Harris has volunteered extensively for many organizations, including Unicef and the Kerby Centre. This excerpt from October 2003 is one of her many articles in the Kerby News.

Hello from South Africa
Robin Barclay

Having my sister, Dinah, visit Cape Town after our trip to Kruger provided Robert, Laura and me with a wonderful opportunity to revisit our favorite haunts in and around Cape Town one last time before flying back to Canada after our year long stay during Robert's sabbatical at University of Cape Town (UCT). One morning, Dinah and I rode the cable car to the top of Table Mountain. The ride takes just under five minutes (but feels like an eternity to those of us with a fear of heights!), and the car rotates so that the views change from city to mountain to sea. Quite spectacular! It was a beautifully clear day, so the 360° views of Robben Island, Table Bay, False Bay, and the Peninsula, from the paths which crisscross the summit, were spectacular. We were early enough that, at least initially, it felt as though we were alone on top of the mountain. A rare treat!

From the mountain, we decided to head downtown to Greenmarket Square and the shops and craft markets at the Victoria and Alfred Waterfront, but were stopped en route by the police, who informed us that there was a demonstration in the City Bowl and it wasn't advisable for us to proceed. These noisy and sometimes violent protests by local people against their municipal governments, who the people accuse of not providing even the most basic services (quite rightly, from our perspective), are becoming more common, and spreading throughout the country (having started in the northeast). This was not the first time we had been waylaid by such a demonstration. When returning from St. Lucia in May, we were intercepted just outside Port Elizabeth by the police, who suggested that we detour around the town because of a large, tire-burning, window-smashing mob. Having seen the horrific conditions in which millions of people in this country live, the only thing that surprises me is that the protests didn't start years ago. It has been over ten years since the end of apartheid - a very long time for the people living in such squalor to wait. If the government doesn't act quickly, I fear that these protests will become more common, and news of them will frighten away already wary tourists, who contribute significantly to the South African economy. Instead of the Waterfront, Dinah and I visited Kirstenbosch National Botanical Gardens, where the protea, my favorite flowers, were just beginning to bloom. We did visit the Waterfront and Greenmarket Square on another day, and Dinah and I had fun bartering with the vendors and did our bit to bolster the economy.

Another day, wanting to show Dinah the cave at the top of Table Mountain that is home to the fruit bats that Robert has been studying, we hiked up the mountain along a challenging trail which begins with 532 stairs. Although there are 350 paths to the summit, we like this particular path because the stairs usually ensure that we encounter few other hikers. It was a clear day and, as we climbed, the views became steadily more impressive. Once at the summit of the 1087 m flat-topped mountain, we hiked to the rocky outcrop where the cave is located, and then spent half an hour scrambling over, around and under countless large boulders, until we found ourselves at the cave. By the time we stood in the entrance, some three hours after we set out, we were tired, hot and rather muddy. Fortunately, we had not scared the bats deeper into the cave with our approach, as has often happened, so Dinah was able to have a good look at her first fruit bats, which were considerably larger than any bats she had seen previously. Well worth the effort!

I took Dinah on a tour of the Cape Peninsula, one of my favorite places, which we have visited often in the past year. We drove our usual circular route, stopping on the way south along the east coast to visit the penguins, which were as comical as ever. We wandered through the craft shops in Kalk Bay and Simon's Town, the most charming of the False Bay towns, with streets lined with lovely Victorian buildings. We climbed up to the lighthouse at Cape Point, where the views are always fantastic, and visited the Cape of Good Hope, where we took the requisite photograph of Dinah beside the sign which indicated that we were at the southwesternmost point of the continent. We returned to Cape Town along the spectacular Chapman's Peak Drive on the west coast, just in time to watch the sun setting over the Atlantic. That winding, ten kilometre drive must rate as one of the top in the world, with cliffs plunging straight into the ocean, dwarfing the vehicles snaking along its side. Dinah agreed that it was somewhat of a relief to reach the end of the section where the road winds its way under a massive, gravity-defying rock cantilever that looks as though it might collapse at any moment. After all our talk of pilfering baboons at the various tourist spots along the peninsula, we didn't encounter a single baboon all day. The park rangers and their slingshots seem to have had a considerable impact!

The highlight of Dinah's visit to Cape Town came near the end of her stay. While Laura was on the road with the UCT volleyball team, Robert, Dinah and I took a guided tour of a township. This was something that Robert and I had wanted to do all year but had hesitated, fearing that we would be treating the people who live in the townships like animals in a zoo, gawking at them and snapping photos from behind the windows of a bus. We had read that some township residents see these tours as an intrusion, while others feel that they are benefiting from the financial and cultural exchanges the tours offer. After much debate and considerable research, the three of us selected Inkululeko Tours, a small tour company whose guides are township residents and who encourage their guests to get out of the vehicle and interact with the people. While we all set off with some trepidation, by the end of the day we were very thankful that we had gone. Robert and I agreed that it was another highlight of our year and wished that Laura had been with us.

Our tour was led by Gladstone Pasiwe, a black in his early twenties, who has been a township resident all his life. We were ferried about in a minibus, and our tour companions included a group of six Italians, who spoke little English, and a couple from New Zealand. Our tour began with a drive through District Six, a large piece of vacant land on the slopes of Devil's Peak, adjacent to the City Centre. Originally the sixth municipal district of Cape Town, it was once an impoverished but vibrant neighborhood, which housed people from every walk of life – musicians, traders, teachers, craftsmen, petty criminals, hookers, and pimps. It was one of South Africa's most inspired and creative communities, producing poets, jazz musicians, and writers. Blacks, whites and coloreds lived and worked side by side. However, in 1966, sixty thousand people were forcibly removed from District Six by apartheid hardliners who, wanting to limit interaction among races, passed a law making it illegal for people of different races to live in the same neighborhood. The government declared District Six a whites-only area and renamed it Zonnebloem ("sunflower"). Blacks and coloreds (the apartheid name for people of mixed descent) were forcibly removed, and their houses flattened by bulldozers. When the bulldozers finally moved out, all that remained were a few churches and mosques, which still stand today. In an ironic attempt at morality, religious buildings were exempt from the demolition order. The community was relocated piecemeal to segregated areas – the coloreds to the Cape Flats (a name that accurately describes both the geography and psychology of the area), and the blacks further east to the "townships" or "black suburbs" of Langa, Khayalitsha and Guguletu. Today, District Six remains largely vacant, as even hardened capitalists spurned development in protest. Only the state-funded Cape Technicon was ever built on the land. Restitution is finally underway, and construction of homes for some of the evicted families started in 2003. It is hoped that by returning the land to the original families, the damage done to the national psyche may be reversed. Until then, the vacant land is a constant and sobering reminder of what took place.

After driving through the area, Gladstone took us to the District Six Museum, which is housed in one of the churches that was spared. There, we admired an impressive collection of historical photographs, paintings, books, artifacts, and physical remains such as street signs, most of which were donated by former residents. There was an especially poignant display of the dreaded pass books, which controlled and limited the movements of coloreds and blacks. All non-whites were forced to carry these passport-like books at all times, and were thrown in prison if found without one. David, who is colored, still has his pass book. Also of particular interest was a layout of the streets and buildings of District Six, which was painted onto the floor of the main room of the museum. Former residents had signed their names where their homes or businesses once stood. It was a fascinating museum, and we wished we could have stayed longer.

From District Six, we headed to Langa ("sun" in Xhosa) township, Gladstone's home and Cape Town's second oldest township. We drove into the township through its only entrance, designed that way originally to allow the police easy control of the inhabitants. Once intended for 40 000 people, Langa is now home to over 100 000 blacks. Driving along the main street, my first impression was of an impoverished but vibrant community. Minibus taxis, the only means of transport available to most residents, littered the streets. There were people everywhere, many just standing around, no doubt among the sixty percent in Langa who are unemployed. We passed an odd assortment of small, dilapidated buildings which offered a peculiar mix of goods and services – a grocery store, HIV/Aids clinic (Langa has one of the highest levels of HIV/AIDS in South Africa), library, braiding salon, jeweler, cell phone shop, environmental centre, nursery school, church, high school (there are two high schools and five elementary schools in Langa, all with classes of fifty to sixty students), arts and craft centre, shebeen (pub), and traditional healer. Street vendors, with their wares spread neatly on tarpaulins which covered the sidewalks, offered everything from freshly plucked chickens and firewood to coat hangers and wooden giraffes. Although we didn't see them, we learned that Langa has a sports stadium, several parks, three public baths and a swimming pool.

The first homes we passed were decrepit three-storey buildings, which were originally built as hostels for migrant workers. During the apartheid era, when cities were designated for whites only, workers were forced to leave their wives and children in rural homelands or "bantustans" while they worked in the cities. Since apartheid, some of these former hostels have been renovated to provide dormitory style housing for families. We stopped outside one hostel and Gladstone led us inside. After climbing a rickety, external staircase, we found ourselves in a small living room that was dark, musty and almost devoid of furniture. In one corner of the room was a kitchen, which consisted of a sink with a cold water tap and a hot plate. A small table and a few wooden chairs took up most of the floor space. Off the central living room were four crowded bedrooms. Two of the small bedrooms held two twin beds each, while the other two, slightly larger, bedrooms each held three twin beds. Gladstone explained that each small bed was shared by a married couple. The worldly goods of each couple were stored under or above their bed. What few clothes they possessed were on hangers that were hung on nails in the walls. Needless to say, there was little space and no privacy. The children of the ten couples slept together on the floor of the central room. There was no bathroom. There was electricity, but Gladstone told us that few families in the dormitories can afford it. Many of the adults living there are unemployed. Kerosene lamps, the cause of many tragic township fires, provided dim lighting. Windows were tiny and overlooked adjacent hostels, and it was clear that the rooms would be stiflingly hot in summer and very cold and damp in winter. We were shocked to discover that this small, five-room dormitory was the home of twenty adults and goodness knows how many children. Communal toilets and showers were located in another building. In one bedroom, we found two grandmothers who were babysitting their grandsons while the boys' mothers were at work. When I admired the two toddlers, the grandmothers asked me about my children. I regretted not having photographs of Graham and Laura with me, which would have made communication a little easier. In another, we found an older gentlemen resting on his bed. He seemed glad to see us and eager to talk, asking us where we were from and how we had travelled to South Africa. As I have on a number of occasions this year, I wished I had a small atlas with me. If they felt we were intruding, they hid it well. They were friendly and welcoming, and we enjoyed our visit with them.

Leaving the dormitory, we walked down the street towards another renovated hostel. We were immediately surrounded by children, who were home on a school holiday. Some slipped their hands into ours and accompanied us down the street. I could have taken them all home with me. They were surprisingly well dressed and healthy looking, and their large, dark eyes and huge, white smiles were irresistible. Many asked for money, but we had been given strict instructions by Gladstone not to give them money, candy or any other handout. Apparently, it didn't take these resourceful children very long to learn that tourists visiting the townships were handing out money and food, and the children started skipping school so that they could be the recipients. Tour operators were asked by the schools to put a stop to the handouts. It broke my heart to have to turn the children down.

The second hostel we visited had also been renovated to accommodate families, but was a considerable improvement over the one with the dormitories. It had been modified into small apartments, which offered much more privacy and space. The apartment we visited was the home of a couple and their son and three daughters. The three young girls were there to greet us. The apartment had a small L-shaped living space, with a couch, bookshelves and a kitchen with a sink, two-burner hotplate and small refrigerator. Off this central living area were the parents' small bedroom and a tiny bathroom. The home had cold water only. The children slept in the central living space, presumably on the couch and floor. The apartment was spotlessly clean and tidy. The only picture adorning the walls was a high school graduation photograph of an elder son. The apartment was small and sparse, but it was a big step up from the dormitories. Most of the families living in these apartments have a small but steady income.

Leaving the second hostel, we took the opportunity to wander down the street. Apart from the litter and abject poverty, it could have been any suburban street. A group of teenage boys was playing a noisy game of soccer on the street. Laundry was hung outdoors to dry. Women stood chatting while their youngsters peered out at us from behind their mothers' skirts. Boarding the bus again, we drove to another, more prosperous area of the township. There we found rows of identical, low-cost, matchbox houses. These homes had a front door opening on to a living room, from which doors led to one or two bedrooms. Each house had a small kitchen and bathroom but, in many, there was still only cold water. Gladstone told us that this was his neighborhood.

From the residential area, we returned to the commercial district, where we stopped to visit the traditional healer. The healer's large shack was dimly lit, musty and chaotic. We were greeted by a large tortoise, which was wandering in the entrance way. The dirt floor and several large tables that filled every available space in the dilapidated shack, were covered with all manner of peculiar objects – feathers, potted plants, bones, sea shells, dried flowers, roots, mushrooms, turtle shells, bark, and dirt. We had to duck to avoid seeds, dried plants, python skins, animal skulls and all manner of strange things which hung from the low ceiling. After a brief chat with the healer, who looked ancient, we left, relieved to return to fresh air and sunshine and determined to remain healthy for the duration of our stay. Outside the healer's shack, we were accosted by several street vendors, who directed us to their displays. As always, we sought out vendors who were offering crafts that they had made themselves, as it always fascinating to watch them work and listen to them talk with such enthusiasm about their work. Some of the crafts were quite lovely and, after some token bartering, I purchased a print of an elephant that is pieced from banana leaves.

Our last stop in the township was at a daycare which Gladstone's company sponsors with the fees that it earns from its tours. When we pulled up outside the tiny building which housed the daycare, little smiling faces peered out at us through the large, front window. Twenty-three children were being cared for by two friendly and efficient women. Most were the children of single mothers who work. In South Africa, only the elderly and single mothers receive financial aid, with the result that many young, single girls become pregnant so that they may collect welfare. There were six babies in one small room and seventeen toddlers in a second, slightly larger, room. It was so crowded in the daycare that we had to take turns going inside. Two infants lay sleeping on a blanket on the floor at our feet. There was little furniture and there were no toys or books. It was heartbreaking. I took some comfort in learning that the children are fed a hot breakfast and lunch every day. The toddlers crowded at the window and waved to us as we drove away.

In many ways, the township was far more civilized than I had expected. I was of the impression, from what I had seen from the highway when passing countless townships over the past year, that all township residents lived in crumbling shacks of wood, plastic sheeting and corrugated metal. I hadn't realized that those "informal settlements" (a wonderful euphemism for a slum!) of dilapidated shacks that lie on the periphery of every township are not typical of what lies within. I was surprised and relieved to discover that people in the townships actually live in dormitories, apartments, and houses, decrepit and appalling though many of them may be. The reason for the slums which surround the townships is simple. When apartheid ended and people's movements were no longer restricted, so many blacks flocked to the cities from the bantustans in search of employment, that not all of them could be accommodated in the townships. In desperation, the new arrivals constructed temporary or "informal" shacks next to the townships, where they could live until housing in the townships became available. More than ten years after apartheid, most are still living in those temporary shacks. The government is desperately trying to build enough low-cost housing to accommodate them all, but it is an onerous task, as the need keeps growing. Some estimates put the number of unemployed blacks arriving annually in South Africa from other parts of the continent at well over a million. I must admit that I was rather relieved to learn that our tour would not include a visit to one of the shacks which surround Langa, although we did drive past them. I had seen quite enough deprivation and suffering for one day and, in the informal settlement, it would only get worse.

While our visit to the township was very difficult and left me feeling saddened and helpless, I was thankful that I went. I believe that I have a much greater appreciation of how a large segment of the population of this country lives, and I certainly have an even greater respect for those perpetually cheerful and hopeful people.

It is hard to believe that our sabbatical is coming to an end. The year has passed so quickly and included so many memorable moments. If ever you have the opportunity to visit South Africa, I would highly recommend it. Cape Town is described as one of the most beautiful cities in the world with good reason. The surrounding country is magnificent, and the people are a delight. I would not hesitate to stay longer if it were possible.

Excerpted from Sabbatical Newsletter 16, 23 July 2005

Dog Walking in Calgary
Lynn Williams

When I moved to Calgary in the fall of 2001, I was fortunate enough to join a wonderful group of women who walked their dogs once a week, choosing a variety of parks in Calgary. Although I do not own a dog now, I have in the past and missed the canine experience. So in the five years since I moved here, I have gotten to know various different parks in Calgary, a great group of dogs, and their equally great owners. We have since expanded our repertoire to walk twice a week; though the Tuesday morning walk is officially called the FWC Wiking Group (a wike being somewhere between a walk and a hike), the dogs still join us.

The dogs are all different breeds and therefore sizes. One thing that interests me most about them is their wonderful names: Oggy, Cropper, Braxton, Sport, Stamp (short for Stampede), Alba, and Molly. I think there is PhD thesis lurking in analyzing how people choose the name of their dogs. Each dog is a delight and has a definite personality, but I want to tell you about some of our more amusing or eventful walks.

One day, when we arrived at the park we had chosen, Elizabeth Milner, Stamp's owner, announced that after our walk we were going to celebrate a special occasion as that day was Stamp's birthday. I thought this was a bit unusual but I supposed that Elizabeth had treats to hand out to all of the dogs after our walk. Indeed she had treats but she also had birthday hats and cake and paper horns to blow and we all sang Happy Birthday to a very bemused

Stamp and his dog friends who were happy enough munching on the treats Elizabeth had provided while we munched on the birthday cake she had brought for Stamp's human friends.

When my daughter had her first baby, I was the first new granny in the dog walking group and they decided to hold a "granny" shower for me. But of course there was a twist, it was decided that everyone was to bring a favorite children's book that would be kept at the granny's home to create a library for the grandchildren when they visited. Since then, we have acquired a few more grannies and for each one we have created a new granny library. I perhaps should note that there are a few ex-librarians in our group, and not a few children's books featuring dogs.

As I mentioned, the dogs themselves have some unusual traits. There is Sport who loves to chase stones (not sticks). He gets very annoyed when you don't immediately bend down to pick up stones when they first appear on the path. He knows just when they are first available and if you are too busy talking to notice, he starts pushing them with his nose and looking plaintively at the group. If you are still too absorbed with your conversation, he will politely clear his throat with a single bark.

Oggy and Cropper are the larger dogs in our group and when I first met her, Oggy would not cross over a bridge (fortunately she has since overcome this fear) necessitating at times a change in our path or her owner getting her feet wet. Cropper had an unfortunate puppyhood until rescued by Sally Goddard and her family and gets upset when any change occurs. He expresses this nervousness quite vocally. So at the beginning of each walk, or if Sally is out of sight attending to Oggy, we are serenaded. Cropper has an unusual but x-rated way of expressing happiness as well, so there are moments where we all look the other way to give Cropper some private happy time.

Our dogs are a well adjusted group and greet other dogs in a mostly friendly way, so that on at least two occasions we have had to take a stray dog, who has decided to join us, to a vet to be returned to its owner. These are usually big dogs and even though our dogs have accepted them on the walk, we feel they would not be so accepting of a new dog in their owner's car. As a non dog owner, I have gotten to know where the nearest vet clinics are to several parks.

We have also had some classic misadventures during our walks. The dead fish incident comes to mind as does the time Oggy and Cropper joined a coyote pack chasing a deer. When the pack was unsuccessful in bringing down the deer, poor Oggy and Cropper became the quarry and Oggy lost part of her tail. She is fine now although it took a while for the resulting infection to heal. Fortunately most of our walks are not quite so eventful and we have time to chat with each other as we walk or at coffee afterwards. The women in this group have become my closest friends in Calgary and I feel truly blessed to have found them . . . and their dogs.

A Golden Wike
Maya Aggarwala

Always ready to walk briskly on the dot of 8:55 a.m., our group's Golden Anniversary Event on September 19, 2006 was, appropriately, a guided tour of the University of Calgary grounds. The guide was a very pleasant young woman who took us to the various buildings around the campus for over an hour. Then as usual we all went for a coffee, this time in MacEwan Hall. Going for coffee is a ritual which we just love every time we go for our regular Tuesday morning walk. The smell of coffee and pleasant company of each other keeps us going. We do have a lot of fun.

Broiled Grapefruit
Margaret Johnston

2	grapefruit, halved and sectioned
2 level Tbsp	demerara sugar
½ level tsp	cinnamon or ginger

Spread over tops of grapefruit and broil. Garnish with cherries.

Faculty Women's Club Favourite Recipes (1969). (2)1, p. 36

Looking Up – *Judith Hall*

Celebrating

A Heritage of Giving
Scholarships, Service, and Support

This is really exciting: Who would have thought that over fifty years ago a small group of women would have started such a philanthropic tradition! The Faculty Women's Club has initiated several scholarships and donated far more than $35,000, numerous in kind offerings such as artwork and library books, and literally countless hours of volunteer service and support to the University of Calgary and dozens of other organizations.

Annually, through endowments totalling over $40 000 topped up by dues and directed donations, we provide three main awards:

- $1800   Scholarship for an undergraduate student at the University of Calgary
- $1000   Scholarship for a University of Calgary graduate studen- with dependent child/ren
- $250   Calgary Youth Science Fair Award for Outstanding Academic Achievement

Through direct funds, in kind items, and volunteer time, here is just a sampling of our outreach:

Adopt a Student Family
Alberta Wilderness Association
Alzheimer's Association
Art Collection Donations
Books for Residence Hall Libraries
Building on the Vision - 14 Women's Memorial Award
Calgary Birth Control Society
Calgary Local Council of Women
Campus Food Bank

December 1985 – Newsletter
The club rents out a large coffee urn for only $5.00 per day – contact Beth Davies

October 1986 – Newsletter
The Club has a 100 cup coffee maker that may be borrowed. Call Ches Crites.

Spring 1988 – Minutes
Coffee Maker – Jenny will ask if the Dining Centre would like our large 80 cup perk, or if not donate it to the Red Cross or St. David's Church. Rita has a 30 cup to donate to us.

April 24, 1997 – AGM Minutes
Tannis reminded members to bring mugs at each meeting; coffee urns and "fixings" will go home with a member in charge of the next meeting.

April 21, 1998 – AGM Minutes
Tannis suggested that interest groups take turns animating/finding speakers and/or providing refreshments for the general meetings. The idea was well received, discussion centering on involvement in the club.

April 2000 – Minutes
Jane Steele purchased new coffee urn at a cost of $49.20.

February 2006 – Extraordinary meeting held at Brentwood Coop.
Free coffee supplied but food expensive. The meeting was held to find names of all FWC members since 1956 for 50th anniversary.

April 2008 – AGM Minutes
Refreshments at future General Meetings will now be potluck. However, coffee will still be provided.

September 2009 – Editors' Note
The Club coffee urn needs a new home; suggestions welcome.

Campus Preschool Association
Canadian Cancer Society
Canadian Diabetes Association
Children's Christmas Parties
Convocation Ushers
Discovery House
Elizabeth Schonfield Memorial Scholarship
Faculty & Staff Suppers, Buffets, and Teas
Foothills Creative Beginnings Nursery School
Hosting the early Convocations
Indian Student Scholarship
Invited Speakers, open to the public
Junior League
Kids Help Phone
Kirby Centre
Kosovo Educator Development Project
The Learned Society
Light Up the World
Library Books
Meals on Wheels
Memorial Scholarships, Funds, and Remembrances
Mothers Against Abduction and Murder
Murray and Anne Fraser Endowment
National Council of Women
Pat Buckmaster Memorial Art Fund
Project Ploughshares
Salvation Army
Student Volunteer Centre
Student Tutoring
Undergraduate Bursary for Reentering Student
UNICEF
University Child Care Centre
University Concert Choir
University Jazz Ensemble
University Student Emergency Fund
University Infirmary
University Balls
Volunteer Centre
Welcoming Committees
Women's Athletics Scholarship – Making Strides
Women's Emergency Shelter

Fundraising events have included benefit dinners, auctions, book bins, fashion shows, bake sales, bidding on a box, cookbook sales, anniversary book sales, and even coffee urn rentals! The list could go on and on…. All proceeds continue to sustain our scholarships, awards, bursaries, donations, speakers, and community outreach.

An early example of the Faculty Women's Club's ongoing tradition of compounding thrifty charity is perhaps best illustrated by the following:

When the University Ball Committee found themselves in the black, their first obligation was to return the $100 to Dr. Malcolm Taylor (who had sent the committee a personal check for $100 to provide wine for the dinner). The balance of the monies from the Ball was unanimously voted to the Book Committee and also the extra money made by the committee selling the table decorations.

Dr. Taylor [Principal of the University of Alberta, Calgary], who had always been interested in the collection of Western Canadiana by the Faculty Women's Club, sent the check for $100 and also another check for $100 (making $200 in all) to the Book Committee.

Members of the Book Committee were able to buy all the many books on Western Canadiana at the Philharmonic Book Sale, including a dictionary of the Cree Language [for the University library collections].

FWC Book Committee Report, University of Alberta, Calgary, April 1964
University of Calgary Archives 86.002.04.03

Risking a Commitment of $15
Early Prizes and Scholarships

We started our $400.00 scholarship in a very humble way. After having a $27.27 carry-over from the year before, we felt in 1961 that we could risk a commitment to a $15.00 prize. It was to be given to the top student in any second year in any faculty and the terms are the same today. Three years later we raised the amount to $75.00, thus qualifying for the scholarship category. In 1970 it was increased to $300.00, then to $350.00 and finally, in 1977, to its present amount. A letter from Terence Fauvel, the first recipient of $400.00, verifies how much such help means:

May I extend my sincerest thanks to you and the Faculty Women's Club for your donation to me of the "Faculty Women's Club, Calgary Prize." To be selected for this award from among many hard-working and persevering students is a genuine honour. Since I must support myself, the prize comes during a period of tight budgeting and a continuous working schedule; the added security and encouragement this award brings to my life is timely and very much appreciated.

Of late it has not been easy to allocate the yearly $400.00, but with some help from interest earned on our term investments, we manage.

On a personal level, we have had the opportunity of contributing to two special awards given in memory of Pat Buckmaster and Elizabeth Schonfield. Pat worked on the 1964 Constitution Revision Committee along with Gertrude Baker, Marjory Holland, Betty Brown, Bernice Gibb, Mary Winspear, and me. She used her bright enthusiasm as Chairman of the

1967 University Ball to make working on the Committee more of a pleasure than an onerous responsibility. She transformed her far-reaching concern for the many new staff families coming here as strangers into their first contact with us – the Welcoming Letter. Elizabeth joined our Club upon her arrival in Canada, one year after we had formed, working always with devoted competence for us. Besides being our President in 1970-71, she held many executive offices, applying her special social and administrative talents to our Club projects; to the University Ball Committee and, as Chairman of the Board of Directors, to Meals on Wheels – probably Elizabeth's greatest community interest.

Harvey Buckmaster established The Pat Buckmaster Memorial Art Fund in 1967 as a tribute to her dedication to the arts. Interest earned from the fund is offered as two purchase prizes of $100.00 each. One is for the best piece of functional pottery and the other is for the best piece of non-functional pottery made by a new exhibitor at The Canadian Potters Association National Bi-Annual Show. Originally, only part of the prize was required to purchase the work, the remainder going to the artist. This award has added several fine pieces to the University collection.

Elizabeth helped to establish our own FWC Scholarship, hence a similar one in her own name is an appropriate memorial. The Elizabeth Schonfield Memorial Scholarship Fund was established by Elizabeth's husband, David, in 1979. Each year a scholarship covering tuition and compulsory fees is awarded to a second-year undergraduate who has markedly improved grades. Our Club had the privilege of organizing the fund until it was transferred to the University Development Office. Financial support was indeed generous, for within a few months of its establishment, funds had accrued to $3,600.00.

Norris, p. 14-15

Endowing the Future: $40 000 and Growing
Undergraduate and Graduate Scholarships

By 2008, the University of Calgary Faculty Women's Club had two endowment funds for scholarships, together totalling over $40 000. From $15 in 1961 to $400 in 1981 when FWC turned 25, to the current disbursements of $1800 for an undergraduate student, and $1000 for a graduate student with dependent children, the FWC has always been wise in managing its funds, and ever generous in their allocation.

In the early 1980s, the scholarship moved to $500 per year, still paid out via deposit interest and dues. By 1986 there was a promise of a matching grant from the Alberta Government for setting up an endowment fund, and FWC began to save and raise money in earnest. The first endowment began on July 31, 1986 with an investment of $5500 by FWC, later matched by the government, thus boosting the yield to $700, which the FWC topped up for a $1000 award for the first time in 1988.

This trend of increasing and topping up an endowment to create a greater award continues to this day. However, with the undergraduate fund secure by the turn of the century, in 2001 we started a second annual award, initially as a $500 bursary for a single parent who had returned for a further degree or qualification. As this was also disbursed through the undergraduate awards office, the bursary usually went to a Master of Teaching student in the Faculty of Education.

After a few years we moved this bursary, covered primarily by dues and small fundraisers, to the Faculty of Graduate Studies. In another year or two, we turned it into what it is now: a $1000 Scholarship adjudicated in the Special Awards category, for any graduate student with a dependent child or children.

In 2008, we split our endowment, keeping the vast majority to continue to fully fund our original award at a respectable rate, with the rest for the graduate one. Currently the new endowment, yielding about half of the award, is added to and topped up through dues and donations, as has been our custom.

All along the way, through various amendments to terms, we have regularly consulted our membership and crafted new motions for changing circumstances. We have always tended to the principles of spreading our wealth to others in meaningful ways, and being as inclusive as possible with the simplest of procedures for the hardworking students.

Tax Deductible Contributions to our Scholarship Funds

Did you know that since 2005, donations and bequests may be made at any time directly to our Faculty Women's Club Scholarship Funds? All contributions receive tax receipts from the University of Calgary! Just contact us for further details. Your support is always welcome!

Honoring Calgary Youth at the Science Fair

Polly Knowlton Cockett

At the beginning of the new millennium – depending on when one starts counting – and with the scholarship endowment fund in good shape after a major top up of $700 in August 1999, the Faculty Women's Club was looking around for yet another meaningful avenue for sharing their modest "wealth" with the wider community in the form of our annual donation. I suggested to the rest of the FWC Executive at our January 9, 2000 meeting that we initiate giving an award to a secondary school student at the Calgary Youth Science Fair.

UNIVERSITY OF
CALGARY

U N I V E R S I T Y   O F   C A L G A R Y
Faculty Women's Club

Award for
Outstanding
Academic Achievement

at the

Calgary Youth Science Fair

Executive Director,
Faculty Women's Club

Chair, Science Fair Award Committee
Faculty Women's Club

Having volunteered as a science fair judge for the first time in 1999, I found it to be a wonderful – even privileged – experience to talk closely with individual students who had put so much time and effort into thinking through and presenting an inquiry project. As well, I had been surprised and pleased to find so many others from the University of Calgary's extended family also participating in the fair in some way: as judges, teachers, mentors, or students, or by awarding prizes or simply attending this festive and interesting public event. In fact, it was at a Faculty Babysitting Swap meeting on October 24, 1999 at Maureen Hurley and Harvey Yarranton's home that the idea first came about in conversation with Blanka Kuhnel. She and her husband, Frans van der Hoorn, were also judges, and Frans had just organized an award through his department of Biochemistry and Molecular Biology. Blanka's suggestion to participate through giving an award has turned out to be a significant community outreach opportunity for the Faculty Women's Club.

Our first award for Outstanding Academic Achievement, together with $200 and a special certificate, was given in 2000. FWC moved to commit to this as an annual award, and the following year a travelling trophy was added. In that our membership represents women from diverse backgrounds at all levels of the University, we wanted our award to go to a project in any field that was thoroughly researched and enthusiastically presented. There was of course much deliberation around the tokens of recognition, so we initiated a poll of our members and their children who had been in fairs. It was conclusively determined that a certificate, rather than the traditional plaque, provided the flexibility of either framing it or putting it easily into a portfolio, the latter being useful for high school students venturing forth toward future careers. Following Frans' example, we also had our trophy made on campus by Engineering staff. Thank you in particular to Tannis Teskey for thoughtful consultations on the production of our trophy.

By 2006, our award was raised to $250, and for 9 of the 10 years it has been awarded, our recipients have also taken their projects to greater depths and breadths at the Canada-Wide Science Fair. When we first started our award, there were only a small handful of other awards from the U of C, with barely a mention back on campus. Now we are one of 11 awards, and all were recently featured in a U Today article on the U of C website, April 8, 2009, including in an interactive slide show. We were also pleased and proud that our 2009 winners, two girls from Sir Winston Churchill High School, were shown holding our trophy and certificate in The *Calgary Herald* article on April 5, 2009, page A9, "Junior scientists impress at city fair."

The Star Attractions
Children's Christmas Parties

We held our first Christmas party on December 7, 1957. From the outset, a children and staff Christmas party was seen as an excellent way of enabling our offspring to meet each other and for parents to make favorable comparisons. The key figures in the whole show, and closely tied to our economy, was Santa Claus. We had to rent a suit (which cost money) and to find a Santa to match any child's fancy (for free). Logically, the field of candidates narrowed to unknown strangers who were great entertainers. Our first was a Tech instructor. When we discovered that Sid Lindstedt was one who could fool his own flesh and blood, the Faculty Women's Club paid cold cash for a Santa suit, generous size. That suit has been steward-ed so carefully that it lived with Sid in his retirement on Cliff Avenue until very recently.

We soon varied the program to include more than Santa as the star attraction. For example, in 1962 and 1963 he shared the billing with Colonel Lunar and Rudolph – the real live reindeer from the Calgary Zoo. When Christine Abbott and Ruth Friesen convened the 1969 Party, they acquired The Creative Puppeteers Association of Calgary and The Calgary Ballet Company to enchant the children. Pre-schoolers watched hand-pup-pets, older children watched marionettes, and all watched the Nutcracker Suite.

The children's Christmas Party continued to grow over the years until by the seventies it was indeed a major event. One of the more tremen-dous ones was held Sunday afternoon, December 7, 1975, in the Medical Mall. Almost 100 parents helped conveners Sandra Nichols and Peggy Watson with the festivities. The follow-up report of the event conjures up the scene and masterful timing:

"2:30 – Children (over 200 of them) began to arrive en masse. They were given their name-tag, and chose a party hat, hung up their coats and placed their gift (for the Salvation Army) on the mitten tree. The clowns greeted the children, and helped them find their appropriate craft. This happened theoretically only. Note: It would be a good move to give the clowns a noise maker to attract attention. Movies were begun, band began playing.

3:15 – Small children brought up for snacks to avoid crush, older ones followed. They were kept in a specified area at this time to confine spills. This had been firmly requested by Mr. Wallace (Administrative Officer).

3:30 – Children urged to return to the mall area as Santa was soon to arrive. Enter Santa. Descending steps on east side. Clowns (4) passed out candy canes from baskets. Children thrilled to be addressed by names spontaneously (name tags or magic?) by Santa.

3:50 – Balloons freed. Santa departed.

4:00 – A Good Time Was Had By All."

With all the work involved, it is understandable that eventually, in 1979, the Children's Christmas Party was discontinued. Hopefully, not per-manently!

Norris, p. 6-8

A Suite of Sweet Memories
Santa Suit for Sale

The Faculty Women's Club is selling their Santa Claus suit for only $50. It is for a tall person and carries with it many fond memories of when Sid Lindstedt was such a wonderful Santa for our Children's Christmas Parties. The suit can be seen at Ches Crites.'

FWC Newsletter, December 1985

Santa Claus suit sold. $50 to Petty Cash

FWC Treasurer's Ledger, November 27, 1985

Photos from Marg Oliver's Scrapbook

I Remember

Marg Oliver

My memories of the Faculty Women's Club go back almost to its beginning. In 1957-58, while working at Chevron, my husband Tom began teaching Geology in evening classes and Saturday labs, in the day of "The University of Alberta in Calgary" on the campus of the Institute of Technology and Art. Therefore, I was the wife of a faculty member.

I REMEMBER the fall of 1957 that Madge Aikenhead, then president of the FWC, called and asked me to join the club. I happily did so, and have been a member every since. In those days our meetings were held in the Wauneita Lounge in the Tech. I don't remember the "business" transacted, but I do remember that we took our knitting or sewing to keep our hands occupied – I took my husband's socks to darn!

I REMEMBER Convocation Receptions in the early days. After having attended the convocation ceremonies at the Jubilee Auditorium, seated in a special section reserved for us, we were the hostesses at the following reception, held in the lower foyer. I recall Elizabeth Schonfield being prominent on these occasions, manning the coffee urns.

I REMEMBER the children's Christmas parties which I helped organize at least once, and attended many times in the 1960s. Sid Linstedt played Santa a number of times – over the ensuing years I always called him "Santa."

I REMEMBER some of the Potluck Suppers way back when. I think it was at one of these events that Pat Judge (then a Reverend) was asked to say Grace. To call the chatting crowd to attention, he picked up a spoon and "'tapped" a nearby glass (crystal?) bowl of salad, which shattered!

I REMEMBER the first University Ball in February 1964 – getting ourselves all outfitted in a new gown (which I made), gloves, corsage, and a rented tuxedo, all for the sum of $75.00 (including babysitter)! It was a grand affair!

I REMEMBER other university parties held at the RCAF Officers' Mess, arranged by Frank Anton – in the days when alcohol was not available on the university campus!

I REMEMBER many of the once-monthly, and then less often, FWC meetings, and many of the speakers and presentation. Two come readily to mind: the diminutive Mrs. Eileen Fish who pulled out a chair to stand on so that she could be seen by all. Dr. Peter Craigie who spoke eloquently on the Dead Sea Scrolls, several times saying that he didn't want to talk too long – I could have listened to him all night!

I REMEMBER being auctioneer at our first few money raising auctions, of the "stuff" brought from home. I think the current "silent auctions" are a better idea, even though we end up taking home half of the things that we've brought!

I REMEMBER the introduction of the Interest Groups into the FWC agenda. I started the Hiking Group in September 1971, with only 5 of us. After a short fall season, we recessed until spring, when we "took off" with ever increasing numbers each week to tackle hikes and scrambles in the mountains and halls, recessing again for that summer. From the fall of 1972, we continued hiking or cross-country skiing weekly until the spring of 1976 when, with a steady and active membership of twenty-five, we seceded from the FWC to become a private club. A new "Thursday Group" was formed, which continues to the present.

I REMEMBER the 25th Anniversary Celebration of the FWC, held in the University Dining Room (Blue Room) – the fun we had, the visiting with long time members, many of whom had come long distances to join us, and the sharing of our memories over twenty-five years.

Mine has been a long and pleasant relationship with the Faculty Women's Club of the University of Calgary, and it has been nostalgic looking back over the long years of my association with it.

Written September 2000

Proudly and Specially Prepared

Potluck Suppers

The same year that we held our first Christmas Party we also entertained the adults in November with a Pot Luck Supper. This is the one special event which has survived the years. Although the name has been changed from plain "pot luck" to "buffet supper" to "buffet dinner and dance," the occasion is still the one where we share proudly our specially prepared food favorites with our staff and friends. This is not to say that our start was smooth sailing. For the first pot luck supper we allocated casseroles, salads, and desserts, impartially amongst the membership. There was a brief squall when a delegation to our President Margaret Finn cleared up a misconception: staff wives were the ones who had time to prepare home cooked food; staff appointments did not. They would bring store items – coffee, pickles, butter. At that time no staff wife was also a permanent academic appointment.

After our Club decided to discontinue the University Ball, the significance of the buffet supper grew because it filled the social void. The one described best in our records was held on Valentine's Day in 1976 with the Faculty Club decorated in that theme. All tickets were sold a week before the function with those on the waiting list pleading their special case. This supper will go down in history as the one where President Louise Guy made 200 chocolate éclairs as her contribution to gourmet dining. Loraine Seastone, in charge of door prizes, collected an abundance. For originality, the first door prize was a door!

Norris, p. 8-9

Chocolate Éclairs
Louise Guy

Choux Paste

½ cup   butter or margarine
1 cup   water
1 cup   flour
4   eggs

Boil water and fat together.
Add flour and beat well.
Remove from heat and beat in eggs.

Shape by piping strips with a large nozzle, or drop in mounds.
Bake at 450°F for 20 minutes until well risen, then 350°F for 10 minutes until dry.
Split and fill with whipped cream or custard cream.
Cover with melted chocolate or chocolate icing.

Custard Cream

Boil together 1 cup milk and ½ cup sugar.
Mix ½ cup flour, 1 tsp vanilla, ¼ cup milk.
Beat in 1 egg and 2 yolks.
Pour into the boiling milk and cook until thick.
Cool while beating.
Whip 250 mL cream and fold into cooled custard.

Chocolate Icing

Boil 2 level Tbsp cocoa with 2 Tbsp water.
Beat in 2 Tbsp butter, 1 cup icing sugar, 1 tsp vanilla.
More water if too thick; more sugar if too thin.
Keep warm while using.

Report on the Buffet Dinner
Rita Smeaton

The Ethnic Evening, held Saturday, March 3rd in the Faculty Club, was a fun evening. The food was delicious, and represented an international cuisine. Tom Crites was an effective M.C., ably assisted by Cheslyn.

Following dinner, there was dancing from 9 p.m – 1 a.m. to the music of the Blue Tones. The enthusiastic response of the dancers was evidence that the band was a real crowd pleaser. They played waltzes, foxtrots, shottishes, polkas, and rock and roll. During the "spot" dance, lucky couples won a loaf of Vreni Gretener's homemade bread. The winners of the doorprizes, two bottles of fine wine, were Louise Guy and Carol Grant. The other doorprize, a $15 Gift Certificate from Safeway, was won by Allan Gray.

The theme was carried out in the decorations. Cleverly handmade dolls, dressed in ethnic costumes, and also flags of many nations formed table decorations. Travel posters completed the décor. Many of the guests wore national costumes, which added to the festive atmosphere.

Sarah Glockner and Karen Roth deserve great credit for a well planned party. They were given invaluable assistance by Francis McLaughlin, Vreni Gretener, Daphne Bayliss [the artist that did the raspberry colored flyer for the Buffet Dinner], Vera Simony, Sudha Joshi, Esti Menipaz and Sue Chivers. Thanks to all of these hard workers and everyone who attended, the party was a success.

- Cost: Gentlemen – $5.00; Ladies – a food dish
- Bar: Operated by the Faculty Club Staff. A one hour cocktail period preceded the dinner. Wine was also available.
- Music: Blue Tones: A wide variety of music was played by this four piece orchestra and those attending enjoyed the selections. The cost was a reasonable three hundred dollars.
- Invitations and Tickets: Four hundred flyers were made.
- Food: Guests were requested to bring: casserole for 10 (an ethnic dish) or dessert for 12 or salad for 12 and buns for 10.
- Meat: Committee members paid $5.00 each in lieu of a food dish. This money was used to purchase meat. We bought 18 lbs. of beef hip cut in two, nine pound roasts and twenty-five pounds of ham (bone in) also cut in two roasts. Meat was bought at the Safeway on Elbow Drive and 75th Ave. S.W. on sale and kept in Committee members freezers until preparation time. Safeway also gave us a 5% discount on the meat and sliced the cooked beef.
- Serving: There were two serving stations south of the bar and a dessert table outside the kitchen door. Casseroles were kept hot on the hot plates in Dr. Len Hill's lab on the ground floor. Two committee members were there to receive the food and a Faculty Club employee took them upstairs.
- Recommendations: Request that wine and liquor glasses are not removed quickly from the tables.
- N.B. A bottle of wine was given to Dr. Len Hills.

FWC Newsletter & Minutes, March 1979
University of Calgary Archives 86.022.04.04

Enjoy an

ETHNIC EVENING

Hosted by the Faculty Women's Club at

THE FACULTY CLUB

on Saturday, March 3", 1979 at 7:00 P.M.

Dance to the Music of the BLUE TONES

TICKETS (limited)
Couples $5 + Buffet Dish
Singles $5

CASH BAR / INTERNATIONAL FOOD

* Here is your chance to wear your national costume. *

| TICKETS AVAILABLE FROM FRANCES McLACHLAN 282-8351 | MAIN MEAL (TO SERVE 10) SUE CHIVERS 282-8380 | SALAD + ROLLS (TO SERVE 12) SARAH GLOCKNER 282-6438 | DESSERT (TO SERVE 12) ESTI MENIPAZ 259-4758 |

FOR YOUR TICKETS, SEND THIS SLIP, ALONG WITH YOUR CHEQUE - PAYABLE TO FACULTY WOMEN (BUFFET) - to

SUDHA JOSHI
7216 SILVERMEAD RD. N.W.
CALGARY T3B 3V2
PHONE 288-6940

NAME: ....
ADDRESS:..............................
....
PHONE: ....

Dance to the Music of The Blue Tones

In the News!
Local Newspapers Cover FWC Suppers

On Wednesday, March 22, 1961, when Mrs. Lou Goodwin was President, *The Albertan* newspaper reported on page 6:

> The Faculty Women's Club entertained the academic staff of the University of Alberta, Calgary, at a pot luck supper Saturday in the cafeteria of the university. The supper has become an annual event at the University and consists of a buffet to which each of the members of the

Faculty Women's Club contributes one dish of a favorite recipe. The social convener for the occasion was Mrs. F.D. MacIntosh assisted by Mrs. A.D.Winspear, Mrs. J.D. Anderson, Mrs. J.A. Stewart and Mrs. T.A. Oliver. Tables were decorated with a St. Patrick's Day motif by a committee under the joint chairmanship of Mrs. J.D. Aikenhead and Mrs. A.S.B. Holland.

The Calgary Herald, on the same day on its page 13, further reported:

The tables "were decorated in a St. Patrick's Day Motif". . . . Held for the past five years, the pot luck supper has now become a regular institution. . . . The club has a membership of 50, drawn from four different countries, making [for] a varied and interesting menu.

University of Calgary Archives 86.022.05.06

University Choir Gets Boost
Benefit Supper Aids Travel to Expo '67

The University of Calgary Concert Choir received a shot in the arm in the amount of more than $500 Saturday when the Faculty Women's Club held a benefit supper in aid of the choir's travel fund for its trip to Expo in May. The choir will be publicizing W.O. Mitchell's play, *Wild Rose,* during its tenure at Expo and Mr. Mitchell [looked] pleased as Mrs. J.D. Aikenhead, president of the Faculty Women's Club, present[ed] the cheque to Dr. Malcolm Brown, musical director of the choir.

The Albertan, Tuesday, April 11, 1967, p.5
University of Calgary Archive 86.022.05.07

First Donation to the University's Art Collection
A Centennial Project

The Faculty Women's Club of the University of Calgary recently presented a collection of eight works of Canadian Art to the University, for inclusion in the permanent art gallery. Included in the donation are two oils by J.D. Turner; five woodcuts by W.J. Phillips and one etching by J.K. Esler.

This is the first donation to the collection and the members of the selection committee were, Mrs. J.D. Aikenhead, President of the Faculty Women's Club, Mrs. H.S. Armstrong, wife of the President of the University, Dr. A.M. Brown, Head of the Department of Fine Arts and Fine Arts Education, R.B. Baker and H.J. Baker of the Art Division.

The University's art collection now totals some 30 works of Canadian Art.

University of Calgary Faculty Gazette March 27, 1967, p. 4
University of Calgary Archives 86.022

Mrs. Aikenhead Presents Paintings to Benefit Campus Gallery
(left to right) R.B. Baker, Mrs. Aikenhead, H.J. Becker, and Dr. Brown
Image courtesy of the University of Calgary Archives UARC 86.002.01.05.01

Of Immense Benefit to Students

The Book Committee

Although it only operated for four years, our Faculty Women's Club Book Committee achieved a great deal. Early in the fall of 1962, Principal Malcolm Taylor suggested that, as a project, our club might collect books, pamphlets and other documents dealing with Western Canadiana to commemorate the official opening of the new library scheduled for the autumn of 1963. Under chairman Mary Winspear and her committee (Lorna Wright, Dornacilla Peck, Shirley Goodwin, Mary Humphries and Joy Nichol) 90 letters were sent to the weekly newspapers in the Province; 300 form letters for distribution to chapters of the Women's Institution of Alberta and a book display was arranged at Woodwards. Two years later, Shirley succeeded Mary as head. Madge Aikenhead remained from the original group, with the new members being Gertrude Baker, Louise Bresky, Rita Smeaton, and Kay Armstrong. Specifically, the committee asked for histories of towns; families who pioneered in Western Canada (especially in Calgary); and works by Alberta authors. . . .

After four years of operation, the committee had collected over 600 books and pamphlets, some of them not Canadiana but welcome additions to the fledgling library. Our individual members gave both money and books in constant support of the project. In a letter dated November 1964, William H. Magee, Chairman, Canadian Studies Committee, assessed, ". . . These books help to form a foundation for our growing collection and will be of immense benefit to students of this and future generations."

Norris, p. 16-17

Special Concern for Students and Children
Book Bins, Child Care, and Tutoring

A brief examination of the [Book Bin] is appropriate. For six years, beginning in 1964, our Club operated a Book Bin where used pocket books, donated by friends or bought from the students, were re-sold at a small profit. By 1966 we were able to purchase a T.V. set (black and white then) for the University Infirmary. Besides giving . . . $50.00 to the Child Care Co-op, in 1967 we also presented a $200.00 cheque to the University for purchase of additional books for libraries in the two residence halls. However, within three years the Bin closed down because the University needed our location for expansion and the students were now operating their own.

In the summer of 1975, we gave $450.00 to the University Day Care Center established in that year by the University of Calgary as phase 1 of an Early Childhood Development Center. Our money purchased a used piano, an item which will bring years of enjoyment to the children. Of the $450 donated, $270 came from the final proceeds of our Book Bin (accrued interest included) and $180 from our Club auction.

While citing our assistance to students, it is appropriate to mention our Indian Student Tutoring Service Committee set up in 1962. Members tutored high school students individually on a voluntary basis. This program was a first for a club of this kind in Canada, a testimonial to the special concern we felt for students.

Norris, p. 19

Coaxing and Cajoling Us to Part With Our Money
April Auctions

One program idea, the auction, has been our annual fund-raising effort for almost ten years now. It is an April event appropriately scheduled for our last meeting of the year, after election of officers and at a time where we can assess suitable uses for the proceeds. First Marg Oliver, then Betty Schofield, and now Madge Aikenhead, have coaxed and cajoled, to help us enjoy parting with our money. We part best for baking, having paid up to $5.00 for a loaf of Vreni Gretener's bread. So this year, our auction night became a bring-your-own baking and buy-somebody-else's event. In the past the funds have been given to city needs – Meals on Wheels and The Women's Emergency Shelter; to campus needs – The Campus Day Care Center and to defray travel expenses for Ward Cole's student jazz ensemble. They are at present designated for our own needs to supplement our funds.

Norris, p. 23-24

9/11 – It Has Changed Us All

Ilse Anysas-Salkauskas

94 cm w x 144 cm h Cotton and tulle fabrics, leather, beads, cotton and synthetic threads

In 2001 the Alberta Society of Artists invited its members to create art work in response to the 9/11 US tragedy. Not only was "9/11 – It Has Changed Us All" chosen for the exhibition, but the title was used as the exhibition's name. The Province of Alberta TREXS program also chose to travel this exhibition around the southern part of the province for three years to a number of venues.

Madge's Bench

Kate Bentley

The founding member and first President of Faculty Women's Club, Madge Aikenhead, passed away during my tenure as President. I knew that we had to do something special to honor Madge and her countless hours of work for the organization. So at the AGM in April 1993 we started planning what sort of tribute would be appropriate. Various suggestions circulated the room and finally it was decided that the nicest way to honor Madge would be to acquire a park bench and place it somewhere on campus.

Little did I know at the time that this was not necessarily an easy task, since I then had to work with the Grounds people at the University. They were not at all happy to have a bench placed on campus, since other people might want to follow suit: it wouldn't look right; the design would be wrong; what sort of message would we be making!!! Since it is some time ago, I really can't remember some of the negatives I received. However, spurred on by the Executive, I kept on pushing and I am fairly certain that I got a little bit of help from Anne Fraser, who whispered in Murray's ear, who sent a little message to Grounds, and finally we were given permission to purchase a bench.

So on a very cold November 8, 1994, we had the Madge Aikenhead Memorial Dedication ceremony around the bench, which is located just outside of the MacKimmie Library Tower on the east side. I still see the bench whenever I am on that side of campus and fondly remember the wrangling with Grounds and am so glad that we were able to honor Madge in this way.

Remembering Nichola

Brentwood Community Mural Committee

There is a very special remembrance painted into the Brentwood Community Mural, found in the foyer of the Nose Hill Public Library on Northmount Drive just northwest of the University of Calgary. The parents and sisters of the late Captain Nichola Goddard, who died serving our country in Afghanistan on May 17, 2006, lived in Brentwood at the time, and Nichola's mother Sally, an FWC member, was a frequent visitor to the nearby library. In June, the creation of the mural was well underway when the committee of five decided to find a way to remember Nichola within the design.

The Goddard's home is painted into the spring section of the mural, below the setting sun, with three poppies growing beside the blue front doors. In the red-white-red order of the Canadian flag, two Remembrance Day Poppies support a central White Poppy for Peace.

Mural Design: Kirsten Horel, daughter of FWC Alumna Carol Marica; Painters: Kirsten Horel and Cheri Macaulay; Additional Committee Members: Lee Hunt, Polly Knowlton Cockett, and Ann Lidgren, Nose Hill Library Branch Manager. All live and/or work in Brentwood.

Light Up Papua New Guinea
Captain Nichola Goddard Projects and Books

Sally Goddard, former FWC President and now Alumna in Prince Edward Island, regularly keeps FWC informed of books, projects, and fundraisers for her late daughter, Nichola, who was born in Papua New Guinea. A major project is run by The Light Up the World (LUTW) organization, which provides innovative renewable energy and lighting technologies to developing countries. LUTW states that:

The objective of the "The Nichola Goddard Light Up Papua New Guinea" project is to improve the quality and functionality of health care facilities in rural PNG by installing solar powered LED lighting systems so that health facilities can be used in the evening. Light Up The World believes that bringing light to aid posts and rural health care centres will contribute to an improvement to the quality of health care provided in PNG.

The first Light Up Papua New Guinea fundraiser was held at the University of Calgary's Red and White Club, with Christie Blatchford of the *Globe and Mail* and author of *Fifteen Days* as the guest speaker. Val Fortney of *The Calgary Herald* now has a contract with Key Porter books to write *Canada's Daughter*, a story about Nichola. Further details can be found at www.nicholagoddard.com.

The Faculty Women's Club donated funds to purchase environmentally friendly LED lighting for a first aid post in Papua New Guinea in the name of Captain Nichola Goddard. Nichola's father, Dr. Tim Goddard, donated a book, *Facilitating Change*, to the Faculty Women's Club as a thank you for the FWC donation to the Kosovo Educator Development Project which is highlighted in the book. The FWC in turn donated this book to the growing library at the University of Calgary Women's Resource Centre where we hold our general meetings. You may check it out from there. This and two other books are recommended by Sally, as they may be of interest to many:

- Anderson, G. & Wenderoth, A. (Eds.). (2007). *Facilitating change: Reflections on six years of education development programming in challenging environments.* Montreal, QC: Universalia Management Group.
- Patterson, K. & Warren, E.J. (Eds.). Foreword by Romeo Dallaire (2007). *Afghanistan in the words of its participants.* Random House Canada.
- Blatchford, C. (2007). *Fifteen days: Stories of bravery, friendship, life and death from inside the new Canadian Army.* Doubleday Canada.

Light Up Papua New Guinea
The Captain Nichola Goddard Project
Gala Fundraiser
Friday, May 2, 2008

Nichola Goddard as a child in Papua New Guinea

LIGHT UP PAPUA NEW GUINEA

A Lovely Setting for Sitting
One and Only 1950s Spring Tea Sortie

The mid-fifties was still a time when a club's social status could be suitably displayed through the medium of a fancy tea. We therefore decided our social debut should be one such event scheduled for the spring of the year. Putting on a tea in style to impress our chosen few guests involved a total effort from our small membership. On the fated afternoon we arrived all hatted and dressed in our best, carefully carrying sandwiches and squares (some chocolate) which we had made with our own little hands (some of them now gloved). The locale for this gracious occasion was the Wauneita Lounge in the Tech – a lovely setting for sitting but lacking any kitchen facilities. In our innocence of the limits of electrical power, we plugged electric kettles into all outlets we could locate by crawling daintily around and below furniture. The fuses blew and so did the janitors who marched up and shooed us off elsewhere to make connections. The disarrayed tea committee regrouped in time for the 3:00 p.m. opening, presenting themselves to the guests as elegantly unflappable hostesses. But the total effort just wasn't worth it – we served tea mainly to each other (there were five guests). Historically, we had had our one and only Spring Tea sortie!

Norris, p. 3-4

Our 25th Anniversary Reunion and Dinner
Fran Davies

In the words of the famous song – THE PARTY'S OVER! And wasn't it a great party? From the moment when the first few guests began to arrive at the Blue Room, even before 6:30 p.m., until the last lingerers reluctantly left at about 11:30, it was a huge success! It really was a delightful and very memorable evening, an evening to go down in the history of the Faculty Women's Club as one of it's finest ever.

As our guests arrived, they were welcomed at the door by our elegant hostess and very first President, Madge Aikenhead, and by Fran Davies. Wearing pretty silver and white name tags, specially designed and lettered for the occasion by Daphne Bayliss, our guests were escorted to sign the guest book and then to two enormous punch bowls for cocktails. The reception area, which was tastefully decorated with colourful balloons, soon became noisy and crowded, as old friends enthusiastically greeted each other!

At 7 p.m. the guests moved into the dining area, where dozens of silver and white balloons and silver ribbons were floating high above each table (thanks to Chris Bewley's genius). So simple, but so effective as an appropriate centrepiece for a Silver Anniversary! Another interesting and thoughtful touch was the conversation point placed on each table. This was a carefully mounted selection of newspaper clippings and other items from the FWC's past, all of which stem from a period when we made headlines in City and Campus newspapers! During the course of the evening, these memories were seen changing tables frequently, and as a result, I'm sure many people learned a lot about the work of the Faculty Women's Club which they had not been aware of before. Pinned to the curtains of the dining area were about twenty letters and cards from former members who were unable to attend the party but had sent their greetings. These too provided interesting news for us to share.

Before dinner was served, Madge drew our attention to the fact that it was exactly 25 years to the day since the Faculty Women's Club was founded – a lovely coincidence, carefully planned! A message of greeting and congratulations from Dr. Norman Wagner was read to us by our Honorary President, Mrs. Catherine Wagner. Fran Davies then welcomed everyone and, with fellow guests, paid tribute to Madge Aikenhead. For it was Madge who first recognized the need for a social focal point for Faculty women and who originated the idea of the Faculty Women's Club. In a touching gesture of friendship and fellowship, the guest all joined hands as Grace was said by Dorothy Krueger.

Our dinner was delicious. The menu included: tomato juice; tossed green salad; a tasty and tender chicken cordon bleu with mushroom sauce, green beans almondine, polonaise tomato and duchess potatoes; strawberry sundae; beverages and white wine. It was beautifully prepared and served by Ethel Lang and her staff at the Dining Centre.

Interspersed throughout the meal was the presentation of five door prizes by Marg Oliver. These were especially purchased for the occasion and – with that fine attention to detail that was so typical of the work of Madge and her committee – they were gaily wrapped in the university colors of gold and red. The award of prizes was based on the 25th theme. For further light entertainment, Vreni Gretener circled the tables playing her recorder to encourage us to table-hop for a short visit after the dessert. Then, in came the surprise! A blue and white iced birthday cake, surmounted by 25 glittering sparklers. So, appropriately enough, we all sang "Happy Birthday to Us" and Cathy Wagner proposed a toast to the Faculty Women's Club.

While the cake was being cut and served, Madge personally introduced to us our original Charter Members, 18 of whom were able to be present at the reunion! It was lovely to see so many of our Charter Members there and for us to have the opportunity to show them how much their continuing interest in the Club means to us. Madge then recalled the memory of some of our members who are sadly no longer with us and who once worked so hard in the interests of the Club. She continued by presenting apologies from members who were unable to be present because of distance. However, some people *did* come from great distances, so Madge introduced us to all of those from out-of-town.

In a short and witty speech that followed, memories of the F.W.C. were humourously presented by our official historian, Marjorie Norris.

Reading from her Commemorative History, Marj described some of the Balls and some of the publicity we attained in years gone by! She graciously thanked those who had helped to produce the history in its latter stages.

Fran Davies complimented Marj Norris on the great success of her History, and on behalf of the Club, presented her with a dried flower arrangement in sincere appreciation for all her extensive research and hard work. Incidentally, over 90 copies of the History were sold at the Dinner. We shall soon be into a second printing! The history is a delightful book, full of charm and humor, anecdotes and facts and beautifully written in Marj's inimitable, distinctive and very literate style. Thank you again, Marj, for your dedication to duty and to the cause! Fran then presented Pamela Harris with a copy of the history and thanked her for her advice and excellent typing of the book. Finally, Fran thanked Madge and her committee for the wonderful evening, and introduced each member of the committee to the guests: Ruth Armstrong; Beth Davies; Ute Dilger; Vi Doucette; Ches Crites; Bernice Gibb; Louise Guy; Vera Simony; Penny Storey; Rita Smeaton and her decorating committee, Daphne Bayliss and Chris Bewley; Cathy Wagner; and Marg Oliver. On behalf of us all, Fran presented Madge and her committee with a box of chocolates, a bottle of sparkling wine and a copy of the History.

Then, it was on with the show, presented by Marg Oliver in her own unique way. She and some of the "Tuesday Hikers", all sporting Madge's best Sunday hats, joined together to provide us with a hilarious review of the F.W.C.'s work over the years, with a skit on the song "Memories, Memories". The words speak for themselves, and we thought you would like to hear them so they are reproduced at the end of this newsletter! This was truly one of the highlights of a marvelous evening. One that deserves to be recorded for all posterity! The 125 of us who were there and who listened to the evocative words and joined in the choruses at the end will understand what I mean!

Nor did the evening stop there! Several members got up to provide their own memories of the Faculty Women's Club. And so the evening went on, with individuals sharing reminiscences with each other. We chatted and gossiped for another two hours or more, and only persuaded the last few to leave by taking down the decorations around them!

Well, Madge, thanks are not enough. Words cannot adequately convey our gratitude to you for what you have done for the Club since 1956. The party is surely your crowning glory! It was organized so very well down to the very last detail. All the months of work finally came to fruition in a most exciting way. Thank you, Madge and all of your committee. The warmth and friendship engendered at the party will be with us for a long, long time. From it, perhaps, will come a sense of renewal and even greater vitality as we enter our next 25 years!

So, girls, in the words of another song "THANKS FOR THE MEMORY."

FWC Newsletter, October 1981, p. 3-4
University of Calgary Archives 86.022.04.04

Turning the Big Four-O
Toasting Forty Years

The Faculty Women's Club is calling on all past and present members to come out and toast the club's 40th anniversary at a dinner at the University Club on October 23, 1996.

The group has about 100 members right now, but has had up to 200 at various times, says club president Tannis Teskey. The club's primary purpose is to welcome incoming female faculty or the spouses of male faculty. It has special interest groups that partake in babysitting swaps, quilting, hiking, or other collegial activities. Members are also involved in events, including the Adopt-a-Family program, as well as supporting scholarships and other worthy causes such as the Campus Food Bank and the University Library.

In the past the club also organized an annual gala ball. However, as Teskey says, "with all the changes at the university, a ball isn't feasible anymore. Now our social events are on a smaller scale."

The club, open to all female faculty or the spouses of male faculty, is holding its 1996 annual meeting on Thursday, September 26.

Reprinted with generous permission from the University of Calgary Gazette, September 1996

Parade of Past Presidents
Presidential Tidbits Back Through Time

This year, as a special tribute to the 40th Anniversary of FWC, Tannis moved back through time and introduced all the Presidents starting with most recent one. Each president who so desired mentioned an interesting tidbit from her year in office:

Linda Crouch 95, Lorri Post 94, Kate Bentley 93 each had funny anecdotes to report (for example, the double booking at Anne Fraser's for a September General Meeting). Dorothy Krueger 92 mentioned the influx of new Faculty and the rejuvenation of FWC, Ruth Armstrong 91 spent most of her year away on sabbatical, and Marilyn Bratton 89 reminded us hers was the year FWC history and papers were put in the U of C Library Archives. Elizabeth Challice 88 has one word to qualify her presidency "Doldrums," echoed by Louise Guy 87. Diane Zissos 1986.

Cheslyn Crites 85, 84 talked about the University Balls and Vera Simony 83 about the Constitution being revised to annul monthly meetings. Interest groups of which there were seven then took over more. Frances McLachlan 82. Fran Davies 81 showed the 25th Anniversary book published by Marjorie Norris (that year's celebration had been organized by Madge Aikenhead). Beth Davies 80 went to U of A to meet her counterpart there and Barbara Laurenson 79 took office with Joe Clark. She mentioned the silver plates presidents received as a thank you gift after their term. Rita Smeaton 78 sent greetings from the Nursing Home. Carolyn Cole 77; Loraine Seastone 76.

Louise Guy 75 mentioned friendships struck at FWC and Betty Schofield 74 presided over the last "Town and Gown" University Ball. Berta Fisher 73 commented on the arrival of new faculty and the opportunity to meet people from all over the world. Dorothy Vernon 72. Dorothy Groves 71 showed photos from her presidency and admitted this was the year FWC lost its privileges from the U of C. Elizabeth Schonfield 70. Vreni Gretener 69 read a delightful poem about the Ball and emphasized how uncomfortable husbands were, playing second fiddle for a change! Gene Williams 68; Jennie Brown 67.

Madge Aikenhead 66. Marge Fauvel 65: she enjoyed meeting people from other Faculties and reminded us that year saw the beginning of Interest Groups to meet different needs as the Club reached a plateau. Lots of energy went to help women in trouble. Elizabeth Challice 64 showed us her second FWC pin and shared her emotion at being given the first one made (left to her by Madge Aikenhead when she passed away). Elizabeth also mentioned that spoons were given in 64, 65 and as we know the last few years past presidents have received a beautiful pottery dish with the FWC logo glazed on. We were delighted to hear details about Colour Night when Sports letters and spoons etc. were given and about Convocation Teas hosted by FWC members in hats and gloves. As we were reminded, the smaller Faculty enabled members to do more entertaining at home, everybody knew everybody else. Marj Norris 63 eventually wrote our 25th Anniversary commemorative book. Joni Chorny 62; Mary Winspear 61; Shirley Goodwin 60; Barbara Guy 59; Margaret Finn & Mary Graham 58; Vi Doucette 57. Our first president and a Charter member was Madge Aikenhead 56.

Faculty Women's Club Archives, General Meeting Minutes, September 26, 1996

Thank You, Anne Fraser and Sue White!

Farewell Teas for Honorary Presidents

The
**University of Calgary
Faculty Women's Club**
announces
an
Honorary Tea
for

Sue White

our
Honorary President, 1996-2001

Sunday 27 May 2001
2:00 to 4:00 p.m.
at the White House
4528 Varsity Green NW
Calgary, AB, T3B 3A5

Please bring a contribution of food or beverage.
Thank you, all! Farewell to Sue!

Farewell Tea for Anne Fraser, Honorary President from 1988 to 1996, held at Kate Bentley's home: a potluck, of course!

Welcoming the New Millennium: Potluck Tea and Reminiscences
Golden Threads: Humble Beginnings

Another Millennium: Another Tea. We all met in February at the White House, potluck contributions in hand, carrying our memories of FWC and friends in our hearts and minds. Many memories came out in conversation; a few even came in on paper! These humble offerings were the beginnings of the trickle that led toward the Millennium Memory Book which evolved into this Golden Threads anthology. The first inklings of an idea gathered into the grand finale in a mere decade in the lives of multitasking women.

Editors' Note: Photo of U of C President Terry White loading the dishwasher after the Tea is not included.

Magnificent and Delightful – *Jennifer Bushman*

Faculty Women's Club Turns 50

Group Connected to Community, Raised Funds, Helped Families

While the University of Calgary celebrates its 40th year, a group of women on campus is marking the golden anniversary of a club that's impacted both university life and the community at large.

Founded in 1956, when the U of C was known as the University of Alberta at Calgary, the Faculty Women's Club had a simple goal.

"The organization originated to provide the opportunity for friendship and social interaction amongst women faculty and wives of faculty, and to support the university in any appropriate way," says Polly Knowlton Cockett, one of the club's directors.

The club laid the foundation for today's fundraisers, alumni and faculty associations, support services, counsellors, day cares and more.

The original members raised money through book sales and bake sales, and contributed to the university libraries.

They also organized "town and gown" balls, bringing faculty and spouses together with the community as an external relations venture, which evolved into fundraising partnerships.

At convocation, the members volunteered as ushers; work which continues to this day.

"When the university was very small, the women were the ones who made all the sandwiches in their own kitchens and poured the tea at convocation," Knowlton Cockett says.

Over the years, working at convocation called for a cool head, as one volunteer knows. Eileen Lohka, a professor in the Department of French, Italian and Spanish, has attended 89 convocations.

"No convocation ceremony is complete without the rebel who lifts his gown to flash his fellow graduands, the sentimental who sneaks her cat under her gown so her beloved pet can share the moment, or the grateful who spells 'Hi Mom' in masking tape on her mortarboard," she says. "We have seen it all, and more."

Club members established a support group for women and newcomers to Calgary, and in 1966 founded Campus Preschool, still a thriving parent co-operative, helping provide childcare for parents while they attend university classes.

Members also pooled their money to start a $15 prize in 1961 for an undergraduate. Now endowed, the fund generates a $1,500 scholarship. The group now also provides a graduate bursary for a student with dependent children, and a youth science fair award.

The club has several events for its golden anniversary, and is collecting submissions for an anthology describing the women who helped develop a sense of place and community, on and off campus.

"These women, I'm sorry to say, will not be here forever, and we need their stories," Knowlton Cockett says. "They really tell a facet of the university's history which isn't coming out any other way."

Reprinted with generous permission from the University of Calgary: Carpenter, E. (2006). Faculty Women's Club turns 50. On Campus, (4)3, 8

May the Spirit of Love Dwell
Within our Hearts Forever More

Golden Anniversary Banquet
Edgemont Room, Village Park Inn, Calgary

Programme	Menu
6:30 Reception	Fruit Punch
7:00 Welcome and Grace	
	Butternut Squash Soup
May the love we share around this table with friends renew us in spirit.	
	Tossed Garden Salad
	Caesar Salad
May the spirit of hope, joy, peace, and love dwell within our hearts this day and forever more. Amen	Assorted Vegetables with Dip
	Whole Decorated Salmon
	Roast Turkey with Sage Dressing
7:15 Dinner	Lasagne Florentine
8:30 Reflections	Potatoes and Seasonal Vegetables
Honorary Co-Presidents	Cheese Tray
Dr. Ethel King-Shaw	Fresh Fruit Mirror
Mrs. Marjorie Norris	Decadent Chocolate Dessert
President - Arlene Kuchurean	Fancy Pastries
9:30 Farewell	Coffee or Tea
University of Alberta, Calgary	University of Calgary
Faculty Women's Club	Faculty Women's Club
Established October 23, 1956	50th Anniversary, October 23, 2006

Our Golden Anniversary Year
Program of Events: 2006-2007

All Golden Special Events are open to all past, present, and potential members. Join us!

2 0 0 6	SEPTEMBER	14	**Golden Larches Hike,** All day hiking in the mountains; Carpooling available RSVP Mary Vermeulen or Verna Sorensen
		19	**Golden University Grounds Wike** [between a walk and a hike] Meet 8:55 a.m. sharp at Scurfield Hall Parking Lot #34, RSVP Maya Aggarwala
		24	**Golden Family Potluck Picnic, Open House, and Reunions** **Faculty Babysitting Swap, Mothers and Youngsters Group, & Campus Preschool** 4:00-7:00 p.m. Knowlton/Cockett home, 5:30 p.m. Welcoming Remarks
		26	**Golden September General Meeting,** 7:30 p.m. Oslo Room, Olympic Volunteer Centre *Inscribing Memory... in Bits and Pieces* **Speaker: Eileen Lohka**
	OCTOBER	23	**Golden Anniversary Banquet** 6:30 p.m. Reception, 7:00 p.m. Dinner Village Park Inn, Edgemont Room, 1804 Crowchild Trail NW, RSVP Ann Elliott Meal Cost: $35; or Celebration Rate '$50 for 50 years' includes Charitable Donation
	NOVEMBER	14	**Fall Convocations** *Ushers Required* 9:30 a.m. & 2:00 p.m., Contact Judy McCaffrey
		25	**Golden Revolving Potluck Lunch Reunion** Theme: American Thanksgiving, 11:30 a.m. at Eileen Lohka's home
	DECEMBER	10	**Golden Festive Evening and Cookie Exchange and Golden Newcomers Plus Reunion** 7:30 p.m. at Kate Bentley's home
2 0 0 7	FEBRUARY	21	**Golden Quilt, Art, & Craft Show** 1:00 – 4:00 p.m., Hosts: Quilting and Coffee & Chat Celebrating 50 years of Creativity & Friendship, RSVP Lynn Williams
	MARCH	9	**Golden Story Storming Potluck Wine and Cheese,** 7:30 p.m., RSVP Monica Paul Brainstorm and/or Share your Story Ideas for our upcoming Book!
		17	**Calgary Youth Science Fair & FWC Award Presentation,** *Join us!* 9:00 a.m. – noon, Big Four Building, Stampede Grounds, Awards Ceremony: noon.
		23	**Golden Arts Sampler Outing,** Museum of the Regiments and Calgary Farmers' Market 9:30 a.m. – noon, Guided tour focusing on Princess Patricia's Regiment (Nichola Goddard's regiment) and the Battle of Vimy Ridge. Contact Elizabeth Milner or Jane Steele
		29	**Golden Anniversary Campus Tea,** 2:30-5:30 p.m. Women's Resource Centre Faculty Women's Club, Academic Women's Association, & Women's Resource Centre Inaugurate a new era of collaboration amongst U of C women's groups, on and off campus! BRING: Book Donation for WRC on behalf of FWC
	APRIL	10	**Golden University Unitarians Reunion Meeting:** *Revisiting Principles* 3:30 p.m., Anne Severson Room, U of C Arts Parkade, Contact Jennifer Eiserman
		17	**Golden Annual General Meeting,** 7:30 p.m. Oslo Room, Olympic Volunteer Centre Program: *Dress Through the Decades,* Bring/Wear: Clothing from last five decades! Agenda Discussion: **Membership - Eligibility, Process, Bylaws** *Attend/Discuss/Vote*
		22	**Golden Sitting Swap Earth Day Evening,** Contact Polly Knowlton Cockett 7:30 p.m., Wine and Cheese for Swap; Final Business Meeting after 40 years of Service
	MAY	10	**Spring Convocations** Ushers Required, Mornings and/or Afternoons, Please contact Judy McCaffrey
	JUNE	11-15	

Hail, Hail! The Gang's All Here
Sure is Good to See Ya!

Hail, hail, the gang's all here –
Sure is good to see ya – Happy Anniversaria!
Hail, hail, the gang's all here –
To celebrate our FIFTIETH

Hail, Hail originally written October 1981 for 25th Anniversary
Updated for 50th anniversary October 2006: both by Marg Oliver

FWC Memories in Song and Verse
Marg Oliver

Memories, memories – friendship, service, fun –
Give three cheers for fifty years –
We've mem'ries by the ton
   Memories, memories – now let's recall the years:
   We've changed and evolved since Madge was resolved
   To start up this club of her peers.

Constitutions, resolutions, lots of friendly talk
No time a-flitting, we brought our knitting
Or darned our husband's socks!
   One purpose was service to the University
   At Spring Convocation, with much dedication,
   baked and served with felicitation.

Scholarships, kid-care co-op, and tut'ring Indian youth
Let it be writ, we've done our bit
"Don't forget the Daffodil booth."
   Activities so varied, the years have seen them grow –
   With tours, crafts and talks, and concerts and auct-ions,
   And cookbooks and fashion shows.

Parties, parties, enjoyed by one and all –
The kids had Santa, adults had Fanta,
Or went to Field McCall!*
   Welcome teas, buffet sprees, we've done them all with skill –
   The food was great, but if you were late,
   You'd find that the food was nil!‡

Int'rest groups, splinter groups, ansome are going still –
Bridge, Antiques, and Books, Musique,
And Hikes and Language Skills
    A highlight in the early years, was the Univers'ty Ball –
    We were coiffed, gloved and gowned, dined with city folk renowned,
    Oh – it was a lovely brawl!

Through this stew our numbers grew – we came from far and wide
From o'er the sea, west, north and east,
And south – just like a tide
    A melting pot, a sav'ry stew – a multi-language soup
    From younger to older, some shy and some bolder –
    We are such a wondrous group.

Times have changed and we have too – o'er many passing years
And projects new have joined the slew –
The future holds no fears
    The Lunch bunch and the Theatre Group were added over time
    And the Student Science Fair, with its prizes declared,
    Is a project that we call prime.

Can you believe it's fifty years since FWC was formed?
We've worked and played, and served and made
This group – let's blow the horn!
    Memories, memories, we're here to celebrate
    Our fifty great years, again give three cheers
    For our Club – we are really great!

---

* In the days of no booze on campus, parties were held in the RCAF Officers' Mess.

‡ Remember the time there were more people and bigger appetites than usual, and we had to send out for Chinese food!

Bridging Connections: Creating Communities
Chancellor Joanne Cuthbertson's Welcoming Reception

University of Calgary Chancellor Joanne Cuthbertson and the Faculty Women's Club are co-hosting a Welcoming Reception for women new to campus at Joanne's residence on Tuesday, October 2, 2007, from 7:30-9:30 p.m. Human Resources will provide the Senate office with email contact information for all faculty new hires. Our joint intent is to reach both new female faculty, and female partners of new faculty.

The FWC contribution for the event is to request that any of our members who are attending to please bring a dessert plate, if they are willing and able. New hires will not be asked to bring anything. Thank you for your support for this special fall event which will replace our traditional Wine & Cheese Evening.

Please feel free to pass the attached invitation on to any potential FWC member, whether they are brand new, have been here 50 years, or anything in between. This event will be a wonderful opportunity to do what FWC does best: Create a Welcoming Community.

Faculty Women's Club Newsletter, Autumn 2007

Vi Doucette in Profile
Barbara Laurenson

Many of us know Vi because her husband, Andy was the first president of the University of Calgary and because she is a founding member of our Club. But perhaps fewer people know that she is also linked with the history of the province. She was born in the little town of St. Albert, ten miles north of Edmonton, in the same year that Alberta and Saskatchewan were created out of the former N.W. Territories.

She grew up as an only child on her parents' farm. People got around by horse and buggy and there was only a dirt road leading to Calgary. With no radio or T.V. people made their own amusement and Vi learned to love music and to play the violin with her uncle, also a violinist, and her father who played the french horn. Later at the U. of A. she played with the University Radio Orchestra and sang with the Faculty Women's Choral Group.

Vi met Andy when she was in Grade Twelve at St. Mary's High School in Edmonton. In those days it was a school for girls only, with the exception of Grade Twelve. Andy had come out West from Nova Scotia in 1922 with an Engineering degree, but was teaching science because those were lean times, and he had not been able to find a job in his field. He loved teaching though and took his degree in Edmonton at the U. of A.

They were married in 1929 and had three children, while living in various small towns in Alberta where Andy worked as a Superintendent for the Dept. of Education.

When war broke out in 1939, Andy was sent overseas and Vi returned to Edmonton with the children where they lived happily with her parents until he returned home.

In the fall of '47 they moved to Calgary because Andy had been invited to become Director of the U. of A. Faculty of Education in Calgary. This was the beginning of the U. of C., though it did not become autonomous until 1966. Their offices were in S.A.I.T. administration building until land was finally acquired and University Buildings put up.

Well, the years went by and the children grew up and were married. Their son Frank is now head of the Fund and Development Dept at the U. of C. After Andy passed away, Vi set up an annual award of a Gold Medal and bursary in his name for the outstanding student in 3rd year education, specializing in Practice Teaching.

The Faculty Women's Club Award was also set up by Vi and her Colleagues, and she looks back over the years with many happy memories of a busy and rewarding life. Not that she has retired in any way. Vi has always been a vigorous and happy person and is actively involved with her family, and 13 grandchildren, and volunteer work at the Foothills hospital. Just before Christmas her first great-grandchild was born, much to her delight. Congratulations Vi and best wishes for your continued health and happiness.

Faculty Women's Club Newsletter, March 1980
University of Calgary Archives 86.022

Shrimp Salad

Violet Doucette

1 pkg	gelatin soaked in ¼ cup cold water.
1 pkg	lemon jello dissolved in 1/3 cup boiling water. Add gelatin while jello is hot to dissolve.
1 tin	chicken gumbo soup
1 tin	shrimp (cocktail size)
½ cup	diced celery
¼ cup	chopped green onion
½ cup	mayonnaise
½ cup	whipped cream or 1 small pkg. Ready Whip
	Green pepper (optional)

Dissolve jello and gelatin in hot water.

Add tinned soup when jello is slightly thickened. Add celery, onion and fish. Fold in mayonnaise and whipped cream. Green pepper may be added if desired. Chill. Serve on lettuce. Very tasty with cheese bread.

Faculty Women's Club Favourite Recipes (1969). (2)1, p. 41

Vi Doucette was a Charter Member and the First Honorary President of the Faculty Women's Club.

Just a Few of the Many Who Have Served
Presidents and Honorary Presidents

Madge Aikenhead 1956, Vi Doucette 1957

Vi Doucette 1958-1960, Honorary
Mary Graham 1958a, Margaret Finn 1958b, Barbara Guy 1959

Vi Taylor 1960-1964, Honorary
Shirley Goodwin 1960, Mary Winspear 1961, Joni Chorny 1962, Marjorie Norris 1963

Kay Armstrong 1964-1968, Honorary
Elizabeth Challice 1964, Marjory Holland 1965, Madge Aikenhead (2) 1966
Jennie Brown 1967, Gene Williams 1968

Jane Carrothers 1969-1974, Honorary
Vreni Gretener 1969, Elizabeth Schonfield 1970, Dorothy Groves 1971
Dorothy Vernon 1972, Berta Fisher 1973

Phyllis Cochrane 1974-1978, Honorary
Betty Schofield 1974, Louise Guy 1975, Loraine Seastone 1976, Carolyn Cole 1977

Cathy Wagner 1978-1988, Honorary
Rita Smeaton 1978, Barbara Laurenson 1979, Beth Davies 1980, Fran Davies 1981
Frances McLachlan 1982, Vera Simony 1983, Cheslyn Crites 1984, 1985
Diane Zissos 1986, Louise Guy (2) 1987

Anne Fraser 1988-1996, Honorary
Elizabeth Challice (2) 1988, Marilyn Bratton 1989, Philomena Hauck 1990,
Ruth Armstrong 1991, Dorothy Krueger 1992,
Kate Bentley 1993, Lorri Post 1994, Linda Crouch 1995

Sue White 1996-2001, Honorary
Tannis Teskey 1996, Karen Serrett 1997, Sue-Ann Facchini 1998
Polly Knowlton Cockett 1999, 2000, Jane Steele 2001, Sally Goddard 2002
Lynn Williams 2003, 2004, Arlene Kuchurean 2005, 2006

Ethel King-Shaw & Marjorie Norris 2006-2007, Honorary
Eileen Lohka 2007, 2008, 2009a, Marie Gailer 2009b

Joanne Cuthbertson 2009-present, Honorary